ƒP

KNIVES
AT DAWN

AMERICA'S QUEST FOR
CULINARY GLORY AT THE LEGENDARY
BOCUSE D'OR COMPETITION

Andrew Friedman

Free Press
New York   London   Toronto   Sydney

Free Press
A Division of Simon & Schuster, Inc.
1230 Avenue of the Americas
New York, NY 10020

First Free Press hardcover edition December 2009

FREE PRESS and colophon are trademarks of Simon & Schuster, Inc.

For information about special discounts for bulk purchases,
please contact Simon & Schuster Special Sales at
1-866-506-1949 or business@simonandschuster.com.

The Simon & Schuster Speakers Bureau can bring authors to
your live event. For more information or to book an event,
contact the Simon & Schuster Speakers Bureau at 1-866-248-3049
or visit our website at www.simonspeakers.com.

Designed by Suet Y. Chong

Manufactured in the United States of America

1   3   5   7   9   10   8   6   4   2

Library of Congress Cataloging-in-Publication Data
Friedman, Andrew, 1967–
Knives at dawn : America's quest for culinary glory at the legendary
Bocuse d'Or competition / Andrew Friedman.
p.   cm.
Includes bibliographical references and index.
1. Cookery—Competitions—Florida—Orlando.   2. Cookery—
Competitions—France—Lyon.   3. Bocuse d'Or, USA (Competition)
(2008 : Orlando, Fla.)   4. Bocuse d'Or (Competition) (2009 : Lyon,
France)   5. Cooks—United States.   I. Bocuse d'Or, USA (Competition)
(2008 : Orlando, Fla.)   II. Bocuse d'Or (Competition)
(2009 : Lyon, France)   III. Title.
TX652.F72   2009
641.5—dc22   2009035271

ISBN 978-1-4391-5307-9
ISBN 978-1-4391-5684-1 (ebook)

for David Black

CONTENTS

INTRODUCTION

ONE OF THE HARSH REALITIES OF EVERY CHEF'S LIFE IS THAT, AT the end of each day, he will be judged.

In many respects this is unfair, because the food in most restaurants, even the most eye-popping, palate-dazzling, wallet-busting cuisine, is more complex than all but the most knowledgeable diners can realize or appreciate. Just about anything served in high-caliber establishments is the product of hours—if not days—of effort, the culmination of the strivings of at least a handful of people, and up to dozens: fish, meats, and produce selected in consultation with farmers, fishermen, and artisans; long-simmered stocks, peeled and shaped vegetables, and minced herbs generated by the unsung morning crew; sauces, condiments, purees, and garnishes fashioned by the cooks themselves in the hours before lunch or dinner

Members of a kitchen brigade bring years of hard-won knowledge to bear every time they strap on an apron. But there's no telling what might happen in those dizzying, adrenaline-fueled afternoons and evenings when the components of a dish are fired (cooked or reheated), seasoned, and brought together. Much has to go right for success; much less need go awry to qualify as failure. It's like that old saw about the Central Intelligence Agency: their daily triumphs are unknown; only their miscues draw criticism. Chefs and their colleagues spend every moment of their working lives swinging from one precarious task to the next: a surfeit of salt and a sauce will diminish rather than enhance all that it touches; a minute too little in the sizzle of a sauté pan and a breast of chicken will be worse than imperfect—it will be a health hazard.

And yet, to those who keep chefs in business, none of that matters. From neighborhood eateries to Michelin-ordained destinations, the moment of truth is brutally simple: the final product is presented, a few ounces framed within the confines of a plate or bowl. Fork or spoon is lifted. Food meets palate. Judgment is rendered.

IN LIGHT OF THIS inescapable truth, one might wonder why a chef would throw his toque into the ring of the Bocuse d'Or, the most prestigious cooking competition in the world, and invite the ultimate moment of judgment. In preparation for this literal trial by fire, which has been staged in Lyon, France, every other year since its founding in 1987, candidates devote months and sometimes years to rehearsing an elaborate culinary routine in order to meet the contest's Everest-like challenge: transform a set of assigned proteins (chef-speak for fish and meats), plus whatever supporting ingredients the chefs like, into intricate, impeccably cooked compositions in five and a half grueling hours. Just before time is up, they arrange their creations on two enormous platters—one showcasing their fish and shellfish handiwork, the other their mastery of meat. An international panel of judges scores the visual presentations, then the chefs plate the food and the jury digs in for the most important evaluation: taste. There are no elimination rounds, no time to ease into the rigors of competition: the candidates get one shot to cook and present their creations, and the judges who determine their fate have roughly five minutes to taste and consider it. In the Bocuse d'Or's current form, twenty-four teams (each comprising a chef and a *commis,* or assistant) compete; the only thing they know for certain when they begin is that three of them will emerge with precious medals, while the others will slink home empty-handed.

Despite those odds, the Bocuse d'Or draws professionals, many from top kitchens who already toil in pressure-cooker environments, subsist on precious little sleep, and subject themselves to dozens, even hundreds, of verdicts every working day. Any number of clichés may explain the appeal of the Bocuse d'Or: *Chefs love a challenge! Chefs are competitive! Chefs are masochists!* All are appealing, but none fits the entire field. Just as people get into cooking for different reasons, there's no single motive for pursuing this culinary Holy Grail.

Candidates *are* philosophically unified, however, when they come out on the other side. "I learned a lot about myself" is perhaps the most common sentence uttered by those who have vied for the Bocuse d'Or when asked to evaluate their experience. This doesn't surprise Roland Henin, who coached Team USA at the 2009 edition. "Competition doesn't form character," Henin is fond of saying. "Competition *reveals* character."

An American team has competed at every Bocuse d'Or, but the United States has not yet reached the elusive podium where gold, silver, and bronze medalists are bathed in a light storm of glitter and flashbulbs. In 2008, a triumvirate of culinary figures—Daniel Boulud, Thomas Keller, and Jérôme Bocuse—raised unprecedented support and awareness for the American enterprise. This is their story, and the story of the team that competed for the United States at the 2009 Bocuse d'Or: what they did, how they did it, and what they learned.

TIMOTHY HOLLINGSWORTH, CHEF DE cuisine at Thomas Keller's landmark restaurant, The French Laundry in Yountville, California, calls the highest state of kitchen being The Dance. It's a phrase he learned from Keller himself, described in the restaurant's employee manual as "the way each of us interacts with the other . . . crucial in the flow of a great kitchen."

The Dance, as Hollingsworth interprets it, can take many forms: there's the synchronicity of a kitchen brigade firing on all cylinders, the cooks complementing—if not actually completing—each other's tasks: picking up food, plating food, sometimes even cooking food for the person next to them; it can, and should, look like a naturally occurring phenomenon, but is achieved only with great and sustained effort.

There's also an individual Dance, in which a cook experiences the exhilaration of peak performance, operating on pure instinct, all of his senses integrated seemingly without the middleman of a brain: preparations are stirred, sniffed, adjusted, tossed, approved, plated, and then forgotten as he undertakes the next order. Hollingsworth likens this iteration of The Dance to the quintessential image of a football running back, the ball clutched tightly to his chest, charging past linesmen, spinning and weaving his way around or through an onslaught of defenders. In movies, that moment is often depicted in slow motion—the way it may feel to the athlete, and the only way for an outsider to fully appreciate its intricacies—but time is actually moving faster, as the running back makes a series of nanosecond decisions and infinitesimal adjustments.

Hollingsworth regularly attains The Dance at The French Laundry. But on January 28, 2009, at the Bocuse d'Or, the most pressure-filled day of his young life, Hollingsworth wasn't dancing. He moved with assurance, grace even, but any co-worker would recognize that he wasn't swaying, or ever so slightly swaggering, as he moved from one side of the kitchen to the other, the way he did when he was in the zone. He wasn't quite lost in his work, wasn't flowing naturally from one movement to the next. Instead, he seemed to be thinking about the long list of tasks before him, whether alternating avocado and diced-shrimp shingles atop a rectangle of puff pastry or overlaying a sheet of poached cod mousse with pureed scallop roe.

Hollingsworth was cooking in a box—a three by six-meter kitchen, one of a dozen such culinary cubicles erected in a row, like laboratory pods, for the Bocuse d'Or. He and his commis (assistant), Adina Guest, a fellow employee from The

French Laundry, were cooking in front of several hundred frenzied spectators and the noise was deafening, the crowd separated into cheering sections for each of the twelve nations competing on this day; the one he couldn't shut out was the melodic chant of the Spanish contingent—"Olé. Olé. Olé. Olé."—which he misheard as a taunt meant just for him: "No Way. No Way. No Way. No Way."

Hollingsworth had managed to contend well enough with all of this until four hours into the five-hour-and-thirty-five-minute marathon. That was about the time that he realized he was in the midst of what he would, by day's end, describe as the "hardest thing I've ever done."

His fish platter—which would display his cod centerpiece and three elaborately composed garnishes—was due in the window in just a few minutes, whereupon it would be whisked away and paraded before, then tasted by, a dozen judges from around the world; then he'd have thirty-five minutes to get his other platter ready for the twelve chefs charged with appraising the meat dishes.

"Are the custards ready?" he asked Guest.

"No, Chef."

On the other side of the window, the team's coach, Roland Henin—in his mid-sixties, a veteran culinary competitor and coach, and mentor of Hollingsworth's chef, Thomas Keller—looked on, hoping for the best, but keenly aware that the team, which had been looking pretty good up until then, was teetering on the brink between triumph and, if not disaster, at least disappointment.

Hollingsworth stopped for a moment to administer an internal pep talk. The phrase that came to mind had great meaning for him. It was the one he used when he found himself in the weeds at The French Laundry, the one that had spurred him to success on any number of previous occasions. But he didn't think about the past. He didn't think about anything, really. He just said to himself, instinctively, "Okay, Tim, let's go."

I

"*Oui, Chef!*"

It is better to begin in the evening than not at all.
—ENGLISH PROVERB

THOMAS KELLER JOKED THAT, BECAUSE HIS FRENCH WAS RUSTY, when the legendary chef Paul Bocuse rang him up at Per Se restaurant in New York City in March 2008, and asked him to become president of Bocuse d'Or USA, he didn't quite understand. "Was he inviting me to Lyon to work in his restaurant?" Keller deadpanned. "Was he inviting me to dinner?"

Keller—age fifty-two at the time, and the only American-born chef operating two three-star Michelin restaurants—stands a lanky six feet two inches tall and speaks with the kind of homespun modesty you'd more expect from the proprietor of a general store than one of the supreme culinary talents of his generation. He paused for laughter before delivering the punch line: "I wasn't really sure, but I knew what to say: '*Oui, Chef.*'"

The audience, a congregation of fellow whisks and industry insiders, erupted in laughter. They recognized the truth at the heart of the anecdote: chefs live a hierarchical existence. Even if you attain the status of a Thomas Keller, there will be an elder you revere and to whom you would simply never say *no*. "When a chef of that stature asks me to do something it is automatically *yes*," said Keller. "There isn't any question about it."

Keller and his audience were assembled on a sauna of a September night in the American Adventure Parlor, a reception room done up in eighteenth-century décor at the American Pavilion of Walt Disney World Resort's Epcot theme park near Orlando, Florida. The American Pavilion was situated in the World Showcase area of Epcot, where eleven countries are represented via pavilions (self-contained clusters of attractions, shops, and restaurants) arranged around a central lagoon. Across the lagoon stood the World Showplace, an enormous event space where the next morning, Friday, September 26, four two-person teams, each comprising a chef and a commis (assistant), would begin competing for the right to represent the United States at the next Bocuse d'Or in Lyon, France, in January 2009.

At the outset of the year, Keller could not have imagined that he would be standing in that room, let alone be there as the president of the Bocuse d'Or USA, the organization that coordinates the biennial search for a candidate to represent the United States at the world's most prestigious cooking competition. Nor could Daniel Boulud, the irrepressible French-born impresario behind Daniel, Café Boulud, and other restaurants from New York to Beijing, have foreseen that he'd be on board as chairman. As Keller spoke, Boulud roamed the crowd, attired in a suit and no tie, shaking hands with sponsors, waving to friends and colleagues, and grinning an effusive smile beneath his always perfectly coiffed hair.

Neither Keller nor Boulud had ever paid much attention to the Bocuse d'Or, or to cooking competitions in general. Oh, sure, Boulud had been a guest judge on *Top Chef*, the Bravo network's popular cooking competition program on which unknown or aspiring chefs go head to head in pursuit of a cash prize. And they both knew of other competition shows such as the Food Network's *Iron Chef*, not that either of them had ever deigned to appear on them.

But another species of cooking competition, the most well-known being the *Internationale Kochkunstausstellung* (informally and unofficially dubbed the International Culinary Olympics) in Germany, predates these sensationalist programs. Generally speaking, these competitions are celebrations of craft rather than springboards to fame and fortune. By and large, their participants find that they have tremendous application to their vocation. In the *Guide to Culinary Competitions: Cooking to Win!*, Certified Master Chef Edward G. Leonard writes that "Chefs who can step into the highly charged culinary competition arena with all eyes upon them and perform at their best in unfamiliar circumstances deserve our commendation. Moreover, chefs who compete perform very well in their own kitchens, bringing much to the table in the form of new concepts and ideas."

Hartmut Handke, the Columbus, Ohio–based chef who represented the United States at the Bocuse d'Or in 2003, placing sixth, agrees. "When you do well in a competition, first of all it teaches you discipline and it makes you a better chef," he said. "And if you [compete] a lot I think it's eventually reflected in your everyday work in your own restaurant or in your place where you work . . . it [also] builds confidence."

Richard Rosendale, then chef-owner of Rosendale's (also in Columbus) and a member of two International Culinary Olympics teams, sees even more value in the competition experience. "In my opinion, one year on the Olympic team is the equivalent of five years in the industry," he said. "In doing the team you have obligations to push yourself and research more and do more and learn more than what you normally would . . . I've competed in Germany three times, Luxembourg twice, Basel, Switzerland, twice, and all over the United States. Seeing these other countries and the food they're putting up really makes you open up your mind and see food a little differently. There's no boundaries." Roland Henin, the French-born certified master chef who was set to coach Team USA for the 2009 Bocuse d'Or, and had coached the US Culinary Olympics team, echoes this sentiment, declaring that four years on the Olympics team "are the equivalent of ten or twelve years of life work."

In addition to the International Culinary Olympics, there are other regional and national competitions all over the world that take many forms. Some focus on hot food cooked restaurant style. Others concentrate on classic cuisine and fundamental, sometimes antiquated, techniques: ice sculpting, ornate platter service, and cold food competitions devoted to butchery, slicing, and basic knife skills. (The International Culinary Olympics combines the two formats.) In the cold food arena, the product itself is often evaluated mostly, if not exclusively, on its appearance, such as how perfectly a terrine is composed and even sliced, rather than on its taste. (One reason for this is that the food is typically prepared ahead of time, chilled, and preserved under gelatin or aspic.) These contests are an ingrained part of the culinary culture in many European countries, but you won't see them televised or covered in newspapers or blogs in the United States and they rarely, if ever, draw the participation of brand-name chefs.

"There are many avenues for chefs to take in their careers," said Keller, who gives the impression that he chooses his words as carefully as he sources his Elysian Fields Farm lamb. "The first competition that I saw was at the [International Hotel/Motel & Restaurant Show] . . . the only thing that you see is the finished platters. Everything is covered with gelatin. I was a young chef focused on restaurant *à la minute* cooking and the platter thing didn't really resonate with me. I never found it interesting to be involved with that. That is the path that I took."

Many of Keller's American restaurant colleagues aren't nearly as polite about cooking competitions, regarding them as a curiosity with little real-world value, something that hotel or culinary school guys get together to do, but not *real* chefs. Even Jonathan Benno, Keller's chef de cuisine at Per Se, commented that, "I respect [the Bocuse d'Or's] history and tradition and the skill set involved to create those beautiful platters, but that style of cooking doesn't really interest me. *This* interests me. Working in a restaurant every day with a team interests me."

One reason for the divide between the European zeal for culinary competitions and the dearth of interest in the United States is that many, if not most, European chefs were raised in ultraconservative, traditional cooking environments, whereas many of today's American restaurant chefs came up in the rule-breaking, fiercely forward-looking culinary scene of the 1980s and '90s. The very name of the movement that drew many of them to the kitchen—New American Cuisine—underscores a desire to move on from both the past and the conventions of classic European techniques and dishes. Conversely, their contemporaries overseas maintain, even cherish, a strong connection to centuries-old traditions, which are themselves a source of national pride. As a result, many European teams are lavishly funded by foundations and other support organizations, and competitors' employers are only too happy to give them weeks or months off to devote to their preparation, something exceedingly rare in the United States, where most culinary competitors come from hotels or cooking schools, entities that can afford to grant them the time, and for whom the prizes hold great promotional value. "Because they work in [a private] club," said Boulud of those who populate the ranks of America's competition chefs, "they don't really work in the competitive environment like we have. Often in private clubs, or in a situation where the chef is a teacher in the CIA [Culinary Institute of America], he has plenty of time to focus on that . . . but when you run a restaurant in New York, and you do it day in and day out, you are so busy there is no way to find a break to do it."

Although Boulud had no relationship with the Bocuse d'Or prior to 2008, he did have one with Paul Bocuse, for whom he had briefly worked when he was a wee lad learning his craft in the kitchens of Lyon. Perhaps signaling early that he was destined for anything-goes Manhattan instead of France's more provincial Rhône-Alpes region, Boulud strutted into his first day of work in Bocuse's kitchen sporting sunglasses and a bass player–worthy mane. Bocuse kicked him out, literally. "He kicked my ass and said, 'Go and cut your hair. And we don't need sunglasses here to work!'" remembered Boulud, joyously laughing at the memory of his own impetuousness.

The seeds for this evening in Orlando were planted elsewhere in Florida, on Saturday, January 12, 2008, when Paul Bocuse's son, Jérôme, was married in Palm Beach at Boulud's Café Boulud restaurant at the Brazilian Court Hotel. When Boulud was the chef of Sirio Maccioni's Le Cirque—*the* see-and-be-seen dining destination for the cultural and political elite of 1970s and '80s Manhattan—Jérôme, who had come to the United States to attend The Culinary Institute of America in Hyde Park, New York, visited him often. The fact that Bocuse and Boulud were both Lyon boys determined to make their mark in the States forged a quick and lasting bond; for example, Boulud is godfather to Jérôme's young son. Today, Jérôme Bocuse is an owner of Les Chefs de France restaurant at Epcot, the food and beverage facility his father founded in 1982 along with fellow French icons Roger Vergé and Gaston Lenôtre and which he took over in fall 2008. At a prewedding lunch at Café Boulud, the senior Bocuse asked Boulud to participate in the 2009 edition of the competition by becoming *Président d'honneur* (Honorary President), and to shepherd the American effort—in particular, to help him get Keller on board as president of the Bocuse d'Or USA.

The United States' best-ever showing in Lyon was Handke's sixth-place finish in 2003. Bocuse longed to see that track record improved. His motivation was partly sentimental: as a soldier in the First French Division, he was shot in Alsace. "I was taken to an American hospital in the countryside where I received a blood transfusion from an American GI," said Bocuse, whose eyes moisten when recalling the larger sacrifice America made for his country. Of the American flag that flaps in the wind outside his eponymous restaurant along the river Saône, he said, "Remember the sixth of June, nineteen forty-four. Ten thousand people died at Normandy." All of that he said in French, but then he paused, and said, in English, his voice creaking, "Thank you, America."

Bocuse's fondness for the United States deepened when son Jérôme took on dual U.S.-French citizenship and married a Yankee, and the two produced an American grandson. But Bocuse, the first great chef-marketer, surely also recognized that success by an American team would mean a wider audience for his competition, which is a phenomenon in many European countries: attended by several hundred screaming, flag-waving, noisemaker-wielding fans, the Bocuse d'Or is broadcast around the world via streaming video to 106 countries and covered live on French television, but was scarcely known in the United States, even to many chefs.

Jérôme Bocuse, a fit, bald, perennially tanned man whose Gallic fashion sense makes him easy to spot in the shorts-and-muscle-shirt theme land of Florida, had his own vision of what an American victory would mean to the Bocuse d'Or. A sports fan as well as an avid water skier, he had noticed a trend in American television coverage of the Olympic Games: "If the U.S. are not a strong competitor, they don't show the event," he said.

"I am not judging that," he added. "But it's just a reality and a fact."

Translation: if the United States did well at the Bocuse d'Or, there'd be a whole new, massively huge nation of interested spectators for the contest that bore the family name.

When Bocuse made his request, Boulud naturally agreed. That's what you do when you're a chef and Paul Bocuse comes a-knocking. There are no two ways about it.

PAUL BOCUSE HIMSELF, FRESH off a flight from Lyon, sat just behind Keller as he made his toast on that September evening at Epcot. Eighty-two years old, with a persistent tremor in his right hand, he silently scanned the room. At Epcot, with its ersatz nations lined up like department-store windows, one could be forgiven for thinking that this wasn't really Paul Bocuse, but a Disney-engineered mirage. But Bocuse it was, there to help usher in what he hoped would be a new era for the United States in his namesake event.

When it comes to the Bocuse d'Or, chefs have been saying *"oui"* to Paul Bocuse since the mid-1980s. That was the time that the organizers of the Sirha, Europe's largest international hotel, catering, and food trade exhibition, which is held at Eurexpo, a Lyon convention center gargantuan enough to register on satellite images, were looking to add a culinary competition to their roster for the 1987 show. They approached Albert Romain, director of the Parc des Expositions venue of Lyon, who turned to his good friend Bocuse, and suggested attaching his name to it because of the worldwide clout it would automatically confer on *le concours* (the contest).

There are many immortals in Bocuse's kitchen generation—Vergé, Alain Chapel, the Troisgros brothers—but the respect and affection of the world's chefs for Bocuse is a little special. He is widely recognized as the first of his comrades to march proudly into the dining room to commingle with the clientele, an act of emancipation that helped his professional brethren migrate from the heat of the kitchen to the glare of the spotlights.

"We chefs and celebrity chefs owe so much to Bocuse; we were *domestiques*, now we are nobility," said Alain Sailhac, who was present at Epcot to act as a judge for the next two days. Formerly the chef of Le Cirque and now executive vice president and senior dean of programs at The French Culinary Institute in New York City, Sailhac remembers that when he was a young cook in France, before the Bocuse reformation, he would conceal his profession from young women he was courting; if forced to confess that he worked in a restaurant, he would claim that he was a *chef de rang*, or dining room captain, which had more cachet.

In time, Bocuse's prominence extended around the world. The promotional copy on the back of the menu at Paul Bocuse sums up his contribution: "More than anyone else, it is he who rendered eminence and dignity to chefs, making them the undisputed stars of the professional food establishment. Yesterday's employee (or, worse, yesterday's lackey) is today's entrepreneur, restaurant owner, concept designer and marketing specialist—exactly like Bocuse and in large part thanks to Bocuse." That sounds awfully boastful, but few in the industry would dispute the claim.

The irony of his gift to the profession isn't lost on Bocuse. According to son Jérôme, he ventured outside the kitchen not exclusively for personal fame and glory (though he has reaped plenty of both for decades), but to elevate the appreciation for his craft in general, and for French cuisine in particular. Many of today's young chefs crave a permanent relocation to the artificial world of a television-studio kitchen, but Bocuse points with pride to the fact that when he returned home from his globetrotting, he always parachuted right back into the kitchen. To this day, though he requires an afternoon nap in his home above his restaurant, and retires most evenings while guests downstairs are still slurping tastes of his famous *Soupe aux truffes noires V.G.E.* (a hearty broth of black truffles and foie gras created to honor President Valéry Giscard d'Estaing in 1975) or nibbling on other signature creations such as red mullet with potato "scales," when he's not traveling, he's in the restaurant.

"Now it's time for everybody to get back in the kitchen," he joked about today's young talent.

Memories differ slightly over exactly how the Bocuse d'Or's format came to be. Albert Romain recalls coming to Bocuse with the concept of an international cook-off already in mind. Bocuse's recollection is that, presented with the opportunity to dream up a cooking competition, he envisioned the Bocuse d'Or as a response to what he considered a lamentable state of affairs on the global table. In his travels during the 1970s and early '80s, he had noted, sorrowfully, that food everywhere was "becoming the same. It was the time of broccoli, kiwi, and avocados." He conceived the Bocuse d'Or as a competition in which young chefs from around the world would come to Lyon and cook the food of their homelands for a panel of judges. In short, the unofficial ambassador for French cuisine was conferring ambassadorships on others.

To help bring the event to life, Bocuse enlisted the assistance of a handful of acclaimed local chefs who were more than colleagues. Every morning for decades they had socialized with each other at the Halles de Lyon marketplace. After rising before the sun and loading up their little trucks with livestock and produce, the gentlemen would sit down to a *mâchon*, or feast, at one of the little cafes situated in the market, fortifying themselves for the day ahead with a steady diet of pig's feet, charcuterie, sausage, coffee, and—why not?—white wine before sputtering off to their respective restaurants. (For a sign of Bocuse's eminence in Lyon, look no further than the fact that in 2006, after a renovation, the market was renamed "Les Halles de Lyon—Paul Bocuse.")

That year, twenty chefs came to Lyon to compete, and before long the Bocuse d'Or had become the preeminent cooking competition in the world. Such is its reputation that casual observers often refer to it as the Olympics of cooking, even though there is an actual International Culinary Olympics, the aforementioned *Internationale Kochkunstausstellung*, which was first held in Frankfurt in 1900. It seems safe to assume that one reason for the Bocuse d'Or's lofty status is that, of the two reigning competitions, it is the only one in which the French participate.

Among the American culinary competition cognoscenti, it is taken as gospel that the French stopped going to the International Culinary Olympics because they couldn't stomach a third-place tie with the American team in 1976, the last year they attended. "France, Germany, they were always the top countries," said Roland Henin, who would coach Team USA for the 2009 Bocuse d'Or. "Then comes this newbie in the picture with [Ferdinand] Metz as the captain—USA. They come in the late 1970s . . . and they do well. So then France becomes *execo* [tied] with the U.S. And the French were in an uproar. 'How could that be? We have been cooking for centuries! This new country that can't cook anything but a hamburger! And now they are *execo* with us.' So they quit."

In 1980, Paul Levy, food correspondent for *The London Observer*, suggested another rationale for the French retreat: that differing sensibilities among various French chefs' organizations, some of which found the Olympics "old-fashioned, even reactionary," led to their opting out. Because "a food competition without French participation would lack legitimacy . . . the organizers hinted that the fact that in 1976 France had tied with America . . . had left the taste of sour grapes in French mouths." (Ferdinand Metz, captain of the 1976 United States team, does not recall any visible outrage from the French team when the results were announced that year. "All I can tell you is that we were there in '76, we tied France for third, and they didn't show up any more," he said.)

The most seismic shift in the Bocuse d'Or since its debut has been the food, which has become increasingly ornate with each passing contest. The cuisine presented in the first few Bocuse d'Ors might have come straight from the pages of *Larousse Gastronomique* or one of the other bibles of classic French cooking—a whole salmon sliced open at the back, gutted, and decorated with compositions of roe and vegetables, truffle-topped suprêmes of fatted Bresse hen, glazed vegetables, and so on. In 1989, Luxembourg's Lea Linster, the lone woman champion in Bocuse d'Or history, made the centerpiece of her meat platter a saddle of lamb in a potato crust. The recipe, published in the book *Gourmet Challenge* (Glénat, 2005), is scarcely more complicated than that for a standard-issue potato pancake wrapped around a portion of lamb saddle, briefly grilled and finished in the oven.

Linster, who was on hand in Orlando and still serves her Bocuse d'Or menu today at her self-titled restaurant in Luxembourg, claims that she had never cooked all of her components at the same time until she was actually in the competition kitchen in Lyon, an approach that would all but cinch a last-place finish today, as many teams execute scores of practice runs to master ever-more-elaborate compositions. Modern Bocuse d'Or platters resemble little culinary circuses, showcasing bits of derring-do that food enthusiasts would associate more with sweet than savory cooking: pastry cups, tuilles, and the like. The Bocuse d'Or's own Web site marks 1991 as the dawn of "artistic" dishes, with special reference to France's gold medalist Michel Roth's jewel egg with truffle garnish, but in stylistic terms, that was just the beginning. The complexity of the food has steadily been ratcheted up year after year. The 2003 silver medalist Franck Putelat's beef platter counted among its garnishes artichoke hearts filled with a foie gras "crème brûlée" and shingled with hand-cut zucchini petals. Serge Vieira's winning 2005 fish platter was anchored by a monkfish loin filled with a porcini mushroom saveloy sausage, ringed with batonnets of black truffle, celery, and carrot, held in place with scallop mousse, all bundled up in pork fat, seasoned with *piment d'Espelette* (a mild pepper popular in Basque cooking), steamed in the oven, and finished in a frying pan.

Assemble four or five dazzling components like that on a custom-designed platter and the effect suggests a dance sequence that Busby Berkeley might have dreamed up had he gone to sleep on a woefully empty stomach. These visual pyrotechnics must be largely responsible for the popularity of the Bocuse d'Or. After all, spectators can only look; they can't taste, and that's just as true for those who follow the event on television or via the Internet. But for all the allure of the presentations, there's a potential downside: If the food weren't so technically sound and didn't taste so good, it would qualify as a parody of the excesses of fine dining. And it's so expensive to produce—requiring huge investments of money and time—that many feel it still has very little application outside of competition.

"It's like the haute couture fashion shows in Paris," said former White House chef Walter Scheib. "The stuff may look great but nobody's ever going to wear it."

But the organizers and supporters of the Bocuse d'Or passionately believe that the event's value transcends the superficial, combining the showstopping presentations and technical rigors of cold-food competitions with the insanely high pressure and, most important, taste expectation of a world-class restaurant kitchen. Bocuse *himself* insists that taste—which accounts for two-thirds of the score, forty of sixty possible points from each judge—must always be front and center. To illustrate his point, he likes to tell the following story: "A maitre d' comes into the dining room with a dish from a chef. He shows it to the guest and says, 'Look at what the chef did. The architecture! This is a work of art.'" Bocuse then pantomimes the customer handing the dish back to the maitre d'. "The guest says, 'Can you frame it for me, please?' *The cuisine is first to be tasted, not to be framed.*"

Eventually, in an attempt to reign in the preoccupation with presentation, and because it had gotten to the point that, according to Bocuse, some teams "were coming with [platters the size of] soccer fields," Bocuse and his colleagues imposed a size limit on the platters: no larger than forty-three by twenty-seven inches, *including handles*.

Yet the Bocuse d'Or hasn't become the platform for world cuisine that its founder originally envisioned. After a few years, most competitors, no matter from where they hailed, began cooking in a classic French style, perhaps because in 1987, the first, tone-setting year that the Bocuse d'Or was held, it was won by French candidate Jacky Fréon.

"They saw that France and the people that were cooking a little more traditional had more chance of winning," said Jérôme Bocuse, who acted as the English-language emcee for the past several Bocuse d'Ors. A number of observers, Thomas Keller among them, have concluded that when you bring together judges from twenty-some countries, the food most will understand is classic French. "I don't know if a single man can have that knowledge of twenty-three different cuisines and . . . how they should taste," said Jérôme Bocuse.

Incidentally, the Bocuse d'Or wasn't Jacky Fréon's first time in a cooking competition; he had participated in several others, including the International Culinary Olympics. In 1976.

CONTINUING WITH HIS REMARKS at the American Adventure Parlor, Thomas Keller introduced Gavin Kaysen, "a young man who I just met recently, but who I have enormous respect for, not only for what he did for the Bocuse d'Or in 2007, but for what he has done working for Daniel, because I know how difficult he can be."

Kaysen, a wisecracking, thirtyish fireplug of a chef with ink-black hair turned up in a wisp, prompting one friend to nickname him Jimmy Neutron, laughed at the joke and gave a little nod to the crowd. But in spite of his good humor, there was nothing lighthearted about this endeavor for him: Kaysen's eyes were trained on the horizon, at the last week in January, when the United States would learn how it had fared at the Bocuse d'Or for the first time since he had cooked for the Stars and Stripes.

It was Kaysen who initially whetted Boulud's appetite for the Bocuse d'Or. The two met in 2005, when Kaysen came east from El Bizcocho restaurant at the Rancho Bernardo Inn in San Diego, California, to *stage* (that is, work for a period of time, usually as an unpaid learning/growing opportunity) for Boulud in New York City. Later, whenever he came through town, Kaysen made a point of connecting with Boulud at Daniel, where Kaysen regaled him with tales of his Bocuse d'Or adventure.

Kaysen is a rare bird, a true-blue American restaurant chef who happens to have a passion for the Bocuse d'Or. He all but stumbled into the competition world at age twenty-three when the chef of El Bizcocho asked him to compete in the United States edition of the National Trophy of Cuisine and Pastry.

"I can't do this because I am French-born," the chef told him. "You have to be American-born."

Kaysen didn't have to think about his answer. "He just handed me this piece of paper and told me to do it and he was my chef so I said 'yes,'" he recalls. In time, though, Kaysen decided that the competition would be "a great opportunity to challenge my creativity and energy."

Kaysen won the contest, held at Johnson & Wales University, which qualified him for an international competition in Paris. He trained intensely, even flying in experts to help him hone his craft. When he got overseas, his first exposure to the international competition scene was intimidating. He remembers that the captain of the Norwegian culinary Olympic team "looked like Ivan Drago in *Rocky 4* . . . I was terrified. But I knew what I had to do. I had practiced it so many times and I knew what I was up against."

Kaysen placed third in the event, making him the first American to reach the podium in twenty-six years. (He also took first place for his fish platter.) This is where his Bocuse d'Or commitment began: Acclaimed French chef Pierre Gagnaire approached him and suggested that he compete in the Bocuse d'Or. "I was, like, 'That's a good idea,'" remembers Kaysen. "And that was it."

In those days, the Bocuse d'Or USA was under the stewardship of Michel Bouit, a French-born, Chicago-based chef and businessman who had served as executive director from 1991 to 2008. Kaysen enlisted a commis named Brandon Rodgers and the two practiced more than thirty times in their run-up to the American finals. In those days, teams first had to compete in one of three regional semifinals before a competition at the National Restaurant Association Show in Chicago in May 2006, at which the national team was selected.

Kaysen and Rodgers made it to the finals where, despite their preparation, they were thrown a few curveballs that tested their ability to adjust— the same way restaurant cooks have to do throughout their day, often during service. When the slicing machine they ordered didn't show up, Kaysen borrowed one from the Hobart booth at the trade show. Then, just before the competition began, an overhead light shattered, raining molten glass down on Kaysen, Rodgers, and their prepared ingredients.

Kaysen, a sports-movie fan and former high school hockey player, turned to his commis and said, "Have you ever seen the movie *The Natural*?"

"No."

"It's this baseball movie and what it comes down to is that at the end of the movie he hits this baseball and it goes so far that it hits these lights and the lights shatter. So, if that is the worst thing to happen to us today, we are going to win. So now we have fifteen minutes to clean up and go."

They cleaned up what could be cleaned up, replaced what needed to be replaced, and were up and ready again just in time for the official start. They won the event, earning the right to represent the United States in the Bocuse d'Or.

Becoming the American candidate to the world's most prestigious cooking contest was a gut-check moment for Kaysen. His life for the next eight months had changed dramatically. It wasn't just that he had to get ready for the competition: Because the Bocuse d'Or had never garnered much attention in the United States, the U.S. team had very little support.

So while many European countries buttressed their representatives with the equivalent of more than $1 million, Kaysen had to raise his own money and support, cold-calling potential sponsors and organizing fund-raising dinners in San Diego.

In retrospect, this aspect of his Bocuse d'Or campaign infuriates Kaysen, who points out that in the past, the *first* query on the questionnaire submitted to U.S. candidate finalists by Bouit was, "How do you plan to secure the funds needed to finance your training and participation in the Bocuse d'Or World Cuisine Contest?" The form went on to indicate that "Past candidates have needed as much as $150,000." ("I won the competition and was given a check that said 'minus $200,000,'" says Kaysen of his selection as the U.S. candidate, adding $50,000 to the estimate. "Dig yourself out.")

It also rankled Kaysen that, of the $150,000 mentioned in the old application, $15,000 was paid to Bouit as a management fee. In time, Kaysen developed the opinion that, rather than focusing on the financial needs of the candidate, Bouit used the Bocuse d'Or primarily as a wagon to which he could hitch his touring business, The World of MBI, which he runs with his business partner Liz Bergin (also his life partner), every two years. But Kaysen does not speak for everybody: Best-ever U.S. candidate Handke, on hand to act as a judge in Orlando, praised Bouit's organizational skills, Lyonnaise network, and deep-seated grasp of the ins and outs of the Bocuse d'Or, all of which he found indispensable when he competed. Handke enjoyed fundraising and points with pride to the fact that he helped Bouit round up his biggest posse of spectators. "Naturally, Michel is also a businessman because that is where he makes the money, when he brings a lot of people," he said.

Despite his growing discomfort with the business structure of the enterprise, Kaysen immersed himself in his preparation, engaging in more than fifty full practice sessions of more than five hours each. The attention to detail was staggering: in addition to rehearsing the preparation of the food—his platter included a Norwegian halibut torte, a Louisiana chicken pot pie, and a BBQ chicken wing served with butter-poached potato, barbecued baked beans, and a California tomato tuile—the team also packed boxes of ingredients and equipment (in the same way they would have to do in Lyon), stashed them in their cars, and orchestrated the unloading and unpacking of them.

Kaysen and Rodgers also embarked on two three-week trips to France as part of their training. (One reason for the trips was that the primary meat for 2007 was *Poulet de Bresse*, a breed of chicken from the Rhône-Alpes region that was essentially unattainable in the United States.) Bouit organized these jaunts, and even though Kaysen continued to resent the expense, he found Bouit, with his Rolodex of contacts in Lyon as big as the Ferris wheel that turns behind the statue of Louis XIV in the town's central Place Bellecour, invaluable overseas.

The trips were both productive and enchanting: when the coach that Bouit enlisted for the team proclaimed their ballotine (roll) of chicken not good enough, Bouit arranged for the team to spend a full day at Le Porcelet Rose (The Red Pig) outside of Paris. They spent hours making ballotines and videotaping the seasoned cooks making ballotines, picking up tricks for keeping the chicken intact and a methodology for adjusting the recipe based on the weight of the individual bird. At the end of the long day, they had a bottle of Champagne and ate a ballotine in the kitchen. Bouit also arranged a dinner for Kaysen and Rodgers in another kitchen, at Restaurant Paul Bocuse, and Kaysen retains a unique souvenir of the evening, one of the restaurant's spoons. (Kaysen has a technically criminal but ultimately harmless pastime—pilfering spoons from as many restaurants as possible; they are collected at home in a drawer, or mounted and framed in his living room.)

On the day of the competition in January 2007, for the first time all week, it snowed. At four-thirty in the morning, Kaysen—aided by his food and beverage director from the hotel, his father, his brother, and a friend—rode to the competition site with Rodgers in the same passenger bus that had been transporting Bouit's spectators around town. In the dark, nearly empty behemoth of a vehicle, with the Dave Matthews Band jamming on his headphones, Kaysen watched the white particles trickle down from the heavens, and steeled himself for the hours ahead.

Kaysen remembers the competition itself as "intense." As seems to be the case for just about everybody who's ever cooked in the Bocuse d'Or, he was struck by the crowd's decibel-level, especially the different noise-makers many teams' supporters brought along to demonstrate their enthusiasm. His kitchen was near the Swiss team's, and their fan base banged on cowbells for the last several hours of the contest. The noise and the stress produced some minor missteps: for all their planning, Kaysen and Rodgers were always ahead of schedule, and they forgot to stay hydrated by drinking water frequently or to pop the energy bars they'd brought along into their mouths.

Team USA was also dealt a devastating blow at the last moment. When the time came to prepare the plates that would be paraded before the judges, Kaysen couldn't find the sheet pan that held his chicken wings.

"It's on my cutting board," said Rodgers, but Kaysen still couldn't find it. He asked the commis from the Institut Paul Bocuse if he knew where they were. (The Institut Paul Bocuse provides an extra commis to each team, somebody to help them with rudimentary tasks.) The commis said, "I ate them." He claimed to have mistaken them for garbage, but Kaysen privately wondered if it was sabotage.

"I wanted to stab him in the face," Kaysen said. "[But] at that point there [was] nothing I can do."

Kaysen called over Jérôme Bocuse (a stranger to him at that time), who acted as the English-language emcee through 2007 and also represented the Bocuse name at the event, but was told that nothing could be done.

When the winners were announced, Kaysen and Rodgers ended up placing fourteenth. The chef was crushed. "I felt like someone ripped my heart out of my chest," he said.

Rodgers, too, was in a state of disbelief. All that work, and they had the least successful result of any American team. Kaysen's only consolation was that the lack of attention the United States effort received would ensure that nobody noticed their failure. "Whether we got first or fourteenth, nobody would have paid attention to it in the U.S.," he said.

For Boulud, who had heard all these stories, supporting the Bocuse d'Or wasn't just an opportunity to pay homage to Paul Bocuse; it was also a way he could belatedly support something important to Kaysen, who in the intervening years had come on board as chef de cuisine of Café Boulud in New York City. Kaysen enjoys a unique relationship with the French superstar; unlike many young chefs who put on airs in hopes of currying favor or merely gaining acceptance, Kaysen was intense and irreverent. "My grandfather always told me to be myself with everybody," said Kaysen, who possesses enough confidence to have flourished under that advice. With Boulud, Kaysen's natural persona made quite an impact: "I found Gavin very cute and very young and enthusiastic, very driven, and yet I wish at the time I could have done more for him," said the chef.

Kaysen wished others could have done more for him, too. Minutes after learning his result, his resentment at the lack of financial support for Team USA boiled over. How much more could he have achieved if only he hadn't had to worry about the money as well as the food? How much mental focus could have been preserved and redirected? Standing there in the competition hall, he fumed to his friend Eric Brandt, managing partner of Brandt Beef who had journeyed to Lyon to cheer him on, that he'd never again allow the United States to be so underfunded.

"This will never happen again," he vowed.

PAUL BOCUSE HAD PICKED the right man to realize his United States dream: Daniel Boulud has a gift for getting people together socially, often with an eye toward some larger goal. "That's a fair statement," he said. "Because I think we all belong to the same fraternity, but there are different branches and some people don't always know each other . . . so when there is an opportunity to be able to bring the two together, I think it is important."

And so Boulud arranged a trip to San Francisco the first weekend of March 2009 to attend La Paulée, a Grand Burgundy tasting that draws chefs from around the world. He had Kaysen join him, and the two of them planned a visit to Yountville on a Friday afternoon, along with 1995 Bocuse d'Or winner Régis Marcon, Marcon's son and cochef Jacques, and a few other friends and colleagues.

The Napa jaunt was vintage Boulud: ostensibly, its purpose was to follow through on Boulud's casual and exuberant suggestion, "Let's show Régis The French Laundry!" But in reality, it was a carefully orchestrated series of "coincidences" that brought together Keller, Marcon, and Kaysen. Marcon's presence was especially important to Kaysen because he wasn't just a past winner of the Bocuse d'Or, but also president of *L'Académie des Lauréats Bocuse d'Or*, the association of previous champions. If Keller could witness Marcon's passion and dedication to the Bocuse d'Or himself, perhaps it would entice him to join the cause.

On their arrival at The French Laundry, Keller greeted the visiting contingent in his whites. Keller always wears his whites in Yountville, where his restaurants dot the main thoroughfare, Washington Street, like properties on a Monopoly board. The French Laundry occupies an unassuming stone building at the corner of Creek Street, its Garden (typically modest Laundry-speak—except for the capital G—for the restaurant's own farm) right across the street; down the road is Bouchon, his Adam Tihany–designed dead-on replica of a French eatery with Bouchon Bakery right next door, and about half a mile down the road is Ad Hoc, which serves a set four-course menu every night.

When he's not in New York keeping tabs on Per Se and the Manhattan outpost of Bouchon Bakery, Keller lives in a house adjacent to The French Laundry property, and also—either via The French Laundry or jointly with his partners—owns the house next to The French Laundry on Washington Street and the one next to that, a 1940s ranch-style house with two bedrooms where his father, Edward, a retired Marine Corps captain, lived until his death in 2008.

Keller had his VIP guests seated in the Courtyard outside The French Laundry, and stole Boulud and Régis Marcon away for a tour of the restaurant. Then he served the group canapés, including two French Laundry classics—cornets (little ice cream-style cones) filled with salmon tartare and topped with sweet red onion crème fraîche, and oysters and pearls, a dish of lightly poached oysters atop a sabayon of pearl tapioca custard that's garnished with osetra caviar—and champagne. Afterwards, Keller himself led the group as they strolled along Washington Street to Bouchon, where he left them to enjoy lunch, returning at its conclusion.

Following the meal, over espressos in California, Boulud began chatting up his old friend from New York about the Bocuse d'Or. Keller, whose cautious, analytical nature is among his most defining attributes, wasn't unmoved by the passion on display, but he confined himself to practical questions, such as "What would my role be?"

Boulud's answer, as it often is to these kinds of things, was "Don't worry about it, Thomas; you won't have to do anything." But Keller was wise enough, about Boulud and life, to know that more due diligence was in order. Among his concerns was the fact that they were already into March, and his calendar, kept by his assistant, Molly Ireland, did not have the Bocuse d'Or factored into it. With less than a year to prepare for the contest the next January, this was no small matter; the reservation book at The French Laundry is opened just two months before a given date, but Keller's dance card has commitments up to twelve months away. In addition to being a chef, said Ireland, "he's also the executive of a 900-plus person company." Ireland also said that it's important to Keller that no matter where he is in the world, he be available "to keep mentoring staff and be available to them, and that requires a lot of time as well."

Kaysen didn't say much at the meeting, but he was—figuratively if not physically—at the edge of his seat, and he welcomed it when Keller turned to him and asked what he thought of the competition. He told Keller that the only way to secure the sponsorships required to fund a legitimate U.S. effort was to have the best chefs in the country, if not the world, on board.

Keller nodded his understanding. "I'm sure," he said. But he didn't say any more than that.

And so, on the drive back to San Francisco, Boulud told Kaysen that the time had come to unholster the big gun. The necessary next step in a series of diplomatic gestures and maneuvers required to fulfill Paul Bocuse's request was to have Monsieur Paul, as Bocuse is known in France, give Thomas Keller a call and formally ask him to take over as president of the Bocuse d'Or USA. Boulud felt that the wheels had been sufficiently greased. He would call Bocuse himself and let him know the time was right to make his overture.

Keller might not have given his "yes" just yet, but with a request on tap from Bocuse himself, everybody already knew what the answer would be.

As KELLER WOUND UP his Epcot remarks, introducing the chefs on hand to serve as judges in the coming days, Jennifer Pelka, an exceedingly extroverted twenty-six-year-old brunette, watched from the back of the reception, savoring a rare break and a sorely needed glass of wine, a respite from a summer of late nights worthy of a political operative.

With no support staff and precious little direct experience, Pelka had spent the past several months obsessively coproducing this weekend, helping bring to life all aspects of the Bocuse d'Or USA finals from her headquarters in the bowels of Restaurant Daniel, down below East Sixty-fifth Street in midtown Manhattan. There, Pelka operates out of a glass-walled office she shares with A. J. Schaller, Culinary Communications Director for Dinex Group, Boulud's corporation. The two face each other across two long and cluttered desks, a near-avalanche of reference books bending the shelves built into the wall behind them. A former cook and caterer, Pelka has the title of research assistant to Daniel Boulud, a job that can mean anything from writing the daily menu at Daniel (which can devour up to five hours on some days), to coordinating packaging and messaging with the manufacturer of Daniel Boulud Kitchen Spices, to conducting research and honchoing specific projects related to new restaurants and charity events.

"When something creative pops up in Daniel's world, and he wants to work on it, then he will often call me in and then set me off on it," summarized Pelka.

While Pelka spends her days below ground, Boulud hovers above it. He shares an office over the kitchen at Daniel with his assistant, Vanessa Absil, herself a native of France, a willowy, bashful woman in her mid-twenties who once studied in Lyon. The office is awash in energy, heightened by the steep, submarine-like steel stairway that ascends to the space, and by the room in which Boulud takes his meetings, called the Skybox: a windowed pen, separated from the office by swinging vented doors, and festooned with framed photographs of Boulud with everybody from Andy Warhol to Robert DeNiro to Barack Obama in his senatorial days—snapshots of more than twenty years in the public eye. The Skybox overlooks the expansive kitchen, all steel and copper by day, a swirl of white jackets by night—an odd, majestic cross between a grand, turn-of-the-century galley and an operating-room theater.

In March 2008, after a brief stint working in the kitchen of Daniel, Pelka had recently returned to the company in a nonkitchen capacity, and her job description was still being formulated. As the chef was between assistants, Pelka took a turn at the assistant's desk in Boulud's office.

Boulud's first impulse to move the Bocuse d'Or USA forward had been simply to tap Kaysen for an encore effort, but when he mentioned it to him, his protégé's response, delivered in his typically quotable style, was a conversation killer: "No problem, Chef," said Kaysen, "I'd love to do it. I'll just need six months off and three hundred thousand dollars." Boulud also found out from Bocuse d'Or Contest Manager Florent Suplisson that the organization prefers that candidates be selected via some form of competition, as was now the case on three continents with the Bocuse d'Or Europe, Bocuse d'Or Asia, and the Copa Azteca in Mexico City.

On March 7, Boulud, commonly referred to as DB among his staff—a casual touch that undercuts the chef's French heritage and the formality of his flagship restaurant—told Pelka they were going to need to find a candidate. By her own admission, Pelka knew nothing about Paul Bocuse beyond his famous moniker, and had never heard of the Bocuse d'Or. But before she could do the necessary Googling, she and Boulud had relocated to the Skybox and set about hatching a plan.

In many ways, Boulud is the unofficial mayor of the New York City chef community. Not only is he one of just a handful of them to hold a coveted four-star *New York Times* rating, but he also relishes socializing and networking in addition to empire building. From 2000 to 2009, at an age when many chefs are plotting their retirement, he added seven restaurants to his portfolio in locations as diverse as Beijing, and Vancouver, British Columbia. His boundless energy is legendary, as are the occasional late-night dinners he throws, welcoming fellow chefs to an after-hours feast. "Daniel is the life of the party," said Per Se's Benno, who worked for Boulud in the 1990s at Daniel, then located in its original space on East 76th Street (now home to Café Boulud). "[He] is up on the bar at four in the morning, dancing, screaming at the top of his lungs, and is back in the kitchen at seven the next morning."

Boulud and Pelka created a network of possible "committee" members to help with "influence, expertise, [and] fund raising," and a list of possible sponsors, which Pelka divided into cash and "see above potential committee members," meaning for in-kind contributions of products and services. Having expedited these first tasks, Pelka recognized that the job she had just been given was colossal, but she wouldn't have had it any other way. She found Boulud's enthusiasm and go-for-broke impulsiveness contagious, and always had.

THE FRENCH TERM *MISE en place* refers to having everything in its place. In American kitchens where French terminology still rules, it describes the order a chef or cook desires before service begins. *Mise en place* means that you are ready to perform, everything is a grab away, and just the way you want it. You are set up for success.

During the rest of that March, Boulud, Pelka, and Kaysen, with intermittent participation from Keller as his schedule allowed, established what the ideal mise en place would be for Bocuse d'Or USA success. Boulud conceived the plan of action the way a chef approaches a dish, building a base, then adding layers in a carefully considered fashion, each following logically the one that preceded it.

A few pieces had already fallen into place: once he was on board, Keller had offered up his father's old house in Yountville, which he had been planning to convert into a research and development facility for his company, as a training center. His vision was to install equipment identical to the competition kitchen so Team USA could practice with the same stoves, ovens, and other equipment that they'd be cooking on in January. The house also had two bedrooms where the team could stay while they trained. Jérôme Bocuse, meanwhile, had suggested making the team trials part of the Epcot International Food & Wine Festival, a forty-five day celebration that takes place in the late summer and would provide a built-in audience to cheer on the competitors as they vied for the honor of representing the United States. He phoned Nora Carey, director of the event, who had *just* left a planning meeting for the next year when he reached her, and had no room in her budget for another event. But this was the Bocuse family asking; she just couldn't say "no." So she forged an alliance with some like-minded members of the Disney food and beverage team, and made the rounds until they had secured all the necessary executive buy-in. (For Keller, it would be the second "collaboration" with Disney. The creative team behind the Disney-Pixar film *Ratatouille* spent time working with the chef at The French Laundry as part of their research, and Keller designed the *confit byaldi*—the elegant interpretation of ratatouille assembled in thinly sliced concentric rings instead of rough-cut vegetables—that Remy the Rat prepares at the film's climax.)

Boulud's next step was to approach a who's who of famous American chefs—or at least chefs who worked in America—to ask them to become members of the "US Committee for the Bocuse d'Or." In the last week of the month, Boulud sent out e-mails, "signed" by himself and Keller, asking fellow luminaries to affiliate their names with the effort. "By having your association as a US Committee member," it read, "we will gain leverage to:

> Support fundraising and sponsorship efforts

> Increase awareness of the Bocuse d'Or among our peers

> Encourage young chefs to apply to compete

> Honor Mr. Bocuse with your affiliation."

With the request coming from Boulud and Keller—and with the reference to paying homage to Bocuse himself—the response from many of the country's most celebrated chefs was—what else?—*"Oui, Chef."* Boulud also pulled off the rare feat of convincing the editors of the three top competing American food magazines—Dana Cowin of *Food & Wine*, Ruth Reichl of *Gourmet*, and Barbara Fairchild of *Bon Appétit*—plus Martha Stewart to sign on as the Media Advisory Board.

In mid-April, with the first members of the committee (in time it would be renamed the Advisory Board) secured, Boulud approached the all-important sponsors with a letter inviting them to participate in the undertaking. Again, the yeses came fast and furiously: All-Clad Metalcrafters LLC, Krups, Diageo, Enodis, and Moët Hennessy USA all ponied up what Pelka refers to as "substantial financial support" as well as in-kind contributions of goods and services, for either training, hospitality in Orlando, or both. For example, Enodis, the company that installs the competition kitchens in Lyon, would furnish the equipment for the team trials and the Yountville training facility. Other sponsors followed in waves: Avero, which sells data-tracking software to restaurants, and American Express made financial contributions; Brandt Beef, a Brawley, California-based purveyor popular with top American restaurants, provided meat for the candidates to train with, and Pierless Fish, also a favorite among acclaimed U.S. chefs, did the same with the seafood; Rougié, the Périgord, France, foie gras company and a sponsor of the Bocuse d'Or mothership in Lyon, provided foie gras for events; Chefwear came through with jackets for candidates and judges; Petrossian Caviar provided caviar for a planned gala dinner at Epcot; and on and on.

Finally, after nearly three months of accelerated preparation, the Bocuse d'Or USA went public on May 28, 2008, with the launch of a Web site that greeted visitors with thunderous music (a hymn composed especially for the Bocuse d'Or in Lyon by Serge Folie in 2003) and a video montage of Bocuse d'Or moments. It was more ESPN than Food Network, depicting screaming fans, a media pit packed with photographers, and a medal ceremony.

Press attention was swift: By two thirty that afternoon, *New York* magazine's Grub Street blog was up with a post entitled "Everything You Wanted to Know About the Bocuse d'Or Competition But Were Afraid to Ask" detailing the involvement of Boulud and Keller, partially listing the Advisory Board, and linking to the application. "If you think you have the stuff to represent the United States in the so-called cooking Olympics," wrote blogger Josh Ozersky, "just fill out the application, send it in to Bocuse d'Or USA, and cross your fingers. You might be the one who brings the glory back home."

Not all members of the inner circle welcomed the attention. Kaysen, who knew what was required to win, place, or show at the Bocuse d'Or, was concerned that it raised expectations that would be difficult, if not impossible, to meet. "If we didn't walk out of that stadium with first, second, or third, people were going to take their shots at it," he recalled later. But Boulud insists that publicity was essential to raising money and attracting the best candidates. To that end, the same day the Web site launched, a call for applications went around as Boulud disseminated e-mails and letters to about three hundred restaurants—James Beard Foundation award winners, top *Zagat*-rated restaurants in key markets, possessors of Michelin stars, and so on—not necessarily urging the executive chefs themselves to apply, but rather asking them to encourage a talented staff member to get in the game.

The application itself was much more than a name-rank-and-serial-number affair—it was the first elimination round, contested on paper, and it was a daunting document comprising several parts: biographical information on the candidate and the commis, plus a one-page resumé, a four by five-inch matte-finish recent photograph (in chef's whites), two letters of recommendation, and a "letter of motivation" (750 words or fewer) described as "a personal statement for representing the United States at the Bocuse d'Or World Contest."

The applicants were also directed to share descriptions of the food they planned to prepare for the competition if they were selected: fish and meat dishes, each featuring the main protein plus three garnishes. "Harmony of flavor will be deemed very important, but we impose no constraints on competitors' creativity in terms of preparation or presentation."

So that the Orlando event would double as a dry run for the Bocuse d'Or in Lyon, the teams were to use many of the same proteins that would be used in France. The selections change every two years. In 2009, they would be seafood from Norway (Norwegian fresh cod, Norwegian king scallops, and Norwegian wild prawns). The beef would be Scotch Beef Aberdeen Angus (oxtail, *côte de boeuf*, beef cheeks, and one whole fillet [tenderloin]). The Bocuse d'Or USA candidates would not be using the same brands of fish and beef, but they would be required to employ a similar combination of types and cuts.

The last page of the application was a pledge form in which the candidate promised to be available for all events related to the Bocuse d'Or, and to "train intensely" for the Bocuse d'Or, working "closely with chef coaches (provided by Bocuse d'Or USA) to perfect all aspects of my dishes, including their timing, presentation, and taste."

———

ON COMPLETING HIS REMARKS, Keller turned the floor over to Michel Bouit, the man who had served as the executive director of the Bocuse d'Or USA for the past twenty years, and whose energetic stride to the center of the room concealed a bruised ego. If the new Bocuse d'Or USA had jettisoned anybody on its way to the future, it was Bouit, who was not consulted about the change of stewardship until things were well under way. Although he later said that he had no hard feelings about how things played out, Bouit didn't appreciate that the first moves were made without his knowledge while he and Bergin were gearing up for the selection of the next American team. He was also outraged when he found his name slotted in alphabetically with the other members of the newly formed advisory board, which he took as a slap in the face, albeit an unintentional one, after twenty years. According to Bouit, he made his upset known and was elevated up away from the pack and listed as "Honorary President," a role in which he would advise the new guard and assist with logistics and lodging on the ground in Lyon.

French-born but an American citizen since 1975, Bouit put the politics of the past few months aside as he greeted the room with the unbridled enthusiasm of a ringside announcer: "Good evening!" he exclaimed. "Are you excited?" Then he summarized the twenty-year history of the American effort at the Bocuse d'Or. In 1987, there was no competition to represent the United States; Chef Fernand Gutierrez of the Ritz-Carlton Hotel in Chicago had simply tapped a sous chef from one of the hotel's cafés, Susan Weaver. "Fernand went to her and said, 'Susan, guess what, you are going to Lyon.' That is how it happened."

In reality, Weaver's Bocuse d'Or saga was a bit more complicated than that. According to Weaver, who today is chef-partner in several restaurants owned and operated by Lettuce Entertain You in Chicago, Gutierrez's vision "was for me to be able to prove myself as a woman." To avoid any pushback from the event organizers in those unenlightened days, Weaver and Guitierrez filled out all of her candidate paperwork under the name S. Weaver.

"It was the only way to do it," recalls Weaver. "Because if they had known that I was a woman chances are it never would have happened . . . they did not know I was a woman until I went."

In preparation for the Bocuse d'Or, Weaver did five practice runs of her fish platter (salmon was the main protein selection) but only three of her meat (Bresse chicken), because "I never expected to go to the final." (Whereas today all teams present both fish and meat platters, in the first year the fish platters served as the initial round, dubbed the "semifinals", and only the top eleven chefs went on to prepare their meat platters in the finals the next day. This was changed after many eliminated candidates groused over rehearsing two courses only to serve one.)

"Honestly," Weaver said, "I thought, *Okay, this is the semifinal; let's really work this and make it really strong and if by some fluke I get into the finals I have something prepared.* But it wasn't detailed and finessed."

When she arrived in Lyon, although nobody outright dissed her, Weaver remembers that she wasn't treated seriously. "But I think at that point in my career, it wasn't new to me. It was part and parcel of how things were. For me, it was put your game face on, put your head down as best you can, and try not to embarrass yourself. At that time I was a sous chef at the Ritz-Carlton. I was making burgers and French onion soup. I was up against the top chefs in the world . . . I was working hard. I did not have the experience or the position of the [other] competing chefs."

When Weaver shocked the Sirha and landed in the top five on Day One, qualifying for the finals, "all hell broke loose. . . . It was hilarious. It was almost like—*gotcha!*" she laughs today. "Paul Bocuse and all the disciples were all of a sudden with me, getting their pictures taken with the utmost respect." For Weaver, the mission was already accomplished. "I wasn't doing it to win; I was doing it to gain credibility and validity as a woman chef, and sticking my head outside of the kitchen."

Of the first Bocuse d'Or, Weaver recalls that at the time, it was a bigger food event than anybody had ever staged. "It was more like a hockey game," she said of the bleacher seating and boisterous crowd. There was even a home team—the French, in the person of candidate Jacky Fréon. Weaver didn't mind at all; because all eyes were on him in the final, virtually nobody noticed when an oil spill in her kitchen caused a *fire*.

"Once they got past the fact that I was a woman and that I could actually cook and beat out the majority of these guys, they had a twinkle in their eye for me. They were like, 'Okay, then!' They nicknamed me *La Petite Américaine*. If you see Paul Bocuse today, and ask him about *La Petite Américaine*, he remembers."

Weaver was followed by Jeff Jackson from the Park Hyatt in Chicago in 1989, then by George Bumbaris from the Ritz-Carlton, who placed seventh and received the prize for Best Fish in 1991. (Best Fish and Best Meat are Bocuse d'Or consolation prizes, somewhat misnamed because they are handed out to the top-scoring platters in those categories *outside the top three*.) In 1993, the first non–Windy City candidate was fielded, Ron Pietruszka from the Hotel Nikko in Beverly Hills, California, who placed ninth. From there, the results were an up-and-down affair: in 1995, Paul Sautory from The Culinary Institute of America placed thirteenth, and the next three candidates placed eighth, ninth, and tenth, in that order.

In 2003, Handke's sixth-place finish (and Best Meat booby prize) set the high-water mark, but the Sisyphean American history next logged an eleventh-place finish by Fritz Gitschner in 2005, followed by Kaysen's fourteenth place result.

Bouit concluded and proceeded to introduce the chefs and commis who would be cooking and competing over the next two days . . .

AMONG THE APPLICANTS WAS Rogers Powell, for whom the Bocuse d'Or represented an opportunity to sweeten a sour moment from his past. An instructor at The French Culinary Institute (FCI) in New York City, Pow-

ell was one of the few who wasn't immediately put off by the rigorous nature of the application and the short turnaround time of just four weeks.

In 1996, Powell had found himself in a perhaps-permanent hiatus from
his culinary career. To pay the rent, he worked for his uncle's business, pro-
moting a man-sized robot with a pivoting head at trade shows around the
world. (The robot was immortalized in cinema when Rocky Balboa gave
one to brother-in-law Paulie in *Rocky IV*.) One day, while waiting to board
a flight to an expo in Portugal, Powell's friend Jean-Jacques tapped him on
the shoulder.

"Look who's over there!" he said.

Powell turned to see Paul Bocuse and another legendary chef, Joël Robuchon, recognizable even without their chef's whites and toques. "We all
knew Bocuse," said Powell, whose childhood was spent shuttling back and
forth from New York to France. "When you go to culinary school, you
study him."

Deciding to have a little fun, Powell discretely worked the robot's con-
trols, causing it to slide across the terminal's slick floor and up to the chefs.
Arriving at Bocuse's side, the robot (actually Powell via a tiny remote microphone that he cupped in his hand) spoke to them in its tinny, electronic
staccato: "Hello, Mr. Bocuse. Hello, Mr. Robuchon. I like my steak medium rare."

The chefs and fellow passengers chuckled agreeably, then boarded the
flight. Powell took his seat in first class, disassembling the robot and parking its torso in the seat the company purchased for it. Hours later, waiting
for the other passengers to deplane in Portugal, Powell felt a hand on his
shoulder. He looked up and saw Bocuse staring down at him, a friendly
smile forming beneath his hawk-like eyes.

"Good luck, *l'artiste*," said Bocuse, having determined that Powell was
responsible for the preflight entertainment.

Powell almost told Bocuse that he, too, was a chef, but it felt a bit silly
under the circumstances. In time, he found his way back to the kitchen,
and eventually to a role helping to train future chefs. Now, he explained

in his letter of inspiration, he was eager for the challenge presented by the Bocuse d'Or, and to meet Bocuse himself "as a chef, not a comedian."

About forty miles away from Powell and the FCI was John Rellah Jr. Even devoted foodies haven't heard of Rellah, but years ago he cooked in the rarefied air of Gray Kunz's kitchen at the opulent restaurant Lespinasse, working as a *chef de partie* (station chief) alongside future celebrity chefs such as Cornelius Gallagher and Rocco DiSpirito. There are plenty of men and women out there who, like Rellah, flirted with big-city gastronomy but ended up leaving the metropolis for the quiet pastures of suburbia or the country. By 2007 Rellah had become the chef of Hamilton Farm Golf Club in Gladstone, New Jersey. He saw the Bocuse d'Or as a challenge into which he could pour his amassed knowledge, much of which was gathering dust in some nether region of his brain, and set about preparing an application.

In Philadelphia, twenty-nine-year-old Kevin Sbraga, culinary director of the Garces Restaurant Group, heard about the Bocuse d'Or USA from a weekly e-mail he received from StarChefs, an online magazine for foodservice professionals. He had recently seen a documentary on Food Network about Tracy O'Grady, the American who competed in 2001, and remembered it well. Sbraga, a former high-school wrestler from Burlington County, New Jersey, who attended Johnson & Wales University on scholarship, had participated in three small-scale cooking competitions as a student and enjoyed it, and this seemed like the ultimate culinary throwdown. "It was almost like magic," he said. "I thought, *I've got to do this*."

One of Sbraga's competitors had experience in a different type of culinary competition. In June, at the *Food & Wine* Magazine Classic at Aspen, Hung Huynh, the season three winner of *Top Chef*, picked up a piece of literature from an American Express booth that alluded to its sponsorship of the Bocuse d'Or USA. *Top Chef* viewers will remember Hyunh as the ambitious, unapologetically intense Vietnamese American with mad skills; even host Chef Tom Colicchio was left speechless at the sight of Hyunh breaking down chickens in fast motion. Every reality show has one contestant (cheftestant in *Top Chef* lingo) who says things like, "I'm not here to make friends; I'm here to win." Hyunh was that guy.

Some applicants were prodded by members of the Bocuse d'Or USA organization: Michael Rotondo, the chef de cuisine of Restaurant Charlie, Charlie Trotter's Las Vegas outpost, was encouraged by Trotter himself, who had once been a judge in Lyon; Percy Whatley, the unassuming executive chef of The Ahwahnee in Yosemite, California, was nudged by both longtime acquaintance Kaysen and by Roland Henin, who oversaw him as part of his role as corporate chef of Delaware North Companies Parks & Resorts.

Henin also encouraged Richard Rosendale, chef-owner of Rosendale's restaurant in Columbus, Ohio, to apply. Rosendale, who has a large, flat nose and dark black hair combed back into a near-pompadour, had more culinary competition experience, *exponentially* more, than the rest of the field combined: a member of two United States Culinary Olympic teams, Rosendale had participated in two three-year apprenticeship programs in his young career, including one at The Greenbrier, the fabled hotel in White Sulphur Springs, West Virginia. As part of his education there, he was expected to do competition-like exercises after work such as mystery baskets (cooking spontaneously from an unannounced selection of ingredients) or putting up buffet platters. These sessions lasted until about two in the morning, and included a critique by his supervisors, who offered no leniency. "The expectation was perfection all the time," said Rosendale.

Though the next installment of the Olympics was set to start on October 19, just a few weeks after the event in Orlando, Rosendale was attracted to the opportunity presented by the new Bocuse d'Or USA. "I really want to see an American win," he said. "We have way too many talented chefs not to have placed any higher than we have."

Rosendale could have been channeling Kaysen when he said that the reason the United States hadn't done better in the past wasn't the candidates, but the resources. "People underestimate how much it takes, not just the commitment from the candidate but financial resources. When you're trying to figure out what one of your garnishes is going to be and trying to figure out how you're going to pay for that via a fundraiser, [it's] a very difficult thing to do. *Plus* your day-to-day job."

That's what attracted Rosendale to the Bocuse d'Or USA in 2008: with the involvement of Boulud and Keller, and the attendant money that had rolled in, "the United States has its ducks in a row," he said.

As THE APPLICATION DEADLINE neared, on the evening of June 23, in Yountville, California, in the kitchen of The French Laundry, Timothy Hollingsworth, a sous chef with an all-American visage, brawny build, and tousled sandy blond hair, looked at the ticket in his hand and called out to the kitchen brigade, "Ordering two tasting menus."

"Two!" called back the cooks stationed around the room. It was a uniform response. A military response. The commander had spoken and the troops would execute his order. The immediacy and intensity of the callback—and it *always* came with comparable force—left no doubt of that. As Keller himself says, "It is a command-response environment in a kitchen."

Different kitchens are organized differently, but each of them has a chain of command. At The French Laundry in June 2008, Corey Lee was the chef de cuisine, and Devin Knell the executive sous chef. There were two sous chefs: Hollingsworth and Anthony Secviar. On any given night, any of these men might be expediting—executing "his" menu (more on this in a moment)—and any of the others might be stationed at the SAS (sous chef assistant station), acting as first lieutenant. After that came the chefs de partie. These were the people who worked the kitchen that year, and cooked the food that is almost unanimously considered the best in the United States and among the very best in the world. At the top of the kitchen's unwritten org chart was Chef-Proprietor (Chef Patron in the classic French vernacular) Thomas Keller. Although Keller no longer cooked or expedited in the kitchen with any regularity—a concession, he says, to the toll it took on his body—his restaurants continued to operate in his image, run by people who for the most part idolize the chef and his role in the industry, some of whom had spent years at The French Laundry working their way up from commis to line cook to chef de partie to, in the case of Hollingsworth, sous chef.

The two prep rooms just beyond the kitchen were lit, but nearly silent, the sounds of the hot line echoing against their white tiled surfaces. That was where the meat butcher, commis, and externs toiled by day, under the direction of morning sous chef Walter Abrams, beginning at 5:30 a.m. The commis do the prep work for the restaurant, everything from turning root vegetables (peeling and shaping them into uniform shapes, not unlike elongated footballs) to making pasta to baking melba toasts, and as the evening crew prepares for service, the commis are cleaning up their area, splashing hot, sudsy water around and wiping the surfaces to a shimmer before departing for the evening.

At the end of the night, Hollingsworth and his cooks scrubbed down *their* stations. Everybody who works in Thomas Keller's kitchens cleans; it's practically a way of life. When Hyunh, who briefly worked at Per Se, first met Keller, the legend himself was scouring kitchen shelves.

Hollingsworth and his crew then pulled stools up around the stoves and went through a nightly exercise: creating the menu for the next time Hollingsworth would be expediting. This is a hallmark of both The French Laundry and Per Se: the creation of the menu, daily, by the cooks who work there. According to Hollingsworth, the reason for this is that by helping to conceive the food they cook, each team member will be more personally invested in it, and that will show up in the final dishes.

In these meetings, the kitchen takes on the air of an academy. Every cook contributes ideas to the menu. If Hollingsworth likes one, he'll nod and write it down. If he doesn't, he'll try to help the cook find his way to a better place, offering suggestions or employing the Socratic method. (For example, "Tarragon with that? You sure?" Translation: "Tarragon with that is a *bad* idea.")

The next afternoon, June 24, as Hollingsworth was turning some carrots at the SAS, Executive Chef Corey Lee—a slight, quietly intense Korean American with a shaved head—came up behind him.

"You want to do the Bocuse d'Or?" asked Lee, characteristically dispensing with any small talk. Hollingsworth was used to it. The two young men were good friends and former housemates and had been working long hours together for several years. Hollingsworth knew about Keller's association with this year's Bocuse d'Or, but he himself hadn't taken an interest in it. In fact, he used to make fun of the contest. Years earlier, he had rented a modest house in Yountville, known to insiders as the Pink Place, and took on subtenants to help pay the rent, sometimes housing them on the living room sofa. Most of them were foreign cooks working stages and externships at The French Laundry. (A sign of the uptick in global respect for American cuisine over the past two decades is the fact that European cooks now come to a place like Yountville questing for knowledge, which would have been unimaginable twenty years ago.)

In 2001, a Bocuse d'Or year, Hollingsworth had a Scandinavian housemate, Jonas Lundgren from Sweden, who would talk about the competition—who was competing, who had won in years past, and so on. Hollingsworth had never heard of it, nor did he have any interest in cooking competitions—"not at all, zero" is how he gauged it at the time—but this guy was into it, and even spoke of competing himself someday. Hollingsworth would tease Lundgren, poking fun at the turducken competitions and similar events his roommate described. "I kind of frowned upon it," Hollingsworth says. In the small-world department, by the time Lee approached Hollingsworth, Lundgren had already been selected as the 2009 candidate for Sweden, but that didn't change Hollingsworth's mind. "Nah," he said, "I'm a restaurant chef, not a competition chef."

Lee seemed disappointed.

"Would you do it?" Hollingsworth asked.

"If I were going to do a cooking competition, this is the one I'd do," said Lee, referencing the history and renown of the event.

"Let me think about it," said Hollingsworth. Lee had Carey Snowden, the restaurant's culinary assistant, print out the application and some other information for Hollingsworth to peruse.

Hollingsworth spent some time at home that night looking over the material, as well as surfing the Internet at his one-bedroom apartment on Main Street in Napa, about nine vineyard-lined miles south of Yountville, just off Route 29. What he saw didn't particularly interest him: the kaleidoscopic presentations and the fact that there were platters involved seemed terribly old-fashioned, manipulated, and show-offy, not really what one associates with the restaurant where he'd been learning and cooking since 2001. For all of its acclaim, The French Laundry remains a fundamentally unassuming place, where the kitchen's emphasis is on quality, flavor, and the satisfaction of the guest, not on inflating the cooks' egos.

"Should I do it?" he asked his girlfriend, Kate Laughlin, a transplanted Northeasterner who had been culinary liaison at Per Se before moving west and taking up a position as assistant to the chief operating officer and chief financial officer for the Thomas Keller Restaurant Group.

"Do you want to do it?" she asked. "If you want to do it, you should do it. It's a great opportunity."

Hollingsworth looked through the packet that Snowden had printed for him. The idea of completing the application, let alone conceiving the dishes, in the six remaining days before the deadline seemed undoable and unappealing.

The next day, he walked into work, went right up to Lee, and told him he wasn't interested. When Hollingsworth referred to the application as a barrier, Lee took gentle exception.

"We could get it done," he said. "We have Carey to help."

Hollingsworth didn't perceive it at the time, but he later came to believe that Lee, his friend as well as his higher-up, wanted him to apply for the Bocuse d'Or candidacy because it would be a growing experience; after so many years at The French Laundry, Hollingsworth was a prime contender to ascend into Lee's coveted position when the chef de cuisine moved on. He had periodically discussed this with Lee and occasionally with Keller over the prior twelve to eighteen months, though no final decision had been made. In reality, Lee's motives were more abstract than that: "Tim's always been someone who's looking for that next thing . . . I know that for the past couple of years he's been very restless, so . . . it made sense to me to propose this to Tim . . . to take a lot of that anxiousness and filter it into something very meaningful. . . ."

Though he sensed that he was disappointing Lee, Hollingsworth held his ground and begged off.

About a week later, The French Laundry chefs and sous chefs, including ranking members of the pastry team, were gathered around a large round table in the main dining room on the ground floor of the restaurant for one of the periodic meetings that takes place about once a quarter to sync up the various culinary groups. Keller came in during the gathering—squeezing a visit in between a meeting that went long and another that was set to begin imminently.

"I have a few things to talk about, is that okay?" he asked. Keller often waives his own authority, asking permission to speak on conference calls and in meetings where nobody would dream of denying him the floor. The gesture has the effect of shrinking the divide between his godlike stature and that of the people who work for him.

Among Keller's list of housekeeping items to discuss with his team was something new:

"So nobody wants to do the Bocuse d'Or?" he asked.

All eyes went to Hollingsworth, who aired his concerns about the application and the time frame. A bit blindsided, Hollingsworth had thought the issue was beyond moot; the official deadline was now in the past. He didn't know that Pelka, in New York, worried about receiving enough applications, and having received requests from other potential candidates seeking extensions or an okay to submit incomplete packages, had begun granting leniency in both thoroughness and punctuality. (For example,

Hung Hyunh had called that very day asking if he could still apply and was told yes.)

Lee and Secviar commented that they thought Hollingsworth should do it.

"We can get it done," said Keller. "If we want to do it, we can get it done."

For all the respect that Hollingsworth had for Lee, his contemporary and friend, as well as his superior at The French Laundry, hearing this virtually identical statement coming from Keller meant just a hair more. Tellingly, when Hollingsworth saw Lee on the streets of Yountville, or went golfing with him, he'd call him by his first name, but when he saw Keller outside "the office," he still called him Chef, and referred to him in the third person as *The* Chef. Even after almost a decade, he found the prospect of calling him Thomas "strange."

"If he says we can get it done," said Hollingsworth, "then we can get it done."

Moreover, Keller's involvement with the Bocuse d'Or and his personal interest, evident to Hollingsworth for the first time in that meeting, caused him to reevaluate on the spot. "He means a lot to me, so to support him in any way that I could, you know, I would do anything," he said.

"Okay," he said. "I'll do it."

ALL OF THE COMPETITORS and their commis were in attendance at the reception in the American Adventure Parlor, and they got a nice surprise after Bouit turned the stage over to Daniel Boulud, who invited them up to have their pictures taken with Paul Bocuse.

As the impromptu photo session took place behind him, Boulud thanked the sponsors. It seemed perfectly fitting that Keller's remarks had been about chefs, and Boulud's about business. Over the course of the just-completed summer, the two chefs' different personalities had manifested themselves in other ways as well.

Very close friends, the two men are opposites in many respects, although some facts of their lives and careers are similar. They were both born in 1955, and have what Keller describes as "this constant drive. We continue to modify and continue to make our lives better and the lives of our staff better. We hold the same values very dear." Of the pair, Per Se's Benno said that where Daniel is a social animal, "Thomas is that guy that stands off to the side and observes." But in the kitchen, they are kindred spirits: "You put an apron on those two guys and there is an intensity and an integrity and a focus and a desire to push themselves and everyone around them to the breaking point."

About Boulud, Keller said, "His career was far more advanced than mine was when we first met at the Polo restaurant. He was the sous chef and I was the chef de partie and we became friends shortly after I left and we have been in constant contact ever since. Our careers have kind of mirrored one another's. He was on the cover of *New York* magazine one year and I was on the cover the next. He would win this one year, I would win it the next. We were always on a parallel path."

But there are just as many differences between the two chefs, most ironically what Keller sees as the accident of their nationality: "He is French and I am American," says Keller, adding that, "I have always wanted to be French, and he has always wanted to be American." Boulud, who has called New York City home for decades, agrees with this observation wholeheartedly.

Getting together was an idea as irresistible to the chefs as it would be to the dining public, like the All-Stars game or a fantasy football league come to life. Eight years before the Bocuse d'Or entered their lives, they had conceived a joint project in Las Vegas that hadn't panned out, and as recently as February 2008 they'd made a speculative visit to Dubai for another project that ultimately fizzled.

Now that they were together, the differences in their personalities came into heightened relief, not least of which was Boulud's impulsiveness versus Keller's studied caution; Boulud, a fan of Formula One racing and a notoriously adventurous driver ("Don't ever get into a car with Daniel," warns Roland Henin), likes to fling himself and his team headlong into things. Keller likes to look at all the angles, ask questions, reflect, reflect some more, sleep on it, then make up his mind.

"He commits himself 100 percent, sometimes *too* early," says Keller of his friend. But Keller understands the impulse; it's the same one that led him to say, "*Oui, Chef*" to Paul Bocuse. "That is what chefs do. We are not in the industry that says *no*. We always say *yes* to people."

This yin/yang dynamic was on display when Boulud discussed the Bocuse d'Or with Diane Nabatoff, executive producer of his HDTV show, *After Hours*. According to Boulud, on hearing about the Bocuse d'Or, Nabatoff said, "Do you want to do a show?" and the two of them began discussing a limited documentary series tracking the Bocuse d'Or USA.

From that conversation, things progressed rapidly. Pelka recalls being on a ten-day cruise with her family at the beginning of July 2008, during which time she was uncharacteristically out of touch with her e-mail. When she returned, she went through her in-box and found a raft of messages from Nabatoff about an upcoming meeting at the Food Network, the Monday of her return at twelve noon.

"I didn't know anything about the presentation, what we were pitching and where we were going," said Pelka. Boulud was out of town that week, so Pelka wandered into the meeting cold. The show wasn't green-lit, but Nabatoff managed to interest Bravo network, home of *Top Chef*, in a documentary series of eight or twelve episodes (the number would be determined at a later date) for which they were prepared to finance one on a speculative basis.

To satisfy the sudden need for filmable activity, Pelka suggested taping a planned press conference to announce the candidates at db Bistro Moderne, Boulud's casual restaurant on West Forty-fourth Street. She also came up with another camera-ready idea: an orientation session for the candidates to be held on Thursday, July 24, at The French Culinary Institute (FCI) in downtown Manhattan, a briefing followed by an abbreviated cook-off of sorts, but with no winners or losers; rather it would be a chance for the organizers to offer constructive criticism prior to the Epcot event. Arrangements were made with the FCI, the idea being to sit the candidates down and give them a taste of what they'd gotten themselves into.

There was just one problem: Boulud hadn't run the idea of the series by Keller or Jérôme Bocuse, and neither was on board: "I didn't think that it was appropriate," said Keller. "It was our first time. I didn't know how things were going to go. I didn't know how the house was going to turn out. I didn't want cameras in our face at The French Laundry . . . even in Orlando I didn't think it was appropriate. These are young kids that haven't had the opportunity to get the exposure to that kind of environment. Let alone this is their first time in any competition and you are going to throw this in on top of them. Are we trying to sell a documentary on the Bocuse d'Or or are we trying to send a team there?"

Sports-fan Jérôme Bocuse circulated an e-mail making an analogy to the Olympics: "You don't send a TV crew to the training camp before they go to the world championships . . . that kind of stays secret." Like Keller, Bocuse was also concerned about unwanted distractions: "They [TV people] always tell you that they will be a fly on the wall but then they impose their schedule."

Outnumbered by his colleagues, Boulud pulled the plug on the program, and by all accounts did so quickly and graciously, even though a production team was already in New York and in preproduction mode. As a result, the Bocuse d'Or USA ended up reimbursing the producers about $10,000.

Boulud freely cops to his full-steam-ahead modus operandi. Regarding the entire incident, he said, rather cheerily, "That was again me going into overdrive with these things and full throttle trying to really get as much attention as possible." But Boulud hastened to add that he had other reasons: "I was worried [about] what am I going to give to the sponsor. What kind of return can I give besides saying, 'Oh, thank you very much for participating in this Bocuse d'Or competition.' So TV was one way for me to create some good return to the sponsor."

Of *l'affaire du documentaire*, Pelka commented, "That right there is why they [Boulud and Keller] are such a good pair . . . we occasionally jump in a little too deep and then there is the reminder that someone like Chef Keller is there who is more choosy."

THE APPLICATIONS WERE REVIEWED on Monday, July 14, in the private dining room at Daniel. Boulud met with several New York–based members of the Advisory Board and the final eight were chosen from a pool of . . . well, the committee won't say exactly how many. "Fewer than twenty," is all that Pelka will allow, though Henin, who was not present, believes the number must have been much lower.

The eight were set: Hollingsworth, Hyunh, Powell, Rosendale, Rotondo, Spraga, Whatley, and Damon Wise, executive chef of Tom Colicchio's Craft restaurant group.

As planned, the candidates were announced in a press conference at db Bistro Moderne on Thursday, July 17. The night before the press conference, Damon Wise sent Pelka an e-mail withdrawing his candidacy: "After discussion with Tom, and much thinking," he wrote, "it is not going to be possible for me to devote the amount of time needed to compete." John Rellah was slotted in as a substitute just in time for the conference, and the planned visual presentation was updated accordingly. Thank god for PowerPoint.

Though the television project was scrapped, the French Culinary Institute orientation went forward, largely due to Kaysen's support. In one of the increasingly frequent conference calls taking place in the summer of 2008, Kaysen pointed out to the group that when the competition was under the auspices of Michel Bouit, there were three regional semifinals prior to the final selection event, which were useful because they gave the candidates practice for not just the American finals but also the big show in Lyon.

In a poetic bit of misspeak, Kaysen, reflecting on his endorsement of the FCI orientation, explained that the semifinals "let us know if we were going in the right direction or shitting up a creek."

Kaysen also felt it was important that the candidates get used to being around chefs like Boulud and Keller, who might make some of them quake in their clogs when the time came to "bring it" in Orlando, and his colleagues took his recommendation. In a twist on reality TV, an event created for television had become reality. (In a sign of how quickly things were moving and how much Keller was deferring to Boulud and his team, this rationale was never shared with Keller, who couldn't be on the conference call in which it was first floated, and privately wondered if the candidates needed this extra pressure with Orlando shimmering on the horizon.)

And so on Thursday, July 24, the candidates (but not their commis), many of whom had been flown in for the event, filed into one of the demonstration rooms at the FCI and took their seats in the stands. Boulud's team, ever mindful of the value of media attention, had corralled a few journalists to attend: Florence Fabricant of *The New York Times*, Andrew Knowlton of *Bon Appétit*, and (at the urging of Keller's public relations agency) Allison Adato from *People* magazine.

Thomas Keller welcomed the chefs to the Bocuse d'Or USA. As he spoke, Chef Roland Henin stood behind him in a white chef coat with a dress shirt and tie showing between the lapels. Keller explained that the goal of the Bocuse d'Or USA this year was to "establish a strong base to continue to compete in the Bocuse d'Or in the coming years, so we're really establishing that foundation." He thanked the candidates for all their hard work getting ready for Orlando and launched into an impassioned introduction of Chef Henin who, famously, mentored Keller, who makes a point of acknowledging Henin whenever he can, in his books and even in the foreword to other people's books, such as the one he penned for the English language edition of Fernand Point's *Ma Gastronomie*.

"Chef Henin was my mentor," said Keller. "Up until we met, cooking for me was a physical thing. I really enjoyed the physical aspects of cooking, the camaraderie of the kitchen, the high intensity. Chef Henin made me realize what cooking was all about, and that was a connection to another person, nurturing, an emotional connection that really resonated with me and really began my career as a true culinarian."

Ever cautious, Keller said that Henin's role as coach would be crucial in "I don't want to say *winning* the Bocuse d'Or, but in our *progression* to win the Bocuse d'Or someday."

"Thank you, Chef," said Henin as he took the dais.

For all of the dignity on display, these two men's initial meeting, in 1977, on the beach of Narragansett, Rhode Island, was anything but high minded. Henin was the chef of the Dunes Club then, and he and his crew took a break most afternoons to play Frisbee on the beach before dinner service. On some days, he noticed a young, handsome stranger always in the company of one—sometimes *two*—beautiful women.

"I said, 'Look at this guy: He is tall; I am tall. He is skinny; I am skinny. He doesn't have an accent; I *do*.' And here he was walking the beach with these beautiful women, and it was, like, *How does he do it?*"

One late afternoon, with the sun waning on the horizon and the surf breaking on the shore, Henin saw the stranger with two leggy companions and, unable to stand it any longer (and presumably hoping that maybe he could take one of the women off the young man's hands), "accidentally" flung a Frisbee in his direction. When he went to retrieve it, the two men got to talking. The young, skinny stranger was Thomas Keller, and he identified himself as a chef.

"So am I," said Henin and, forgetting his original motives, offered his young colleague a tour of his kitchen, a large, old-fashioned warhorse, with a gigantic rotisserie and an actual office for the chef.

"He was pretty impressed with the size of the kitchen," remembers Henin. "I don't think that he was ever exposed to a kitchen that was like this."

"How does a guy get a job like this?" asked Keller.

"This might be your lucky day," said Henin, whose staff chef had just abruptly quit. The staff meals were a constant thorn in Henin's side because many of the club's employees were children of locals and club members, "brats" who constantly complained about the quality of their meals.

"There is only one rule," Henin warned. "Get them off my back!"

Keller took over as staff chef at the Dunes Club. "Within two or three days, he shut them up," said Henin. "I don't know what he did, but that was it." "The most challenging and amazing part of that job," Keller recalls today, "was my contact with the individuals I was cooking for. I had never experienced that previously and it truly motivated me to be a better cook. There is no substitute for personal contact with individuals you are cooking for. You truly feel that you have nourished them."

Later that summer, Henin's p.m. saucier left his job, and it was too late in the season to make a new hire, so he offered Keller the position.

"I am not too knowledgeable with classical sauces," said the young cook.

" 'Don't worry,' " said Henin. " 'I will work with you.' And I did. I helped him to produce a sauce or whatnot for the rest of the summer . . . I would put him on the track and then he would do the service."

Even then, Henin remembers, Keller "was always very organized, clean and neat."

The two men didn't really hang out together that much outside of the kitchen, maybe just an occasional beer, but Henin became a sort of spiritual and professional adviser to Keller, recommending him to friends in Florida, where they both migrated after the northeastern summer, and eventually pointing him to the right kitchens in France for stages and such. When Keller became the chef at La Rive in Catskill, New York, Henin was teaching at The Culinary Institute of America, and Keller—who decided against culinary school, opting instead for the artisanal route—would occasionally visit and observe a class. By the same token, Henin who was a long-distance runner, sometimes spent weekends at La Rive in order to train on the hills.

Keller remembers Henin as the man he would turn to for advice, saving up questions—such as how to roast a leg of lamb or make *pâte à choux*—for when they next saw each other. Keller has memorialized these moments in his writings, such as the essay on the importance of knowing how to truss a chicken in *The French Laundry Cookbook*. He also remembers a formative moment when they were together at a restaurant in Lake Park, Florida. "I had the book, *The Great Chefs of France*, and I was going through that and I said, 'What makes these chefs so great?' He told me it was dedication, their love for what they do. Their pure dedication and determination. It is a life-style and not a job, and that resonated with me a lot."

Turning his attention to the Bocuse d'Or USA candidates before him at The French Culinary Institute, Henin commended them for putting themselves out there in an "almost naked" way. "Either you're nuts," he said, "or you have a lot of guts."

Then he assumed the persona of a drill sergeant, launching into a crash course on culinary competition and what it demands of participants, a decidedly opinionated view of how to train for the Bocuse d'Or. He described his "three prerequisites" for competition: getting into physical, mental, and culinary condition. The physical preparation would ensure that they would survive the marathon of the competition, which is challenging even to chefs accustomed to working long hours on their feet. Mental preparation, achieved by proper focus and practice, would keep their minds from playing tricks on them—strange things happen under pressure; they might believe that a judge has it in for them, or be unable to shrug off a mistake. Culinary preparation means showing up on top of your game.

"It's not what you cooked five, ten years ago. It's what you're cooking today, for the judge. It's not where you been. It's not who you know. It's what you do today under those circumstances," said the coach.

Henin briefed the candidates on what to demonstrate in Orlando: solid foundation and proper technique, from butchering to knife skills to sauté-ing. He admonished them to have an action plan, on paper, preferably with timing indicated. "It's like a trip on the road," he said. "You need a map."

His list of tips was extensive: watch your sanitation, don't taste with your finger ("Use a spoon!"), show good time management, and coach your commis well; if you don't, "they make mistakes and then their mistakes become your mistakes." To that end, work side by side or front to front "so that you are one." Be efficient: if you go to put something away, bring something back with you. And maximize ingredients—use the trimmings of *everything*, from chickens to mushrooms.

As for the food, in competition a combination of textures is essential:

the three primary ones being "crisp/crunchy, meaty, and soft." By way of illustration, Henin pointed out that apple pie à la mode, which he described as the most popular dessert in the world, has all three: the crust is crunchy, the apple is meaty, and the ice cream is soft.

Proper seasoning is also important, as is being distinctly American. Henin didn't buy into the notion that you had to cook French to win the Bocuse d'Or. He believed that you need to celebrate where you come from. "Maple syrup, wow!" he said. "They don't have that anywhere else in the world." This particular subject is the source of much debate among those who organize, participate in, and observe the Bocuse d'Or USA. To this day, Kaysen, for one, is convinced that a reason he didn't do better at the Bocuse d'Or is that his food was too American.

Kaysen himself followed Henin, joined by his commis from 2007, Brandon Rodgers, who was then working at Daniel. The two talked about their experience, and how important the timing was, and about the noise in the competition hall, specifically the cowbells from the Swiss fans. This aspect of the Bocuse d'Or has attained near mythic status; past competitors and observers alike warn of the earsplitting, rafter-shaking volume of the audience, which is so overwhelming that many participants and observers (including many reporters) routinely refer to "thousands" of spectators when the true number is in the high hundreds. Some even wear earplugs to shut out the noise, though this can impede communication between chef and commis. (In 2007, when coaches were not allowed near the kitchens or to communicate with their team in any way—a rule that was changed for 2009—Kaysen considered using earpiece walkie-talkie setups to shut out the audience while still allowing him to communicate with Rodgers, but he was warned that it might appear he was cheating.)

The candidates were divided into groups of four and given two hours to prepare a fish course. They wouldn't have to present it on a platter, but they would have to serve five plates, to Boulud, Keller, Henin, Kaysen, and Rodgers. As they cooked, Kaysen and Rodgers observed them and Henin roamed the floor taking the kind of notes the technical judges might take in Lyon, about how sound their butchering technique was, and how clean they kept their stations.

When the cooking was done, the judges tasted the food and conferred in private, concluding that it was a mixed bag. To avoid embarrassing or discouraging any candidates, rather than critiquing individual dishes, they offered their commentary en masse, though some opinions were delivered rather bluntly, as when Kaysen told the group that only two chefs' fish were cooked correctly, an especially significant note because proper doneness is a crucial consideration in the Bocuse d'Or; the French have a word for it: *cuisson*.

IN THE WEEKS AFTER the orientation and group-cook at The French Culinary Institute, Kevin Sbraga took Coach Henin's advice to heart—including the part about preparing physically. Sbraga, whose combination Italian and African American heritage lends him a hard-to-place swarthiness, didn't have a regular workout routine, but as a former athlete who always enjoyed training, he rediscovered his inner jock, rising at five thirty every morning and biking between fifteen and twenty miles. He also stopped shaving his beard, a not-unusual tradition for athletes preparing for a big occasion.

For a solid month, Sbraga—who had tapped Aimee Patel, a cook from Amada restaurant, as his commis—spent four or five hours a day, four or five days a week, developing his dishes. The rest of the candidates prepared in their own ways, but with the exception of Rosendale, each of them had to go through a learning process because he wasn't a competition cook. For example, Rellah focused his research on past winners of the Bocuse d'Or, which made him question Henin's go-American advice. "I trained in two French restaurants and have looked at a lot of menus and information about what other teams have done in the past . . . I don't think [acclaimed Swiss chef and judge] Philippe Rochat wants to taste maple syrup," he said.

Jérôme Bocuse agreed: "For me, [maple syrup] is comfort food," he said. "Maple syrup is for the pancakes in the morning for breakfast. Barbecue is for Sunday with your friends . . . I know it is part of the [American] heritage and the culture . . . but can we bring it to a gourmet level? I am not sure. Maybe by tweaking it. Maybe we can bring some barbecue *flavor* into it. But are you going to do real barbecue at the Bocuse d'Or? Certainly not."

Rellah, Sbraga, and Whatley ended up in about the same place, deciding to call on American terminology and reference points, delivering them via classic French technique. Rellah, for example, devised a meat platter he dubbed the Blackboard Special. One component was a tenderloin of beef, split open, filled with a farce or forcemeat (finely chopped, seasoned meat) comprising the scrap and mushrooms ("almost like meatloaf"), wrapped in Swiss chard and sealed with the help of transglutaminase, essentially a "meat glue" that binds proteins together. Rellah planned to *sous vide* (cook in a vacuum pack) the entire composition before presenting it.

Similarly, Whatley planned a deconstructed cod chowder theme for his fish platter, and a Southwestern "Texas ranchers" theme for the beef, including wrapping the tenderloin with chorizo he made himself, roasting it, and saucing it with a "sort-of barbecue sauce reduction." He also planned chiles rellenos stuffed with beef cheeks, and oxtail timbales with pinto beans. Having lived in Georgia, Sbraga eventually settled on a Southern Hospitality theme—his meat platter came complete with candied yams and a maple-bourbon jus that paid homage to red-eye gravy—drawing on his personal history.

Meanwhile, in Yountville, Hollingsworth, who had spent most of his adult life working at The French Laundry, decided to forgo competition style in favor of the understated elegance he lived daily. He drew heavily from The French Laundry's Garden for inspiration, and planned to bring all of his produce from Yountville, leaving nothing to chance.

Hollingsworth found preparing for the Bocuse d'Or USA to be a revelatory experience. "It has made me learn a lot about myself and who I am," he said. "If you come to work and you cook every day, you learn by working with the product. But if you cook with the same product every day and you're doing these different techniques and you're really analyzing the food that you do, then you learn more about the style that you prefer and what better represents you and how you work and how you handle different kinds of stress."

Sbraga reached out to the community of chefs to help with his preparation, starting with George McFadden, a certified master chef he had kept in touch with back in Naples, Florida, borrowing a kitchen at a Philadelphia restaurant school to train in, and even driving up to Johnson & Wales University in Providence to do a tasting for some chefs he knew there, videotaping the practice for his own review.

By Labor Day, Rellah had his themes all set (his fish platter was titled "An Indian Summer in Cape Cod") and he began to consider his platters and other ancillary concerns. He started doing timed trials fives times a week after work, beginning at 10:30 p.m., and going for five hours. That might sound like a lot, but Rellah had no trouble slipping into his old work habits. "I worked in two four-star restaurants in Manhattan for a total of seven years," he said. "That is, like, the pinnacle of pressure."

Where Rellah felt the most pressure was in preparing his commis, Vincent Forchelli, for the challenge ahead. Because Forchelli was right out of culinary school, Rellah felt it was important to create a stressful environment for him, so he'd put him on the line and throw curveball after curveball at him.

The result of that brutality? "He is a different person today," said Rellah. Forchelli agreed: "I think it improved my skills dramatically. Any competition where you push yourself you will always be better than the guy who doesn't do competitions."

For the two weeks leading up to Orlando, Whatley and his commis, Josh Johnson, a chef de partie who had worked with him for two years, performed exhaustive practice runs every day—not just the five-and-a-half hours of cooking, but also another several hours for prep and then a few more for clean-up and debriefing—about a twelve-hour commitment per day. As he practiced, Whatley came to respect the Bocuse d'Or, as opposed to, say, cold-food contests. "This particular competition really makes sense," he said. "You have to be organized. You are on a timeline. You have to work clean. You have to make things sizzle. Smell good. Being in a live stadium with an audience is the ultimate *Iron Chef.*"

Asked what he had done to prepare a week before the competition in Orlando, Hyunh—who was working in the kosher restaurant Solo in midtown Manhattan while its owners got a new project together for him—cackled gleefully. "I'm not!" he said. "This is a kosher kitchen . . . I'm competing against Thomas Keller's guy, Charlie Trotter's guy. They have all the resources in the world. Here I am, I have two vinegars—red wine and rice wine vinegar—and some vegetable stock." He shrugged. "It's very hard."

"I know what I'm going to do," he explained. "But I haven't had time to perfect it. I'm just going to bring ingredients down there . . . and I'm gonna go . . . I'm gonna cook, with proper techniques, and I'm going to hope it tastes good. I don't know if it'll be the most perfected dish of my career—definitely not I would say—but given the circumstances I'm in now and given what I can do and get out of it, I think it's going to be excellent."

"I cook best under pressure," he said, snapping his fingers. "And at the moment. Shit's gonna go down. Things are gonna burn. Things are gonna break. I'm gonna go with the flow, and do what I do best. *Cook!*"

Clearly, this was not the ideal preparation, but in many ways, Hyunh's attitude exemplified the ideal of culinary competitons: He embraced the *experience.*

By the week before the competition, Richard Rosendale, who had been practicing overnight alongside Seth Warren, a string bean of a cook who worked for him at Rosendale's, between overseeing the build-out of a new restaurant and trips to Rye, New York, to train for the Olympics, had stopped rehearsing.

"All of the hard work should have already taken place," he said. "Right now, as we get ready for next week, it's a lot of packing and going through pack lists, making sure shipping addresses match up, all those little things."

Did Rosendale feel like the favorite going into Orlando? "Absolutely not. I know . . . from competing over the years, you can never underestimate any of your competition . . . I hope that I'll win, but I also know there's some very talented people that I'm going against. . . . It's any given Sunday. Anything, and I mean *anything* can happen that can really just throw your game in that five-hour period. The Olympics is a perfect example of that. Four years of preparation comes down to spilling a sauce, or scorching something, or overcooking venison loins."

Rosendale took about twelve hours to pack his toolbox, which was about the size of a chest freezer, in the most efficient way, and the tools and equipment would be set up very precisely according to when and where he'd need them in the kitchen in Orlando, all with an eye toward maximizing time.

"Every second counts," he said. "If you go to reach for something and you bring your hand back without something in it . . . you lose precious seconds . . . you add that up and by the end of the competition you have lost five or ten minutes . . . that might not seem like much, but if that's your window [to present your platter] . . .

"Packing is huge."

ON SUNDAY, SEPTEMBER 21, a bombshell rocked the financial world. Lehman Brothers filed for bankruptcy, the first stirrings of what would quickly reveal itself to be a financial crisis that would alter the world markets and the presidential election. The next morning, Senator John McCain uttered his faux pas for the ages, that the "fundamentals of the economy" were "strong," triggering his downward spiral in the polls; by midweek, he would engage in a game of chicken with the Democratic nominee, Senator Barack Obama, as McCain threatened to pull out of the first planned presidential debate that Friday night so that he could return to Washington, D.C.

Yet all this election-season melodrama was mere background noise at the World Showplace by Thursday afternoon, drowned out by the power tools employed to bring the new Bocuse d'Or USA to life. In the auditorium, construction teams worked furiously to finish the setup for the next two days: a scaled-down facsimile of the Bocuse d'Or space in Lyon.

A staging area had been set aside for the candidates—a large high-ceilinged space with industrial carpeting on the floor and a few long folding tables. As the chefs arrived—some had already gotten there the day prior—they went scavenging around the back corridors of the facility and into the kitchen area in search of speed racks, sheet trays, and other sundry items they needed to transfer their ingredients.

It was Jérôme Bocuse's idea to make the competition hall in Orlando as similar as possible to the one in Lyon, to give the candidates a chance to visualize what the day would be like in January. Smart, because one of the distinguishing challenges of the Bocuse d'Or is that it's a culinary Brigadoon that only exists for the few days during which it takes place. Candidates who weren't selected two years before their entry, or didn't go on their own in years past, simply cannot see or experience it until they get there. To bring Bocuse's vision to life, Nora Carey had worked for months to coordinate the efforts of Disney's Entertainment, Culinary, and Operations teams, reviewing video footage of the Bocuse d'Or for inspiration and accuracy, and holding weekly meetings and planning sessions.

That afternoon, Jennifer Pelka and Coach Henin held a briefing for the candidates at the American Adventure Parlor. With Revolutionary War music, all flutes and drums, wafting in the windows from outside, it was the first time that all of the candidates and commis were in one room. There was the air of a mass blind date about it. Henin, dressed in a camel-colored Ralph Lauren Oxford with the sleeves rolled up and Pelka, in a sleeveless black dress, set up an easel with a giant pad to brief the group on the rules and regulations of the competition: the start times would be staggered by ten-minute intervals; they'd be required to prepare their platters as well as six plated portions; and waiters would take the actual plates to the judges.

The separate preparation of plates and a platter was a marked departure from the standard operating procedure of the actual Bocuse d'Or, where platters are paraded before the judges and the audience, photographed by the media, then delivered to a carving station, where they are portioned out onto plates for tasting and evaluation. This protocol results in one of the more vexing elements of the Bocuse d'Or: it may be the preeminent culinary competition in the world, but after the twelve- to fifteen-minute lag time between preparation and service, the food is received by the judges in a manner that would be unacceptable in any restaurant: it's cold.

When Henin opened the floor to questions, Rosendale's depth of experience became clear, as he peppered the coach with one query after another: Could anything that wasn't connected to plumbing be moved to customize the work space? Would there be a runner and dishwasher the whole time? Would there be an ice machine or a runner who can fill an ice bin?

"Good one!" exclaimed Henin, writing the question on the pad.

After the meeting, the chefs emerged into blazing sunlight and made their way to the French Island, a recessed area alongside the lagoon around which Epcot is centered, where they were met by a humbling spectacle: the chefs who would be observing and serving as judges, many of them members of the Advisory Board. There were old-guard legends such as Alain Sailhac, former Lutèce chef Andre Soltner, and Georges Perrier, chef-owner of Le Bec-Fin in Philadelphia. There were young bucks such as Daniel Humm of New York City's Eleven Madison Park, and Laurent Tourondel, partner in the fast-expanding Bistro Laurent Tourondel (BLT) restaurant group. Jean-Georges Vongerichten, chef and co-owner of restaurants all over the world including Jean Georges and Vong, was on hand. And of course, Daniel Boulud and Thomas Keller. All were dressed in their whites. If there was a chef heaven here on earth, this was it.

Boulud, Keller, and Jérôme Bocuse each spoke, then the candidates drew lots to determine in what order they would compete: on Day One, Rosendale, Sbraga, Rotondo, and Whatley would cook; on Day Two, Hyunh, Powell, Hollingsworth, and Rellah. The chefs were presented with official Bocuse d'Or USA jackets, then Boulud, Keller, and Jérôme Bocuse posed for a picture. Before the photographer could snap the first one, Boulud—ever the showman—looked over his shoulder and realized something was missing. "Get the French Pavilion in the background," he said.

The chefs pivoted, the photographer relocated, and the photo was taken.

Shortly thereafter, at the World Showplace, the chef-judges were briefed. With Henin and Kaysen chiming in, Boulud and Pelka ran through the timing for the two days of competition and how the scoring would be broken down: 50 percent for taste, 30 percent for artistry (presentation of the platters), and 20 percent for "execution/kitchen skills."

AT THE RECEPTION LATER that evening, Dieter Hanning, a vice president for Walt Disney Parks and Resorts, took the floor. An energetic German, Hanning launched into a hilarious recap of the milestones in world gastronomy, with a focus on American dining. Hanning began more than a half-century earlier. "In 1952, Kentucky Fried Chicken opened up," he recounted, his German accent making the factoid sound automatically ironic. "And in 1954, the Burger King." Sensing confused delight in his audience, Hanning said, "You're going to ask, 'Where is that going to fit in with the Bocuse d'Or?' Just bear with me."

He continued: Julia Child's *Mastering the Art of French Cooking* (which he charmingly misnamed *Mastering the French Cooking of Julia Child*) in 1961.

"In '64 to '74 I did some terrible misery," he said, getting personal. "Today they would call it *slavery;* in those days they called it *apprenticeship, culinary apprenticeship.*" This brought one of the great laughs of the night from a room in which so many people had experienced the personal sacrifice it took to become a chef.

Hanning picked up his timeline: Alice Waters's Chez Panisse restaurant in Berkeley and the first-ever Starbucks in Seattle in 1971. From his folder, Hanning produced a menu from L'Auberge du Pont de Collonges, commonly refered to simply as "Restaurant Paul Bocuse." "And here he signed, Monsieur Paul Bocuse, 1971. Eating at his restaurant . . ." The audience was silent, then he hit them with the sucker punch: "That was like taking out a mortgage." Chuckles broke out across the room.

Hanning continued ticking off milestones: the first Spago in 1982, Charlie Trotter's restaurant in Chicago in 1987, and up to the present day. As he spoke, the laughter subsided and the parlor took on a hushed tone, suitable to a sermon. His message was unmistakable: American food had come into its own, and many of the people in that room had been a part of the evolution.

"Then I would also like to thank the *millions* of unknown heroes in this industry, who will never get the recognition, but who help to make us look good. And there's a *lot* of people out there, who wake up every morning, different cultures, different upbringings, different heritages, and we should never forget this."

Hanning again broke the seriousness conclusively with: "We should also never forget all those guests who come and spend all this big money."

It had been the first speech of the night, but it set the tone for the evening and the weekend, putting the mission of the Bocuse d'Or USA in historical context. There would be a battle played out over the next two days, but the competitors would enter—and leave—the arena as colleagues with a common goal: bringing that golden Bocuse home to America.

Hanning's remarks were bookended by the evening's final speaker, Damian Mogavero, CEO and founder of Avero, who recounted the story of the Judgment of Paris, the 1976 blind wine tasting that put ten of France's best wines against ten from California, with a stunning result: California won! (The events had recently been depicted in the movie *Bottle Shock*.) Mogavero, a food and wine enthusiast, had purchased and brought along one bottle of the winning red wine from that long-ago showdown, Stag's Leap Wine Cellars' 1973 Cabernet Sauvignon, and while he couldn't procure any of the winning white—1973 Chateau Montelena California Chardonnay—he had managed to get his hands on a magnum each of the 1971 and 1972 vintages.

Small samples of the wines were poured, and the guests lined up to savor a sip, to experience what victory tasted like. And, for a fleeting moment, the candidates were reminded that, although the odds against them were long, anything was possible.

2

Knives at Dawn

Dining is and always was a great artistic opportunity.
—FRANK LLOYD WRIGHT

K EVIN SBRAGA RAN.

It was minutes before 6:00 a.m. on the morning of Friday, September 26, the first day of the Bocuse d'Or USA competition, and Sbraga wanted to see his physical preparation through to its logical conclusion. Finding the exercise room at Disney's Beach Club Resort hotel (where all competitors were staying) locked and dark, he did what chefs do: he adapted, jogging along the footpath that encircled the resort complex, past the sandy shores of a lagoon, and along the deserted boardwalk on the other side.

Back in his room, Sbraga showered, then treated himself to a room-service breakfast and threw on a baggy white Nautica sweatshirt. He checked himself in the mirror, his face a reflection of all the work that had brought him to this day. Sbraga had shed almost twenty pounds during training. He was an athlete again, a competitor. He was also clean-shaven; he'd shorn off his beard before turning in last night, to surprise his opponents and make them wonder what this guy had up his sleeve.

By six fifty-five, the four two-person teams who were to square off that day had gathered in the lobby: Sbraga and Patel, Rosendale and Warren, Rotondo and Jennifer Petrusky, one of his sous chefs; Whatley and Johnson. The vast, garishly lit space was otherwise deserted save for the desk clerk, and it was dead silent. The teams kept their distance, yawning and pacing about under the seahorse-themed overhead lamp or walking circles around the potted palms on the fringes of the room. On the circular sofa under the seahorses, Jennifer Pelka pecked away on her laptop.

Three thunderclaps, in quick succession, rang out in the lobby, shattering the calm. It was Sbraga, smacking his hands together violently, then plunging them deep into the pockets of his sweatshirt. His eyes were squeezed shut, and he had earphones in, flooding his cranium with the hip-hop group Wu-Tang Clan's greatest hits. Sbraga's high-school wrestling team used to spark up the CD on a boom box before meets, but it was a strangely appropriate selection for this day as well; just as many rap and hip-hop songs are about the rhyming prowess of the singer, cooking competitions—certainly one with a visual component like the Bocuse d'Or—are about the chef's showing off his skills, making lyrics like "I be tossin', enforcin', my style is awesome," the perfect underscoring of what was about to go down at the World Showplace. As others watched Sbraga, he again yanked his arms free of the sweatshirt and clapped his hands loudly, looking fierce, ready to rumble.

Just a few feet away stood Richard Rosendale. His overnight preparation was different from Sbraga's: after touring their kitchen the day before, he and Warren convened in Rosendale's hotel room. Working off a digital photo he'd snapped at the Showplace, Rosendale sketched out how they were going to rearrange the equipment to create a more optimal layout. (He'd also taken the step of speaking to one of the electricians to be sure he wouldn't trip a circuit breaker and to see if there'd be enough cable, although he'd brought plenty of heavy-duty extension cords along, just in case.) Then Rosendale quizzed his assistant, quick-firing questions about the sequence of tasks he had to execute over the five-and-a-half-hour battle. If Rosendale noticed Sbraga's theatrics, he didn't let on. And even if he had noticed them, they would not have made an impact. Rosendale was in familiar territory, and his philosophy was that it's all about what you do in your own kitchen that wins the day. Any energy directed outside those four walls was wasted.

Minutes later, the teams had split into two chauffeur-driven vans and were rumbling along the back roads of suburbia to the World Showplace. In one of the vans, Pelka swiveled around in the passenger seat and asked Percy Whatley about his preparation.

"The garnishes took a long time," said Whatley.

Pelka nodded. On the radio, The Romantics sang "That's What I Like About You."

"Played around with the cod," Whatley continued.

At the mention of the cod, Johnson, who had seemed dead set on *not* talking, interjected: "It sucks."

"Water. No fat. Big challenge," Whatley explained, summarizing the prevailing opinion about cod.

As morning broke over Lake Buena Vista, the vans arrived at the World Showplace and the teams, their moment of judgment at hand, filed into the facility with all the joie de vivre of prisoners on a death march.

A soaring, Western movie–like instrumental theme washed over the hall, which had been brought nearly to completion since the day prior. Gone were the cherry pickers, but one ladder remained, from which a stagehand was hanging long rectangular signs bearing the names of the candidates and their commis over each kitchen. Another member of Disney's Entertainment crew was touching up the kitchen window frames with an odorless red paint.

The teams had fifty minutes to set up their kitchens and the time flew, in part because there were some surprises in store. In Kitchen 4, Whatley discovered that the All-Clad roasting pans didn't fit into the Convotherm oven, a problem because, to roast veal bones for stock "classically, culinarily, you need to use a roasting pan." He opted for a shallower pan and hoped that the proctors wouldn't dock him for deviating from tradition.

As in Lyon, the teams would commence cooking in an empty stadium; audiences wouldn't wander in until the doors opened at eleven thirty. Henin gathered the hopefuls together in a line and reminded them that they'd start at ten-minute intervals, which would create the ten-minute window between each team's fish platter and five minutes between their meat platters.

Henin dispatched them to their kitchens: Rosendale in Kitchen 1, Sbraga in Kitchen 2, Rotondo in Kitchen 3, and Whatley on the end in Kitchen 4. Rosendale again exhibited his competition experience: he banished the hand sink to the corridor; commis Warren's task list was color coded; and photographs of the finished dishes—the ultimate in aided visualization—were taped to the wall for reference.

One by one, Henin visited the kitchens, counting down the staggered start times: "Five, four, three, two, one. *Go!*"

The chefs jumped right in: Rosendale began butchering his meat and fish, while in Kitchen 2, it was Sbraga's turn to be surprised: why were the veal bones and oxtail still frozen? He roasted the bones and prepared an ice bath to thaw the oxtail, then, scrambling to recapture lost time, he butchered his beef tenderloin too quickly and stabbed himself in the hand. Improvising for the second time that day, he taped a napkin over the wound and wedged it in place with a latex glove.

For Michael Rotondo, the drama had come the day before: because his shipment from Las Vegas had arrived several hours later than expected on Thursday, he was not able to organize his mise en place as thoroughly as the other competitors had during set-up time at the Showplace. But the chef took it in stride. At a Charlie Trotter restaurant, where many VIP guests are treated to a new menu every time they come in, "We do a lot of spontaneous cooking . . . cooking on the fly . . . [so] are used to working in an environment that is pretty intense and under pressure."

In Kitchen 4, Whatley and Johnson had misplaced one of the essential elements of their game plan: their rhythm. Whatley fell behind almost immediately. He had no idea why, but by one hour and twenty minutes into their time, he was still butterflying prawns that should have been finished more than a quarter hour earlier.

"I'm fifteen minutes behind and I don't know how I'm going to make it up," he whispered to Johnson. He didn't have to say another word: his wingman immediately put the pedal to the metal, going into full-on octopus mode, doing three or four things at once instead of just one or two: chopping faster, stirring sautéing vegetables while setting peppers to roast, kneading a dough in between other tasks—all with the goal of freeing up time to receive whatever jobs Whatley needed to hand off.

Judges, in their whites, began filing in around nine o'clock. With coffee and Danishes in hand, they strolled around the kitchen, watching their young colleagues toil, often admiringly so. Georges Perrier took note of Rosendale's technique of soaking the cod for twenty minutes in cold salted water, which would cause the notoriously watery fish to firm up, making it easier to manipulate. "Very smart," enthused Perrier.

As 10:00 a.m. approached, all of the kitchens were in full swing, with proteins being boned, liquids being stirred, vegetables being chopped, but to what end nobody knew. In this regard, the Bocuse d'Or resembles the American version of the television show *Iron Chef* in which narrator Alton Brown can often be heard attempting to deduce what the two competing teams are preparing, but usually fails to put it all together until the final minutes. So it is with the Bocuse d'Or. Through much of the five and a half hours, the chefs and commis are creating pieces for a puzzle known only to them. The end result isn't clear to the audience until the cooks are barreling down the homestretch.

———

"IT'S HARD TO TELL chefs who own empires to 'Get over here,'" said Gavin Kaysen as he marched around the Pavilion attempting to herd all the chef-judges together for a briefing in the back of the hall where café tables, couches, and a flat-screen television had been set up to serve as the VIP lounge when the doors opened to the public.

When he finally gathered them there, the sight was surreal: all those famous chefs—the group now included Patrick O'Connell from The Inn at Little Washington and from California, David Myers of Los Angeles' Sona restaurant and Traci Des Jardins, chef of three San Francisco restaurants—gathered in their whites in the back of a gargantuan black box amphitheater at Epcot at ten in the morning.

Coach Henin described what the technical judges, or kitchen proctors, would be looking for: efficiency of movement, logical procedure of steps (for example, butchering the fish first to get the bones simmering to make stock), whether or not the candidates work side by side or face each other to facilitate communication, and so on. Kitchen management would factor into the Bocuse d'Or USA tallies, but in Lyon those points—rendered by past winners who serve as technical judges—are only used in the event of a tie.

"Talk about your experience judging end product," Keller asked Henin.

"Well," Henin said, "Does the food say, 'Eat me,' or does it sit there like a dog poop?" The chefs laughed. Henin went on to describe the desired visuals: Is everything accessible to the judge without having to move things around? Is the high point in the back of the plate [as it would be classically]? Regarding texture, Henin outlined the marks that the chefs have to hit in competition, offering the same commentary he had at the FCI briefing. And of course, the flavors had to mesh. "I like to taste meat with sauce and without sauce," he said. "Then, I taste the pieces [main proteins and garnishes] together."

He also warned everybody to be careful to not eat too much, lest they become sated before they'd tried all the food.

Boulud jumped in to describe the awards that would be handed out in Orlando: Gold, which came with a $15,000 cash prize (it also came with a three-month paid training sabbatical that had already received a fair amount of media interest); Silver ($10,000); and Bronze ($5,000). (The Bocuse d'Or itself also awarded cash prizes: €20,000 (euros) for Gold; €15,000 for Silver, and €10,000 for Bronze.) There would also be awards for Best Fish and Best Meat, which would be divided between the fourth and fifth finishers, Best Commis, and other "surprise prizes," each of which would come with an attendant reward, such as time in a three-star Michelin restaurant in France, or a three-day tour of Brandt Beef's headquarters in California.

Boulud also asked the chefs to display poker faces as they tasted and made notes, in order to maintain maximum suspense until the winners were announced. He then turned to his friends and colleagues, all these chefs who had come down to Orlando at his behest, and—although it was only about half past ten—sent them forth with one final instruction: "Enjoy lunch!"

JOHN BESH, NEW ORLEANS chef and former marine, opened the public portion of the Bocuse d'Or USA at eleven thirty that morning, functioning as emcee along with a male-female team provided by Disney. He oriented the audience, letting them know which judges would be evaluating fish (Kaysen, Des Jardins, Vongerichten, Sailhac, O'Connell, and Humm) and which would be on meat detail (Tourondel, Perrier, Handke, Bouit, Myers, and Soltner).

Besh introduced many of the Advisory Board's great transplanted French chefs (who were "guys I grew up reading about") to the audience and held a microphone up to Soltner, who was plainly awestruck at the morning's demonstration.

"I am amazed," he said. "I came here in 1966. When I see these guys, how they work and what they do . . . American chefs are the equal of European chefs. They are just as good."

Sailhac was only too happy to keep the pro-American beach ball in the air: "When I came to this country forty-three years ago, there were no Americans in the kitchen," he said. "What they are doing here is a great spectacle."

Over the next few hours, as the chefs cooked in their pods, the proctors made notes, and the emcees explained the proceedings to the audience— all was as it would be in Lyon, minus the fervor of the international fans and their noisemakers, such as the cowbells wielded by the Swiss or the clackers smacked together by the Japanese.

At about 1:00 p.m., Rosendale, who would be the first to present his dishes, set a gleaming triangular silver platter on his workstation. He and Warren looked calm, even though things had been very tight; he'd gotten his tenderloin into the circulator (sous vide bath) just in the nick of time: fifty-five minutes before it had to go up in the window (fifty minutes for cooking, and five minutes to rest), and was still putting the finishing touches on the components of his fish platter, seasoning the sauce and assembling individual garnishes.

Rosendale put the platter in the window. Titled "Modern Cod and Seafood Preparations," it was a quintessential competition display with lots of layers and work on it (more than thirty individual recipes had gone into its production): the centerpiece was an imposing cylinder of gently cooked cod wrapped in a lobster coral mousse flecked with bits of dill and saffron; behind the cod, arranged along the short rear side of the triangle were a half-dozen scallop croquettes, a saddle of fern-colored celery gelée flopped over their centers. In formation along one long edge were blue prawn timbales topped with cabbage and, opposite them, charlottes of white asparagus velouté ringed with alternating segments of green and white asparagus. All was accompanied by a prawn Américaine sauce.

Next from Kitchen 1 came the plated fish course, whisked by waiters to the jury. The chef-judges took knives and forks to them, but betrayed nothing, per Boulud's instruction.

Alain Sailhac was impressed with Rosendale's food: "Only a clean, precise mind . . . [could] realize that plate," he wrote on his score sheet, awarding Rosendale 9 of 10 possible points for Originality and Creativity. He continued: "So many details well realized. Great techniques." But not everybody was won over by the taste: "Flavors were bold & a bit bland at the same time," scribbled Traci Des Jardins, also commenting that "dishes were on the edge of being too salty." Perhaps summing up the marriage of world-class presentation and imperfect flavors, Jean-Georges Vongerichten wrote "Classic cold preparation for hot food."

While he was still chewing on Rosendale's fish course, Vongerichten rose to snap a picture of the platter that had come out of Kitchen Number 2, bearing Kevin Sbraga's fish offering: medallions of cod loin topped with pecans and tomato marmalade; slabs of Swiss chard–wrapped shellfish terrine, a rectangle of duck liver showing in its center; "shrimp and grits" topped with a fried quail egg; and seared scallops perched atop green-onion bread pudding. The most distinctive component was okra, stuffed with a seasoned bacon mixture, buttermilk-battered, fried, and held aloft on antenna-like stands. Reviews were decidedly mixed: many judges— O'Connell and Vongerichten among them—praised Sbraga's creativity and embraced the Southern theme, but others found the flavor lacking or the overall effect too convoluted.

For all the drama in the kitchens and on the platters, the energy in the auditorium was strangely low. The stadium seating had filled up, but appeared to be populated by Duane Hanson sculptures, as many didn't seem to know quite what to make of the spectacle, staring impassively at the competition floor.

Boulud found Pelka at the edge of the competition space, and decided to pump up the energy by putting Pelka herself in front of them. He ran out to center stage and introduced her to the audience, adding emcee to her list of duties. Even though they had never discussed the possibility of her joining the hosting roster, she jumped right in to educate the turistas.

"What you may not know about the Bocuse d'Or is that it's like a football game," she said, explaining the competition in France and how the chefs had fans rooting for them. She got their energy up, interviewing Daniel Humm at the judges table, and having Sbraga's family and friends hold up their handmade sign, "Sbraga + Patel PUSH."

From Kitchen Number 3, Rotondo and Petrusky sent out their fish platter: a rectangular silver tray with cod wrapped in baterra kombu (kelp) and topped with fermented black garlic and a frizzle of fried baterra kombu slivers. A flotilla of little silver kayaks housed seared Long Island sea scallops topped with a coil of *haricot de mar* (a type of kelp with what Rotondo calls a "fettuccine-like appearance") and a clove of elephant garlic. In the center of the platter, in a triangle pattern, were arranged six servings of Hawaiian blue prawn mousse with molten black garlic in the center, and on the other side were Spanish chorizo profiteroles that resembled small sliders filled with Oregon chanterelle mushrooms. Overwhelmingly, the judges were knocked out by the taste ("Set and leave a great flavor in my mouth," wrote Alain Sailhac), though a few, Kaysen among them, dinged Rotondo for cold food and even cold plates.

Somewhere along the way, Whatley and Johnson found themselves back on track, having regained their rhythm. "It's like at a restaurant," said Whatley. "It can be a little rough, that first seating, but by the time the second seating rolls around you're in it." They were also aided by the size of the kitchen, smaller than the one they practiced in. As Henin had said, seconds and minutes add up; all the time they saved not covering the same amount of turf they'd had to back home put precious minutes back on their clock and they were as synced up as they'd ever been. They reclaimed so much ground that Whatley only had to pass one job to Johnson, asking him to fry up arepas (cornmeal crêpes) for the beef platter.

There were, however, some last-second hiccups: because the oven wasn't calibrated the same as the one back home, their corn custards doubled in size, and because the fryer was smaller, their Tater Tots didn't quite hold together. But the platter, titled "New England Seaboard Flavors," came out on time, headlined by poached cod hugged by a summer truffle mousseline and crusted with shrimp. Garnishes included Ping Pong ball–sized cod brandade fritters topped with squares of ham hock sandwiched around a piece of Vermont cheddar and held in place with a steel pin, and in the back corner of the platter, a vessel containing sauce Newburg. Comments were all over the map: O'Connell, in a sheet littered with nothing but 8s and 9s, rhapsodized about all aspects of the platter, while Vongerichten awarded a measly 6.8 for Originality and Creativity saying "safe combination."

At the end of the first round, only one thing was apparent to those who couldn't taste: Rosendale's presentations were on another level from those of his competitors, and he didn't let up with his beef platter. On an identical arrowhead silver tray, he presented his "Contemporary American Beef Medley": foie gras–infused beef tenderloin cooked sous vide, with an herb cloud garnished with a beef oxtail and shallot confit with potato chive mousseline and assorted wax beans; chili-braised beef cheeks, tomato, and mushroom inside a pasta timbale; and crêpe-encased white truffle custard with shaved black truffles. An oxtail jus accompanied the goods.

In a score sheet of 8s and 9s (with an unlucky 7 tossed in for perhaps the most unexpected category, Technical Knife Skills), Laurent Tourondel raved: "Perfect Beef Temperature, Right on It, Just the Right Combination of Flavors, Very different, Amazing Details!!!, Top Level." Others, such as Handke and Myers, offered mixed reviews.

In the VIP area, sponsors and visiting dignitaries, such as James Beard Foundation President Susan Ungaro, and Florent Suplisson, Contest Manager of the Bocuse d'Or in Lyon, nibbled on hors d'oeuvres made with Rougié foie gras and sipped spirits provided by Diageo as they watched the action on the television.

Sbarga's meat course, featuring medallions of tenderloin and that red-eye gravy he'd had in mind since the summer, emerged from Kitchen 2, complemented by candied yams topped with orange-blossom marshmallow presented in petit jars with spoons tucked into the clasp, and a lattice-topped pie of barbecued beef cheeks and collard greens, playfully referenced as *"en croûte"* on the team's menu.

He was happy with the platter, although he was a little worried about the cuisson because, ironically, "the oven cooked perfectly and we are not used to a perfect oven."

On stage, Boulud, having reclaimed the microphone, strolled up to Andre Soltner.

"What did you think of that beef dish?" he asked of Sbraga's composition, apparently forgetting his desire for poker faces all around.

"A little sweet," frowned Soltner. "A little modern."

Eager as ever to bridge divides, Boulud smiled up at the audience. "Well," he said. "You are going to have to be a little in the present and a little in the past." Nothing to see here, folks.

As the judges nibbled on Sbraga's meat dish, Rotondo's platter emerged, starring braised beef-cheek rounds topped with grainy preserved mustard seeds and "petite coin" onions. Supporting players included sweet potato custard and crispy okra atop a scroll of black pepper tuile, and confit turnips filled with red wine–braised oxtail and caramelized shallots. (Many American chefs use *confit* to refer to ingredients slow cooked in warm oil, an adaptation of the French word for duck and other proteins cooked and stored in their own fat.)

Comments on the flavors of Rotondo's platter varied wildly, from "Okay" (Tourondel) to "Great-tasting food all around" (Handke). Where Rotondo took a hit was in the presentation scores. "Garniture too small/too simple," wrote Michel Bouit, who should know, while David Myers scribbled, "Somewhat minimal which is ok, but made it look lacking."

Whatley's meat platter came out: beef tenderloin larded with chorizo, corn spoonbread set in tiny skillets, oxtail timbale set atop that pan-fried arepa. Unfortunately, the judges were not kind, with most box scores in the 3 to 7 range.

As the teams finished cooking, they pulled the curtains shut on their pods and set about cleaning them, a requirement in Orlando just as it would be in Lyon to leave everything in perfect order before departing the kitchen. They would also be judged on how well they did this.

THAT NIGHT, BARACK OBAMA and John McCain duked it out in their first televised debate, but in Orlando the fighting had ceased. Day One and Day Two candidates mingled with VIPs at a Chef's Beach Barbecue held on the sandy banks of a lagoon down the footpath from Disney's Beach Club Resort Hotel.

Amidst the bonfire and revelers, Sbraga and Patel reflected on their day: Sbraga wasn't at all relieved that his work was done: "If we *win* then I will be relieved," he said. "If we don't, then I will be disappointed."

"We really wanted this," said Patel. "We were the team that wanted this the most. We want to go to France and represent the United States as a team. It would mean everything."

Standing on the edge of the party, reflecting on the day, Rosendale was haunted by a concern about the jury, composed as it was, predominantly of restaurant chefs: "I hope that everybody is looking at what the actual Bocuse is. . . . It is not restaurant food. *It is not restaurant food.* If this competition today was about your best restaurant dish, we would have a dish that the presentation was completely different. . . . The Bocuse is the ultimate in French finesse and, if we want to win that, then we need to beat them at their own game, and that is just an unbelievable amount of creativity and visual impact and big-flavor profiles. . . . There is an incredible panel of judges, but I just don't know . . . how familiar they are with the actual Bocuse competition."

He shook his head, unsure of what to think.

"I hope it wasn't a twenty-minute orientation," he said.

ROLAND HENIN WAS MESMERIZED.

It was early on the morning of September 27, aka Day Two of the Bocuse d'Or USA, and in Kitchen 3, Adina Guest, the commis of The French Laundry's Timothy Hollingsworth, had gone through a transformation:

casual and carefree at the prior days' events, now her hair was pinned back, she stood at attention, and the affability in her face was replaced with stoic focus. Guest was well aware of the change because she had very deliberately developed her kitchen persona out of a belief that the kitchen is still a different place for a woman than it is for a man. She calls it her "Game Face," and it creates the impression that she is several years older than her actual age of twenty-two.

But that's not what attracted the rapt attention of Henin, as well as that of Hartmut Handke, who stood alongside him. The two competition veterans were impressed that Guest was actually *trimming* the green tape she was using to attach her task list to the glass wall of the pod, ensuring that the border was perfectly straight on all four sides. Had Henin known the reason for the step, he would have been pleased; it was a reflection of the exactitude demanded by his former protégé, Keller. "That's The French Laundry," Guest would later say of the tape-trimming. "The reason that I fit in well at The French Laundry and the reason why we all fit in well is that we are perfectionists. . . . What I have learned from Chef Keller and Chef Tim, it doesn't translate just into food, it translates into everything. The tape, it's major. If I hadn't cut off that little edge, every time I looked at it I would have noticed it and it would have thrown me off."

When told of the slack-jawed admiration his mentor and Chef Handke had demonstrated, Keller was surprisingly *un*happy. "It really troubles me that people found that to be remarkable," he said. "Because cooking is about precision . . . and precision doesn't start when the plate's finished. Precision starts when you wake up in the morning. It is a lifestyle. When someone is trimming the tape it's like that's habitual and that's a habit that we try to propagate throughout the entire group." Indeed, anybody who works at The French Laundry will tell you that ripping tape is strictly prohibited, so much so that on a rare occasion when an uninitiated commis makes the mistake of tearing off a piece, senior kitchen members—even from the next room—react to the noise like fingernails on a chalkboard.

"You can't just say, 'Okay, I am going to rip the tape and put it down,

don't worry about it and then I will be precise when I plate my food,'"
Keller continued. "That is not consistent . . . we are trying to be consistent,
not inconsistent, so everything that you do has to be consistent with the final idea that the plate is going to be perfect. Even though it is never going to
be perfect but that is the goal. So every step before that has to be the same.
You have to take it the same way. You have to feel the same way about it."

It was her love of precision that had landed Adina Guest at The French
Laundry in the first place.

When she was a student at Kapi'olani Community College in Hawaii,
Per Se's chef de cuisine, Jonathan Benno, performed a cooking demo there,
and Guest was the only student who volunteered to assist him. Among the
dishes he demonstrated were Keller's signature salmon cornets, which the
chef famously conceived (originally with tuna tartare) at a Baskin-Robbins
years ago. Guest was charged with folding napkins around the little cones.
She spent thirty minutes on the assignment, an intricate chore that she
treated with painstaking attention.

"I had known about The French Laundry for a long time and it had
been my dream to even eat there and I was super psyched to be helping him
out," she said.

Benno remembers Guest well. "I have been doing this long enough, I
can see most of the time someone who is going to be really, really good and
she was one of those people."

After the demo, she approached Chef Benno and asked if there was a
possibility of doing a stage at The French Laundry. Impressed with her, he
instructed her to e-mail him her resumé.

She didn't hear anything for two months and had pretty much written
off the idea, at least for the time being. But one day, just after winning a
student cooking competition in Idaho, she was in her hotel room checking
her e-mail and performed a routine check of her spam folder. Among the
unmentionable advertisements was an e-mail from the human resources
department of The French Laundry, congratulating her on being accepted
for a stage.

Following on the emotional release of competing, the news was over-whelming: she burst into tears.

DAY 2 OF THE competition had begun much as the previous day had, with the chefs congregating in the hotel lobby. Absent was Hung Hyunh. Given his casual preparation for the weekend, one might naturally have wondered if he had overslept, but when the other teams arrived at the Showplace, he was already there, having driven over with Pelka.

Hyunh and his commis, Girair (Jerry) Goumroian, a Culinary Institute of America student who met Hyunh while working at Guy Savoy in Las Vegas, occupied the same kitchen as Rosendale had the day before. Powell and Kyle Fiasconaro, a French Culinary Institute student who just a year earlier had been cooking at a Red Lobster on Long Island, were in Kitchen 2. In Kitchen 3 were Hollingsworth and Guest, and in Kitchen 4 were Rellah and Forchelli.

Hyunh and Hollingsworth had their eye on each other because they had something in common: Thomas Keller, and each presumed the other to be the favorite for the weekend.

The presence of Hyunh evokes unavoidable comparisons between American television cooking competitions like *Top Chef* and the Bocuse d'Or. But despite surface similarities, the two are actually quite different. Where the Bocuse d'Or follows the same format contest after contest, a great deal of the drama of *Top Chef* is conjured by pulling the rug out from under the cheftestants in weekly challenges, sometimes altering the rules midstream. For example, on one episode in the winter 2009 season, the competitors were charged with cooking a recipe out of the *Top Chef* cookbook. Midway through their frantic improvisation, Grant Achatz, the red-hot chef of Alinea restaurant in Chicago and a former Thomas Keller disciple, emerged in the kitchen along with cohost Padma Lakshmi. "We've changed our minds," said Lakshmi, whereupon Achatz smirked maliciously into the camera and announced, "We want soup." The competitors then had to take what they'd prepared to that point, change gears, and fashion a soup with it, using Swanson's broth. (One thing the Bocuse d'Or and *Top Chef* have in common is unapologetic product placement; the first thing that greets visitors to the Bocuse d'Or Web site is a shot of outer space from which an Eau de Perrier logo rushes up from the distance and explodes like the Death Star.)

After his experience, Hyunh would offer this comparison of the Bocuse d'Or and *Top Chef*: "Bocuse is more like a three-star Michelin [restaurant]. The dishes are perfected before you even do it. You are satisfied, the restaurant is satisfied, and your execution had better be perfect. *Top Chef* is more like when a customer comes in, they are ninety years old and they want this [a special request] *now*. They both reflect reality . . . in *Top Chef* you have to be creative and think on your feet and work fast. Do or die. In Bocuse, you have no excuses because you have time to train."

The morning did not go exactly as planned for Hyunh, but he didn't know that: almost as soon as they started cooking, his commis sliced his finger. Badly. But he bandaged himself up and continued without the chef taking note. As the morning progressed, Hyunh's lack of preparation began to show: his kitchen was cluttered, leftover ingredients were left strewn about, and he violated many tenets of Cooking Competition 101, such as reusing a tasting spoon without cleaning it. Watching him from outside the kitchen's glass wall, one of the proctors shook his head mournfully and muttered, "All day long," as he made a note on his score sheet. (By contrast, Rosendale had gone through more than 100 spoons the day before.)

Hyunh also had a bit of a run-in with A. J. Schaller, who was tasked with making sure the candidates got whatever they needed in the kitchen. When he reached for corn that wasn't where he remembered leaving it during his set up, Hyunh waved Schaller over and accusatorially asked her where it was.

"Nobody touched your corn," she said.

"It was right here," he replied, sounding a bit heated.

"Well, I'm telling you—"

"Never mind," he said, waving his arms. "If it's not here, I won't use it. That's fine."

Roland Henin happened on the scene, watched for a moment, then stepped in. He fished a few ears of corn from a supply box and stuffed them into Hyunh's hands.

"And I don't want to hear nothing more about it," he said, and stormed away.

"There's some hot-tempered chefs in here," said Handke.

"I didn't appreciate the temper," said Henin. "But if you give the benefit of the doubt, there's no excuses."

Asked why he gave the corn to Hyunh, Henin replied, "If there's a problem with him, it will show up in another way before the time is up."

But here was the thing with Hyunh: despite the inefficiencies in his kitchen, his food *looked* delicious; vibrant colors, such as the fiery orange of butternut squash puree or the bright green of creamed spinach, promised big flavors. As the cliché goes, if you eat with your eyes before your mouth, then people would be predisposed to liking his food.

Henin strolled along the windows. In Kitchen 2, Rogers Powell was scraping a fluffy white puree out of a Robot Coupe food processor with a rubber spatula. Perhaps it's a fish mousse, thought Henin. "It will be interesting to see if he makes a test quenelle," he said. That's the thing to do when you make a mousse—quick-cook a small quenelle in simmering water to see how it will taste when finished; then you can adjust the seasoning before it's too late. This should be standard operating procedure in any kitchen, but a lot of cooks don't follow the conventional wisdom. Not spotting a pot of water on Kitchen 2's stove, Henin wasn't optimistic.

Outside Kitchen 3, passersby were focused on how clean Hollingsworth and Guest were working. At any given time, it looked like they had just gotten there; as soon as a piece of equipment was used, it was stashed. But it was nearly impossible to get a sense of what the food would actually taste like as components were neatly assembled, then whisked away to the refrigerator or freezer until the time for service arrived. A number of the chef-judges also took note of a piece of equipment that Guest employed to slice potatoes, a Japanese turning vegetable slicer: the vegetable is impaled on a rod, which is snapped into place at the rear of the device. When the hand crank is operated, the vegetable is spun against a blade, producing long slices that roll out of the front of the mechanism like paper out of a fax machine.

Among the observers was David Wong of Canada, who had been selected almost two years earlier to be the 2009 candidate for his country. Wong was such an earnest soul that while he must have been there sizing up his competition, he seemed as if he were just along for the camaraderie. Wong had been sent to the Bocuse d'Or in 2007 to observe, and had many opinions on how to go about winning: "Every year, there's a half dozen clowns who imitate previous years' France platter," he said. "If you're not yourself in Bocuse d'Or, you lose."

As with so much about the Bocuse d'Or, perceived reality changes from person to person. One past champion who agreed with Wong was 2005 champion Vieira, who had once said, "You have to pursue your own ideas, do what you feel is right, and give it 100 percent during the preparation and the big day, so that you have no regrets." Then again, he *was* the French candidate, so being himself hardly seemed a risky proposition.

When the platters were paraded and tasted, Hyunh and Hollingsworth were the two who most impressed the judges. Neither of their presentations rose to the competition-style heights of Rosendale's, but Hung's seafood leaned that way, headlined by olive oil–poached cod topped with overlapping circles of scallop coins and black truffles. His Hawaiian prawn crêpe with leeks, chanterelles, and prawn reduction was bound up by a Chinese chive, and his ratatouille was deconstructed and topped with zucchini rounds, a peeled cherry tomato, and pepper. (The ratatouille was *not* an homage to Keller's contribution to the Disney-Pixar movie. "That movie actually scared me," laughed Hyunh. "I don't like rats.")

The platter met with approval from many judges. "Good harmony, overall flavors and textures were very good," wrote Kaysen, while Jean-Georges Vongerichten proclaimed the seasoning "perfect." On the other hand, Daniel Humm was underwhelmed, noting that the "execution could be better," and a number of judges commented that the cod was leaching liquid onto the platter.

As Hollingsworth plated his fish, seemingly deaf to the crowd, the emcees were impressed with his preternatural calm. "It's a known fact he's air-dried," said Besh, who was joined on Day Two by television personality Al Roker, who exhibited the ironic delivery that is his hallmark on *Today*. Of Hollingsworth's even keel, Roker exclaimed, "He had his sweat glands surgically removed."

Hollingsworth's fish platter was love-it-or-leave-it straightforward cooking. A sausage-like coil of grilled cod belly occupied the center of the platter. In the corner were browned diagonal cuts of *barigoule* bread pudding (made by pureeing a classic braised artichoke preparation, adding cream, combining with ground bread, baking, and slicing it) topped with San Marzano (a variety of plum tomato) marmalade. The platter also featured an artichoke gratin topped wtih Hawaiian blue prawns, piment d'Espelette, and Niçoise olives. Society garlic blossoms, an edible, faintly purple flower, were strewn about the tray.

The results were, for the most part, unqualified raves. Patrick O'Connell loved it: "Somewhat sleek and elegant in comparison to many of the overwrought presentations of the other contestants," he wrote on his score sheet. Some chefs differed on the same elements; for example, Daniel Humm found the fish "rubbery" and the bread pudding "dry" while Jean-Georges Vongerichten noted "great texture, all cooked perfectly."

In Hyunh's kitchen, order had been sacrificed in favor of getting the job done, but he was really pushing it: where some kitchens looked as though one could eat off the floor, Hung actually had food underfoot. A lone potato had been left to dry out there, along with a spoon and a spider (strainer). By day's end, to nobody's surprise, Hyunh would have accumulated the lowest kitchen score.

As the audience counted down from five to one in anticipation of Hyunh's deadline, he and Goumroian set the meat platter in their window, continuing the slugfest: a potato-encrusted beef tenderloin, the tawny color of a giant knish, sliced open to reveal a mouthwatering, rare-red tint and rings of Swiss chard, braised beef cheeks, and foie gras between the meat and the potatoes. Roasted butternut squash disks were filled with pureed squash and topped with sage toast. The platter was completed with oil-poached potatoes and a creamed spinach tart.

"As chaotic as Hung's kitchen was, who would have thought he could produce such beautiful food?" said Besh.

"Obviously he did," replied Roker as he watched Hyunh jump up and down and punch the air in a manner familiar to *Top Chef* viewers.

Hyunh wasn't winning the same approval from the meat judges that he had with the fish jury: "Very mediocre" wrote Laurent Tourondel in the "sophistication and subtlety" line on his score sheet.

Hollingsworth's beef platter exhibited more showmanship than his fish had, headlined by a rectangular slab of beef tenderloin seemingly upholstered on top with bacon. The unnatural shape of the meat—significantly wider than tenderloin naturally is—was a quietly spectacular touch he achieved by using Activa, a brand-name transglutaminase, to "glue" two pieces of beef together. The Activa also fused the bacon to the beef, even when sliced. The beef was accompanied by bias (diagonal) cuts of potato *mille-feuille;* the name means "thousand sheets" and classically refers to a dessert with many layers of puff pastry. Here it referred to an escalloped potato composition layered with black truffle. The mille-feuille were topped with braised beef cheek balls wrapped in Swiss chard and Tokyo turnips. Little cigars of port wine–braised oxtail in *feuille de bric* (a light, crispy dough) were set directly on the platter, halved Violette figs propped against them, along with a scallion salad.

The judges were blown away: "*Très grand plat,*" wrote Georges Perrier. Tourondel wrote "the best of 4 dish" (sic) on his form, but also noted, "need to be more competition and less restaurant."

For Powell and Rellah, it would be a hard day, their platters received in a lukewarm way by the judges, even though they displayed no shortage of creativity: Rellah prepared all American-French hybrids such as cod cake, *pipérade* (tomato and pepper stew), chowder sauce, and caviar, and a potpie of oxtail and beef cheek, which he'd been developing since the summer, while Powell unveiled a daring platter featuring unpredictable touches such as a lobster-roe-and-squid-ink pasta, black-olive-tomato caviar, and corn-and-seafood-chowder *fondant* on his fish platter. On his beef platter, the tenderloin was set on a bed of vegetable *brunoise* (fine dice) and wrapped in a mushroom–foie gras crust. Unfortunately, despite patches of approval (David Myers appreciated that Rellah's meat dish "really represented what he wanted to achieve," while Vongerichten praised the "great detail" and "good skill" on display on Powell's fish platter), the prevailing feeling was that the dishes were, at the end of the day, unsuccessful.

Powell already knew that he hadn't done as well as he'd hoped to. He had had some technical problems, as just about everybody did, but he also felt he had made a psychological error: on the previous day, he had sought out Paul Bocuse in the VIP area and told him the story of how they'd met years earlier. Bocuse remembered, and Powell told him how happy he was to be able to meet him as a cook. "I was really pleased with that moment," Powell said later. "But I wonder if it [would have] been a better thing after I cooked. Because it is like I already got what I wanted. I don't know. Maybe I am just trying to find excuses."

Other candidates didn't know how to evaluate their own performances. Back in their hotel room, Hollingsworth said to Laughlin that he thought he had done well. He knew he had taken a risk by not doing competition-style food, but was hopeful that even if the old-guard French chefs like Soltner and Sailhac might have been looking for a more ornate presentation, the younger ones such as Laurent Tourondel and Daniel Humm might be more open to understatement.

———

THAT EVENING, THE REAR area of the World Showplace was transformed for a gala dinner. Several hundred guests were on hand for a meal featuring dishes by Patrick O'Connell, Charlie Trotter, and Daniel Boulud. Absent was Thomas Keller, who had had to fly to New York City that afternoon for a function at Per Se that had been planned before the Bocuse d'Or USA came into his life.

The evening was exactly what one would expect of an event combining the worlds of Bocuse, Boulud, Keller, and Disney. At the end of the meal, Max McCalman, *fromager* of Terrance Brennan's Picholine and Artisanal restaurants in New York City, presented the cheese course, but not before Remy the Rat from the movie *Ratatouille*, a chef's toque affixed to his head, burst into the room and romped among the tables.

Dana Cowin, editor-in-chief of *Food & Wine*, announced the winners, consolation prizes first: Best Fish went to Hung Hyunh, while Best Meat went to Kevin Sbraga. Best Commis went to Adina Guest. The French Laundry newbie had to fight back tears because she thought that this award, like the fish and meat ones, meant that she and Hollingsworth were no longer eligible for the big prizes. Most upsetting to her was the feeling that she had let Hollingsworth down. "I was, like, this is Chef Tim's deal. I want him to win. This is all about him, not about me at all. When I got it, my heart sank," she said.

Continuing with the announcements, third place went to Michael Rotondo, who was also named Most Promising Chef, with a potentially bright future with the Bocuse d'Or USA. Second place went to competition veteran Richard Rosendale.

And first place went to Hollingsworth and Guest, who would go on to represent the United States at the Bocuse d'Or in Lyon in January. The audience burst into applause, then quickly filed back out to the reception room for passed chocolates, more cocktails, and dancing.

It felt like the end of something, but the truth was that it was only the beginning. As photographs were taken and interviews conducted, Kaysen sought out Hollingsworth on the stage. To the veteran, his successor seemed happy, but understandably dazed and confused as he processed the mission ahead.

"Get ready for a wild ride," Kaysen said.

3

Three Months in Yountville

We are trying to do the best we can with a piece of striped bass.

—DEVIN KNELL

TIMOTHY HOLLINGSWORTH STARED INTO THE EYES OF YASUJI Sasaki, the Japanese candidate who would be flying his nation's red-dotted sun flag into battle at the Bocuse d'Or. The American didn't know what to make of Sasaki, who seemed the very picture of poise, and whose gaze gave nothing away. Of the twenty-three chefs against whom Hollingsworth would compete, the Japanese was among the handful he presumed to be most formidable. An admirer of Japanese cuisine—its purity of flavor and nowhere-to-hide reliance on pristine ingredients and the cook's fundamental skill, especially with knife work—Hollingsworth trusted that Sasaki would be a fine technician, every bit as devoted to his craft as Hollingsworth was to his. He also took note of the man's age: forty-one, just enough to be experienced without being over the hill.

Hollingsworth wasn't in the same room with Sasaki, or even on the same continent. The Japanese chef was at his home in Kobe, Japan, a sous chef at Restaurant Alain Chapel at the Portopia Hotel, and Hollingsworth was at his home in Napa, scrutinizing the candidate photographs posted on the Bocuse d'Or Web site. Provided for fans and journalists, the profiles were a tantalizing resource for the candidates themselves. Of all the cooks and chefs in the world, just twenty-four would be throwing down in January. Regardless of who garnered the highest marks and who emerged empty-handed, it was an elite club and, for those who didn't already know one another, this was as close as they'd come to meeting until the week of the competition. The site was the only opportunity to size each other up, as best they could based on a photograph and some factoids: in addition to a headshot and date of birth, many of the dossiers, or link-to sites for the chefs' restaurants or national foundations, also featured brief profiles of the chef-candidates describing where they worked now and had worked, as well as statements on their philosophy of cooking.

Based simply on their country of origin, Hollingsworth had ideas about who the fiercest adversaries would be. Those were the profiles he clicked on first. The Norwegians had a fearsome track record at the Bocuse d'Or. Their cuisine may not be as highly regarded as, say, that of France, but their culture of cooking competitions and well-funded effort had produced three gold medalists and two silver. The Norwegians were the first team to beat the French at their home event, which may or may not have prompted a rule change: through 1999, in order to give other countries a chance, the victorious nation was not eligible to compete in the following Bocuse d'Or. Many believe that this demonstrated an air of superiority by the host country, who had won the top prize each time they competed, and are, of course, widely considered the kings and queens of Western cuisine, if not world cuisine. But in 1999, even with the French in contention, Terje Ness of Norway emerged the victor. Shortly thereafter, the Bocuse d'Or organizers announced that the winning country from the 2001 event would be permitted to return for the next Bocuse d'Or. Jérôme Bocuse said the timing of the rule change was a coincidence, but the Bocuse d'Or's own Web site headlines its summary of 1999 as "The Norwegian Lesson" and describes it thus: "The victory of the Norwegian chef boosted the contest by proving that France was not invincible." Since 2003, the French and Norwegians had such a stranglehold on the most precious of Bocuse d'Or metals—splitting the two top honors in three of the past five contests— that the reality of the competition, according to Michel Bouit, was that, "Twenty-two chefs are competing for the bronze."

Hollingsworth looked up the Norwegian, Geir Skeie, whose headshot depicted a wisp of a young man the same age as Hollingsworth, with icy blond hair and laser-like eyes that looked right off the screen and through whoever was gazing at him. In 1993, when he was just twelve years old, Skeie had sat in front of the family television and watched in wonder as his countryman Bent Stiansen, who had won the gold for Norway that year, described his Bocuse d'Or triumph on a cooking program. As he imagined glitter raining down on Stiansen at the Bocuse d'Or, and the crowd screaming for him, Skeie had decided that, according to the Bocuse d'Or press kit, "one day it would be his turn to participate."

These profiles, many of which indicated longtime Bocuse d'Or ambitions, were among Hollingsworth's first indications, other than past conversations with former housemate Lundgren, of what the contest meant to some European chefs. When he had taken on the Orlando challenge, he had no idea of what the Bocuse d'Or itself would be like. "I knew it was a famous culinary competition. Period," he said.

Even now, he barely knew the half of it: in reality, the phrasing of Skeie's profile—his "turn to participate"—was a politic way of expressing what Skeie really meant: it was his turn to *win*. At the age of twelve, he had already decided that he wanted to be a chef. "When I saw this on the TV," said Skeie, who speaks in blunt though not unfriendly proclamations, "I thought that must be the best thing you can do when you're a chef. I wanted to be the best chef, so that was the wish."

Skeie describes himself as highly competitive, a guy who "always liked winning" and, just as importantly, *hated* to lose. As a boy, he played soccer and did some shooting (target practice and hunting), and his lust for victory often led to arguments with his friends and his brother.

Like many of the European candidates, Skeie wasn't new to culinary competitions; if he were, he wouldn't have been taken seriously as a potential candidate to represent Norway. Skeie's competition experience dated back to 2000. He had been a member of the Norwegian national team, won the Norwegian championship in 2003, and placed third in both the Nordic and Norwegian Championships in 2004. To gather intel for the time when his own Bocuse d'Or moment arrived, Skeie went to Lyon on his own dime in 2005 and 2007 to attend the Bocuse d'Or as a spectator. He had not yet been selected as the Norwegian candidate when he attended the second time—that would come about two months later—but he had already made the cut to participate in the national trials.

Skeie had also put himself though physical hell in service of his childhood dream. In 2005, he fractured his kneecap in a car accident in the mountains of Norway, ramming into another car on his weekly commute from Oslo to the hotel where he was employed. He underwent strenuous physical therapy in order to firm up the muscle groups around it for extra support, eventually doing the exercises on his own, without a therapist. His doctors told him that the injury would shorten his kitchen career and that eventually he'd have to replace the kneecap, but these prognostications did nothing to deter him from his goal.

Hollingsworth, who had just learned that he'd be representing the United States, had no way of knowing the details of Skeie's preparation, but the Norwegian had made the most of his long lead time. For more than a year after he was selected to represent his country, he continued to work as chef de cuisine at Mathuset Solvold, where his employer, not coincidentally, was Odd Ivar Solvold, who won the bronze at the 1997 Bocuse d'Or. During that time, Skeie *thought* about his cuisine, not cooking even one garnish, but instead visualizing elements and compositions, imagining their flavors and how they would harmonize, taking them apart and reassembling them in his mind. In September 2008, about the same time Hollingsworth was finalizing his dishes for Orlando, Skeie was taking his actual Bocuse d'Or food out for a test drive in a kitchen outfitted with the same equipment he'd be using in Lyon; he'd have started earlier, but his participation in the Bocuse d'Or Europe in July (one of the continental contests that had been introduced in recent years), ironically, distracted him from the upcoming world competition.

In addition to employer Solvold, who was on board as Skeie's coach, the community of Norwegian Bocuse d'Or medalists and other past participants was crucial to Skeie. "Most important was Odd Ivar, because he was with me all the time," said Skeie. But other past candidates gave him important input: When Skeie and Solvold had the idea of outfitting a van with a training kitchen while in Lyon, so that he would be able to simply cook, without having to lug equipment to and from a training space, Eyvind Hellstrøm, who had placed fifth at the Bocuse d'Or in 1989, offered a hearty endorsement of the notion, opining that it would be well worth the trouble. As his training progressed, Skeie would also invite Hellstrøm and Stiansen (the one he had watched on television as a boy) to taste his food and offer feedback.

In addition to Skeie, Hollingsworth couldn't help but think of Lundgren, who displayed a short and spiky hairstyle in his photo, which showed him holding a spoon and grinning almost mischievously—the very picture of quiet confidence. Lundgren hadn't been selected until February 2008, which was about the time Boulud was courting Keller in the United States, but which Lundgren considered "too late. You should select your candidate as soon as the [previous] Bocuse d'Or is over."

Lundgren is an athlete: he plays soccer and participates in amateur body-building contests, and he likened preparing for the Bocuse d'Or to training for the Olympic Games. Determined to make the most of his one shot at glory, he withdrew from his restaurant work after the Bocuse d'Or Europe in July, though he did take some part-time work for the money, as did his commis, Öyvind Novak.

Like Skeie, Lundgren was able to glean advice and inspiration from former Swedish competitors, primarily Matthias Dahlgren, who brought home the gold in 1997, and 2001 silver medalist Henrik Norström. Though he was wary of being able to incorporate much input from that many chefs, he found the practical information from these *consiglieri* indispensable in preparing for the singular, fleeting demands of the Bocuse d'Or such as that onerous lag time between platter and plate.

"You are not used to working like that," said Lundgren. "Normally, you cook, your ten people plate the plate, and thirty seconds later the guest has the plate. That is the beauty of a restaurant. Here you have to plate something that is going to be fantastic and really good after half an hour on a silver tray. That is difficult."

Denmark was also on Hollingsworth's mind. "I know the way the Scandinavians are thinking and I know how competitive they are and so I thought that they would be a challenge," he said. Recent results bore out his logic: Denmark was on the march in the Bocuse d'Or, having won bronze in 2005 and silver in 2007.

Hollingsworth also took special interest in these candidates because the chefs from these countries were all about his age, with similar kitchen experience. This meant something to him because, while he proffers a great deal of respect for history, he is also a fiercely forward-looking chef; he rarely uses the adjective *traditional* to describe classic cookery, opting instead for the pejorative *old*.

And, of course, he thought about Philippe Mille, the French candidate: in all the years of the Bocuse d'Or, when the French had competed, they had never placed lower than second. But beyond that, he knew the reputation of Mille's employer and mentor, Yannick Alléno, the acclaimed chef who won the silver medal at the 1999 Bocuse d'Or. "I thought he would definitely be a challenge because of France and because of Yannick," said Hollingsworth, who had made a point of picking up Alléno's book *4 Saisons à la Table No.5: Le Meurice, Paris* and was impressed by how "tight" it was, the word Hollingsworth uses to describe a real clarity of vision.

Mille was an unusual candidate for the Bocuse d'Or because, other than the contest to become the French candidate, he had never participated in a culinary competition before. "I am not what we call informally in French *une bête de concours* [a beast of competition]," he said. But, although he had never attended the Bocuse d'Or, he had been attracted to it since observing Alléno's preparation in 1999. "I was quite impressed by his training, his involvement, and even the pressure and the enthusiasm around him," said the chef. In turn, Alléno had proved invaluable to Mille in his preparation, advising him on how to manage the intense media scrutiny the French candidate is subjected to, and helping conceive dishes, such as the caviar pie garnish that would figure prominently in Mille's seafood platter.

AND WHAT OF THE American candidate, Hollingsworth himself, the young cook who would be representing the United States?

The twenty-eight-year-old was born to divorced mom Karen Chavez in Houston, Texas, in January 1980. He was originally christened Timothy Chavez, although Chavez wasn't his biological father's name; it had been his mother's married name. When Timothy was four months old, Karen met Quentin Hollingsworth at the Baptist church they both attended. The two began seeing each other, married, and eventually moved to the town of Shingle Springs, California, when Timothy was in second grade. In time, since Quentin Hollingsworth had filled the role of Timothy's father since before he could walk or talk, the boy took the man's last name, just as his mother had before him. Today, Hollingsworth always refers to his stepfather as his father, and rarely feels the need to explain the adoptive nature of their relationship.

When Timothy was in fifth grade, the family moved to Grizzly Flats,

California, nestled in the mountains between Sacramento and Lake Tahoe, a rural area where the closest sundries shop was a quarter of an hour away, and "our backyard was a national forest." (In truth, the national forest was about one-eighth of a mile down the dirt road from where the Hollingsworths lived in the company of just three neighboring houses.)

His parents recall him as a confident kid, capable in sports, even though their remote location made it tough for him to play on school teams because of the onerous transportation demands it would have put on his family.

His first food role model was his mother, although she was more of a baker. "I never had Oreo cookies in my school lunch. I never had Chips Ahoy," recalls Hollingsworth. He and the rest of his family—Michelle, Brian, Kevin, and Amber, half-siblings all—fondly recall homemade lasagna, pizza prepared from scratch, chicken and dumplings, and beef stew, although Karen Hollingsworth, an exceedingly shy, modest woman, doesn't have much of a memory for her own repertoire.

As a boy, Hollingsworth never envisioned a lifetime in the kitchen. His first work experience was not with his mother, but with his father. When he was in the fifth grade, he began spending weekends working construction alongside his dad, a burly man who sports a goatee and spectacles today. They worked long hours, often spending the day on paid business, breaking for dinner, then helping fellow parishioners renovate or repair their homes, which they did free of charge as members of their church and community. Being reared in such a devout environment had a reverberating influence on Timothy: to this day, though he's capable—as most chefs are—of letting an occasional f-bomb fly in the heat of a dinner service or after work at Yountville's lone late-night watering hole, Pancha's, he doesn't swear in front of his parents. He also prides himself on his integrity, how he treats others both at work and outside the restaurant.

Hollingsworth's father was demanding, described even by Karen as a "perfectionist," and young Timothy learned to be exacting working alongside him. "See there," his father would tell him, stabbing his finger in the direction of a shoddy paint job. "See how they didn't cut in right?" Timothy would study the streaky, uneven coats, nod his comprehension and, in time, the contempt his father felt for a job poorly done became his contempt. If they borrowed tools or equipment from other workers, Quentin Hollingsworth would deep-clean them, dismantling and reassembling the parts if necessary, returning them to the owner in better condition than they had gone out. "See that," he'd say to Timothy, turning a tiller to show him the freshly glinting steel. "Remember how it looked before? It looks better now, right?"

Timothy had an aptitude for construction. Quentin Hollingsworth recalls that, by age ten, he had begun tagging along to jobs, and naturally evolved into an extra set of hands that he could count on. And Timothy wasn't alone; his brothers followed in his boot-clad footsteps. Quentin Hollingsworth's boss was so impressed by Timothy and his siblings' work ethic that he told Mr. Hollingsworth, "When my son gets of age, he is working for *you*."

"I don't know," says the senior Hollingsworth on hearing himself describe the family dynamic. "Maybe I demand too much. They seem to learn. All of my boys are hard workers . . . we have worked twenty-four-hour shifts and [Timothy] is right there working with me."

When he reached his late teens, Timothy decided he wanted to find something he could call his own. He considered becoming a fireman or an EMT (emergency medical technician), which he imagined offered an appealing lifestyle and relatively little risk in such a small town, "the ability to be able to work out and kind of have a good life. Something a little bit exciting."

That might have been his path had his brother-in-law, Aaron, not worked at Zachary Jacques [Country French] Restaurant in nearby Placerville, and had he not gotten Timothy a job there as a dishwasher. The restaurant was a true mom-and-pop operation, owned by a couple, Christian and Jennifer Masse, who ran it after a classic fashion: he was the chef; she was the maitre d' and pastry chef. Before long, Timothy, who had never considered becoming a cook, let alone a chef, was promoted to the restaurant's equivalent of *garde manger*, the cook charged with salads and other cold food preparations. He demonstrated an aptitude for cooking, and in the small kitchen the owners were delighted to teach him as much as he wanted to absorb. He developed into the chef's right-hand man, and picked up some pastry prowess along the way. Their trust in Hollingsworth and his ability were so complete that, when the couple went on vacation, they'd leave the place in his care.

Hollingsworth enjoyed cooking, and had the combination of basic skills that make for, at the least, a successful culinary professional: a good and malleable palate, soft hands, and a tireless work ethic. He also had a flair for cooking instinctually, which was useful in a kitchen where there were a total of four employees and the chef passed his recipes down like oral history. Chef Masse also shared his personal story with his young protégé, spinning yarns of his time in various cities around the world, learning his craft. He talked of the great chefs of France, with a special emphasis on three-star Michelin honorees. Hollingsworth, who had never been across an ocean, was intrigued: the romanticized tales sparked something in him. He'd look at the sauces and salads, pâtés, and plats du jour they were preparing, and envision them in their original contexts; the combination of stories and stimulation created something akin to a chemical reaction: he *had* to know more. To this day, he can't put words to why. The attraction was as unexplainable, and unexamined, as love at first sight.

Masse loaned him the works of Escoffier and Louis Saulnier's *Le Repertoire de la Cuisine*. Hollingsworth read them at home, then would bound into the kitchen the next day, eagerly asking about sauces and preparations, which the chef was only too happy to explain. The next thing he knew, Hollingsworth was addicted to culinary books, buying them up from the nearest Barnes & Noble. "I never stopped reading," he said. "I would read and read. I would wake up in the morning, I would read. Go to the gym, work all day, and then after work sit at the bar in the restaurant and talk and read the books. Then go home and read."

Hollingsworth moved into his own apartment in Placerville, and started trying his hand at cooking beyond the restaurant's repertoire. Sometimes he'd invite his mother and maternal grandmother over and make them simple dinners; his mother recalls fish with "little asparagus and some kind of little potatoes." Following the example of his employer, he rarely used recipes except for formula-like pastry recipes, instead preferring to operate on intuition and instinct.

One of the countless cookbooks he read around this time was Thomas Keller's much-lauded *The French Laundry Cookbook*. As much a biography as a collection of recipes, *The French Laundry Cookbook* depicts, in breathtaking photographs by Deborah Jones, the food and setting that had been slowly but surely earning the restaurant a reputation as one of the premier dining destinations in the country. The book resonated with Hollingsworth more than almost any other. He would experiment with the techniques that author Keller periodically stopped to describe, such as big-pot blanching, his preferred way of cooking green vegetables to preserve their color and uniformly season them by using a lot of water relative to the quantity of vegetables so that the temperature didn't drop significantly when the ingredients were added, and a lot of salt, about one cup per gallon of water. Where Masse only put a modicum of baking soda (rather than salt) in his blanching water for, say, green beans, Hollingsworth tried Keller's recommended method, but only when the chef was away, so he wouldn't get upset at the expense.

The more he read and cooked, the more he found himself gravitating toward Keller and to Alain Ducasse, the deified French chef who had opened a restaurant at the Essex House Hotel in New York City in 2000, and who had himself penned a number of exquisitely produced books. Hollingsworth made a one-man fact-finding trip cross country to check out the nation's preeminent cooking school, The Culinary Institute of America, and dined at Le Cirque and Ducasse. But he decided against both culinary school and New York City, realizing that he'd rather stick close to home.

And so, he set his sights on The French Laundry.

Hollingsworth hatched a plan to gain employment at his target destination, making a dinner reservation for himself, his girlfriend at the time, and two acquaintances who owned a cooking shop in Grizzly Flats. When he booked the table, he confirmed with the reservationist that Keller himself would be working the night of his visit, and told her that he wanted to meet the chef during a kitchen tour—a by-request tradition at The French Laundry dating back to the days when it was owned by Don and Sally Schmitt—and to personally hand him his resumé.

The quartet went to dinner. They were on a budget but wanted to try everything, so they shared the foie gras dish that required a supplemental charge. Hollingworth was "blown away," and after the meal, a manager led him through the hushed corridor known as The Breezeway, where waiters and sommeliers transition from the pressure-cooker setting of the kitchen to the elegant hush of the dining room. Up ahead, in the shimmering kitchen, Thomas Keller himself was standing at the pass, a marble table draped with white linen fastened in place with green tape, and tickets lined up along the edge closest to him. Hollingsworth introduced himself and handed off his resumé.

Back in Placerville, Hollingsworth began a telephone campaign. He rang Keller but declined to leave a message for him, instead calling incessantly until he finally caught the chef at a moment of availability. Keller invited him to come to the restaurant and "trail" for a day, meaning that he would be put to work, observed, and evaluated. Hollingsworth did, but failed to impress the chef de cuisine, Eric Ziebold. Then the funniest thing happened: Keller hired him anyway. "It was really a miscommunication between Eric and me about Timmy's future," recalled Keller. "Eric didn't think that he would amount to anything and I did."

Regardless of how it happened, Hollingsworth was over the moon. He still has the letter from the restaurant's human resources associate offering him the job. "It was the best thing that has ever happened to me," he said.

———

ONCE HE WAS ACCEPTED as a finalist for Orlando, Hollingsworth's first order of business had been to identify a commis, the assistant whose success would help determine his own and, if he won, that of Team USA.

He had heard some buzz about a young cook at Bouchon, Keller's bistro down Washington Street from The French Laundry, and gave the kid a shot, but friction ensued. Hollingsworth is too polite to say much more than "his personality wasn't a good match for me to be working with day in and day out, side by side, for something that was so important."

The one illustrative transaction Hollingsworth did volunteer is what might be aptly dubbed The Turnip Incident. He asked the commis to turn a turnip, a simple enough task—cutting a turnip down to a sharply angled football shape. But turning isn't just about shaping. Even though this turnip wasn't bound for the dining room, a turned turnip, in the chef's mind, has certain connotations *no matter where it is headed*: it should be immaculate, it should be thoroughly peeled, and the edges should be as defined as a D flawless diamond.

Instead, the cook brought him a turnip to which traces of peel were still attached, along with a few coffee ground–sized particles of dirt.

This alienated Hollingsworth. "What you bring to me is a reflection on yourself . . . it reflects on you and what you think of me," said Hollingsworth. This wasn't the first time he'd encountered a cook who perceived a difference between dress rehearsal and performance, but it irked him fiercely. "They show me something and I will be, like, 'You are going to show me something and tell me, "Well, I will do it differently next time?"'"

The monologue was a perfect illustration of the influences of his two fathers—the professional father, Keller, and his talk of precision as a way of life, not something that can be switched on and off, and his all-but-biological father, Quentin Hollingsworth, pointing out subpar workmanship and saying, "We don't do that."

Such is the culture of mutual respect within the Thomas Keller Restaurant Group that, despite his frustrations, Hollingsworth wasn't willing to unceremoniously dismiss the commis, especially since it was he who had invited the cook to join him in the Orlando adventure in the first place. He spoke to Corey Lee about his predicament, then to The Chef. Both supported his need to captain his own ship. At Keller's suggestion, Hollingsworth called Phil Tessier, chef de cuisine of Bouchon, and explained the situation, then met with the commis in what became a ninety-minute conversation that Hollingsworth wanted to be as constructive as possible.

But first, he had surreptitiously begun the hunt for a new commis. One of The French Laundry's chefs de partie, Rodney Wages, who worked the fish station at the time, pointed him toward Adina Guest, a commis at the Laundry who had come on for a three-month externship and was hired as an official employee two months in based on her strong performance and because a position had opened up. Hollingsworth had had very little interaction with Guest, and in fact had only recently realized she was American. Her face, with its round, somewhat sunken cheeks, and the halting cadence of her voice led him to believe that she was European, maybe Swiss. He wasn't too far off: Guest's mother, Katrin, is Swiss by birth and she and her younger sister Arielle had lived in Switzerland for a time. "You looked at her, and the first thing you thought was: *Heidi*," said Frank Leake, who instructed Guest at Kapi'olani Community College, and whom Guest considers a mentor.

Hollingsworth had taken note of Guest before. Believing that you can tell if somebody has the right stuff, or at least the right attitude, almost at first sight he appreciated her head-down determination and respect for the chain of command.

He also believed that she had talent. One of the preparations the commis are regularly charged with at The French Laundry is making chive chips—paper-thin slices of potato fused around a chive segment. The final product is plunged into truffle oil–infused custards served in an eggshell, one of The French Laundry's signature offerings. Hollingsworth often came into the prep area with a linen-lined pan of freshly made chive chips in hand, pointing out why they had to be made over from scratch. There were any number of reasons why they might need to be redone: if there were air bubbles between the layers, if the chive wasn't straight, if the chip wasn't crispy, or maybe the color was off.

One day, Guest made the chive chips: she shaved translucent potato slices on a mandoline, laying them on a Silpat (a nonstick baking mat made from fiberglass and silicone) brushed with clarified butter and sprinkled with salt; positioned a chive segment in the center of each slice; topped it with another potato slice; squeezed out the air; then topped it with another butter-and-salt treated Silpat. She pressed out any air bubbles, weighted the stack with press pans, and baked them in the oven. When they were done, she walked them out of the back into the main kitchen, and up to Hollings-worth.

"Chef, if these are not all right, I'll do them over," she said.

Hollingsworth scarcely looked at the chips.

"Adina," he said, "I can tell from here that those are fine. What I need you to do is show those other guys how to make them like that."

With The Turnip Incident firmly in mind, he asked Wages to take six carrots to Guest and tell her to turn them as fast as she could. When Wages found Guest, it was at the end of her day, and she was scrubbing the windows that looked out on the courtyard.

"Am I going for perfection or for speed?" asked Guest. Ironically, though she had no idea what was behind the task, it was her competition experience that drove the question; she had participated in four competitions, both individual and team events, and the timing component of Wages's command brought them to mind.

Guest stopped cleaning the kitchen, switched gears, and went to work on the carrots, her hands dancing over them with the peeler, the knife cutting them into segments, then both hands working in harmony to turn and shave them down to the desired shape. Guest is an intense person and an intense worker, and her focus, especially when handed a specific task, is absolute. And she is *fast*.

"Done!" she yelled. Just two minutes had elapsed.

Wages gave nothing away, no sign of either disappointment or approval.

"Keep cleaning," he said, and she went back to work.

Hollingsworth didn't really care how many carrots Guest turned. What he wanted to see was whether she *got it*—did she peel the carrots thoroughly before turning them? Were they good and properly turned? Were they clean?

The answer, on all fronts, was *yes*.

Hollingsworth wasn't surprised, because he'd seen Guest's handiwork, and expected the level of perfection that The French Laundry demanded. Thomas Keller, in his introduction to *The French Laundry Cookbook*, set down one of the most famous lines ever inked in a recipe tome: "When you acknowledge, as you must, that there is no such thing as perfect food, only the idea of it, then the real purpose of striving toward perfection becomes clear: to make people happy. That's what cooking is all about."

Keller says that he wrote that line "because everybody says, 'Thomas Keller is this perfectionist.' Over and over again it is what I hear: 'Thomas Keller is a perfectionist.' But I don't necessarily believe that about myself. I am always striving to do a better job in the quest for perfection. Does that mean I am a perfectionist? I don't know. It always bothered me. I wrote that phrase. This is it. This is what cooking is all about. Not to be perfect but to make people happy. At the end of the day that is what it is about. It can come from a quest for perfection in sourcing the best lamb. It can come from a quest for perfection in cutting the perfect brunoise. It can come from a quest for perfection in having the most beautiful china. At the end of the day what is it going to do? The plate is going to come and sit before you and you are going to eat it. And what do I want to have happen? I don't want you to say, 'Well, Goddamn, that Thomas Keller is a perfectionist.' I want you to be happy with what you are eating."

The line is immortalized on plaques in the kitchens of The French

Laundry and at Per Se, and even in Keller's more casual establishments, and there's an air of twelve-stepdom about it—the acknowledgment of a higher power and a lesser-known Alcoholics Anonymous mantra, the desire to achieve "progress not perfection." Keller didn't offer this connection, but any observer of kitchen culture will attest that chefs can be perfection junkies, criticizing themselves and their colleagues ad infinitum. On a day when ninety-nine things go right, they will home in on the one that went wrong. This makes for better cooks, but it can also be devastating to morale, as well as self-esteem.

"We have to be able say we really did a good job," said Keller. "We have to be able to pat ourselves on the back. We have to be able to feel that we have achieved some level of success. We may not have achieved exactly what we wanted to do. We have to be able to feel confident and comfortable, too, and kind of celebrate our successes rather than continuously beating us down. That is my, I don't want to say biggest fault, but I am constantly my worst critic. . . . You give me something that is amazing and I will try to find something wrong with it rather than telling you it is really a great dish. . . . It's a hard thing being hard on yourself and how that translates to everyone around you. I have heard many times throughout my life, 'Chef, can't you tell us once in a while that we did a good job?' "

"All I hear is, 'You are not happy? You are not happy? Can't you say you are happy once in a while?' For the past several years, five years or so, I have been trying to say 'yes' and not at the same time try to encourage people to do better work. But acknowledge our successes . . ."

Despite this philosophy from The Chef, there's no shortage of talk about perfection at The French Laundry. Of those carrots and his selection of Guest to be his commis, Hollingsworth said, "Being in this environment you know the level of perfection that you have to do. You know that if you are turning a carrot or you are shucking fava beans or splitting peas. Whatever you are doing, it better be done correctly or something will be said to you. It's not like you turn a turnip and there is still a little piece of peel. That is absolutely unacceptable."

Guest herself, though still a relative newbie, had already absorbed this aspect of life at The French Laundry. She had already attained a level of authority among the commis that required her sometimes to correct externs, or tell them to do a more efficient job with, say, their brunoise. She would sometimes get pushback, which she attributes to her youth and sex. This used to throw her, but now she has no hesitancy to demonstrate her own lightning-quick technique in order to make her point. She recognizes the importance of at least striving toward perfection because, as somebody once pointed out to her, "People are getting charged $250 [actually $240] per [meal]. You are here to learn. This is how we do it, so I expect you to do it like this from now on and push yourself to do better. . . . It's one of the best motivational things to say. Yes, of course all 100 of those arugula leaves have to be perfect. There is no point in arguing, 'Oh, it's just arugula' or 'That's just a bug bite.' *Pick the better arugula.*"

Minutes after delivering her carrots to Hollingsworth, Wages told Guest to report to the chef's office, a glassed-in cubicle with a sliding door, right next to the kitchen. Inclined to be hard on herself—she routinely sits on the edge of her bed at night agonizing over what she might have done better throughout her day, whom she could have been kinder to, or what she could have improved in her work—Guest naturally assumed that she had failed some kind of test.

"So, I guess you know I'm doing the Bocuse d'Or," said Hollingsworth.

"Yes, Chef."

"Would you like to do it with me?"

"Yes, totally!" she said without hesitation.

The commis could scarcely believe it, especially because she knew there was another commis on board. But more than that, she loved competing. "It is in my blood," she said. "It pushes me to the extremes and challenges me to be a better cook, a better person, a better everything."

She left the office and headed back to work; the Game Face slipped out of place for a moment, but she had righted it by the time she got back to her colleagues.

———

IN PREPARATION FOR ORLANDO, Hollingsworth and Guest practiced in the evenings on days when Hollingsworth worked a lunch service, commandeering the prep kitchen of The French Laundry and starting when the hot line went into dinner service. It made for endless days, which affected them differently: Hollingsworth, accustomed to cook's hours and raised in a double-shift environment, had no problems with it. Guest, who had never worked service and freely admits to needing a full night's sleep, found it tiring, but the adrenaline sustained her.

The intensity of such a working relationship, and the sweet nectar of victory in Orlando, might have made for a quick friendship in other scenarios, but Hollingsworth was careful not to let things get too casual between himself and Guest because, when it was all over, he'd need to go back to being a sous chef at The French Laundry and she'd need to go back to being one of the commis. There was no room for an intimacy that would make it difficult for him to give orders to her the same way he did to anybody else, or for others to feel that there was favoritism in his treatment of her. The chain of command had to be preserved above all else.

Besides, after they'd won in Orlando, they were back home, and weren't spending much time together. Though the Bocuse d'Or USA had publicized a paid three-month sabbatical for the chef-candidate, Hollingsworth wasn't ready to jump off The French Laundry ship just yet. First he wanted to spend some time getting his head around the competition. And while he was prepared to train mightily, he wasn't ready to abandon his job. It might have been different if he'd known back in, say, January, that he was going to audition for the part—then Lee could have taken the necessary steps to prepare for his absence. "If I said, 'Tomorrow I am going to quit my job, I want to give my notice,' my notice is not a month. It's not three months, either. It's *six* months. It's a year. It's a very respectful time that you give to leave your job and your position," he said. Hollingsworth had given this topic some thought about this time because he had privately considered leaving The French Laundry, most likely for an extended stay in Thailand to chill out and recharge, but had decided against it.

About the sabbatical, Thomas Keller said the idea was born out of an abundance of excitement, and because he and other committee members had heard about how intensely some Europeans trained. "We weren't thinking of it practically, realistically . . . we didn't think it out very well," he said. Echoing this sentiment, Corey Lee said, "I think that the Bocuse d'Or organizers highly publicized that there would be this time given to this candidate was a little bit unrealistic and very poorly planned . . . there's no fine-dining restaurant in the world who can replace a significant sous chef in two months. When that came out I think everyone knew that was an unrealistic thing. . . . I don't think there was a question in anyone's mind that he wouldn't have that opportunity to take a full three-and-a-half months off . . . the American selection process was way too close to the actual competition."

For Hollingsworth, staying on was an unspoken expectation. His commitment to his job had always been unflagging; in seven years, he had only asked for an extra day off once, to attend his brother's wedding. So after Hollingsworth won in Orlando, he and Lee hashed out an arrangement for an extra four days off per month for him and Guest in October, November, and December. Conveniently, The French Laundry would be closed for most of January, as it is every year, so the three weeks leading up to the competition were wide open.

The shift in plans was essentially concealed from the public and the competition. "I've been helping out," was how Hollingsworth was directed to answer media inquiries about his schedule. But members of the Bocuse d'Or committee said they were fine with it. "We were thinking like that [having a three-month sabbatical] because we were having a candidate coming from who-knows-where and we had to put him somewhere in a boot camp, but he [Hollingsworth] was already in the camp there," said Boulud.

Moreover, Hollingsworth *wanted* to conceive his Bocuse d'Or food where he'd done just about everything else related to cooking for the past seven years, not just where he honed his craft, but also where he'd helped shape and execute new menus on a daily basis. As a manager-level staff member, he was confident he'd be able to carve out time in his day to devote to the Bocuse d'Or. "Every day that you are in that kitchen cooking, you are training," he said. "I am thinking about the menu when I am turning carrots. I am thinking about the menu when I have free time to try to do something that I want to work on." Hollingsworth also planned to incorporate ideas for his competition food into the restaurant's menu when possible, trying them out in a real-world context.

Hollingsworth also needed time—*a lot* of time—to think about his menu. The style of cooking that wins the Bocuse d'Or and other competitions, with very few exceptions, was almost antithetical to the mindset he'd been honing at The French Laundry, where the daily menu comprises a series of compositions that are elegant but rarely elaborate: the quality of the ingredients and the finesse of the staff are such that a few perfectly cooked vegetables, a piece of protein, and a *jus*, unfussily arranged, are one possible equation for a meat course.

"He knows how to execute *our* food," said Devin Knell, executive sous chef of The French Laundry. "It is a big challenge to learn how to cook [competition food]. . . . Our food is: one, ingredients; two, flavor composition; and three, execution. . . . We don't try putting so many cooking techniques into one dish to show off. We are trying to do the best we can with a piece of striped bass."

Translation: Thomas Keller might just want to make people happy, but when those people happened to be the Bocuse d'Or judges, there would only be one way to achieve that: *perfection*.

ROLAND HENIN, VETERAN CULINARY competitor and coach, understood this only too well. He also believed that Hollingsworth's learning curve would be steep. Henin hadn't tasted Hollingsworth's winning dishes in

Orlando, but he had seen them: "The presentation in Orlando was pretty simplistic, to be nice," he said later. "The taste of the food is what carried them in Orlando and I believe strongly that it is the taste of the food that will carry them [in Lyon]. Whether or not it will carry them all the way to the top it is difficult to call. I am not sure."

With all of that in mind, Henin was fashioning a month-at-a-glance training schedule that assumed Hollingsworth and Guest would be available full time. It was an aggressive plan that called for developing "tentative menus with first and second options" the week of Monday, November 3, then spending the following week honing the fish platter in the kitchen and the week after that doing the same with the meat platter. According to Henin's vision, the team would actually serve guests in January, to provide them essential practice plating from the platters.

Henin made two unproductive visits to Yountville in early November, finding Hollingsworth largely unavailable because, in addition to his working schedule, he was down with the flu for several days. But the two did engage in some tense conversations over the calendar. In addition to the schedule, Henin tried to convince Hollingsworth to employ a grid that would ensure they hit all the necessary marks on both platters: flavors, textures, colors, and so on. Hollingsworth wasn't interested; those were obvious concerns, he said, and ones that he considered on a daily basis when he shepherded a new menu to fruition at The French Laundry. Hollingsworth would later acknowledge that he took the grid suggestion personally, a sign that even though he might have been ignorant of the ways of competition, Henin didn't give him credit for all that he *did* know.

Despite the tension, Henin—who is nothing if not a realist—tried to keep an open mind about Hollingsworth's fidelity to his job, especially if he could weave proteins and garnishes from his platter into the daily menu at The French Laundry, as he planned to. "I am all for it," said Henin. "*If* it can be done. If you can incorporate [the food into the restaurant menu], so much the better, as a practical issue and an economical one, too, because you don't waste the food. You get feedback from the customer and you can pay for the food that you used." But the coach quickly developed the opinion that Hollingsworth was "in limbo . . . neither at work, neither in practice, he was always in between." He also had the feeling that the candidate didn't understand what he was up against. Hadn't Hollingsworth taken those words from The French Culinary Institute to heart, the ones about it not mattering what you've done before, where you work, or who you know? Even to a sous chef from The French Laundry, a culinary competition, especially a five-hour-plus labor of love like the Bocuse d'Or, was something to be respected—the difference between basic training and actual combat, or in Henin's preferred long-distance-running analogy, a sprint and a marathon.

In an attempt to accommodate everybody's needs, a revised monthly calendar was fashioned that included the coach's goals while also showing the days Hollingsworth was committed to working his regular job. One glance revealed a daunting void at the end of November, when Hollingsworth was set to work at The French Laundry Saturday the twenty-second and Sunday the twenty-third, then decamp for Maine and girlfriend Kate Laughlin's family for the Thanksgiving holiday—a week of non-Bocuse time after which he'd be plunked down in December, just six weeks from the departure to Lyon.

Henin couldn't have disagreed more with *that* decision. "Not when you have the Bocuse d'Or in six weeks!" he said.

BEYOND THE SCHEDULING KERFUFFLE, the truth was that Hollingsworth just plain didn't want company yet, not from Henin, not from anybody. He might have been working, but by early November, feeling ready to try his hand at competition platters, he had also been conceptualizing his cuisine and he felt he had to do it on his own, that his dishes needed to flow naturally from him and be given the time and oxygen to grow.

There's no one path to conceiving a dish. But for many chefs, the creative moment—the instant when an idea emerges from the primordial mental swamp, either fully formed or requiring further evolution—often does not involve a protein. The average diner might be surprised to know that the fish, poultry, or meat is frequently the last tumbler to fall into place; as often as not, inspiration offers up a notion for a fresh variation on a familiar theme, a new sauce, or a combination of accompaniments. Even for those chefs who begin the thought process with a protein, it's almost unheard of that they would begin with three or four of them in mind.

This is one of the distinct challenges of the Bocuse d'Or: the proteins are the *only* parameters dictated by the organizers, and both the fish and meat platter demand the harmonizing of several of them. In 2009, it would be Norwegian fresh cod, Norwegian king scallops, and Norwegian wild prawns on the fish platter, and Scotch Beef Aberdeen Angus oxtail, beef cheeks, *côte de boeuf* (bone-in rib-eye, of which each candidate would be receiving three on a "carvery cut forerib"), and fillet (tenderloin) on the meat.

In addition to the assigned proteins, Hollingsworth had imposed some other parameters on himself. Because time was short, he had decided to incorporate preparations that Guest already had expertise in from her work at The French Laundry. Chive chips weren't the only thing she already knew how to do: she also did a lot of Silpat work, such as making melba toasts and *pommes Maxim* (potato rounds tossed in clarified butter and baked together in an overlapping pattern), and adored brunoise for the precision it demanded. To give her a head start, or to help her make up lost time, Hollingsworth wanted to work those elements and techniques into his Bocuse d'Or food as well.

Beyond the hours he devoted at The French Laundry, Hollingsworth began spending personal time on his Bocuse d'Or menu. He'd sit in the living room of his Napa apartment, cookbooks surrounding him on shelves high and low, a steady blend of rap and hip-hop blaring out open windows, and, with the California breeze ruffling its pages, make preliminary drawings in a sketch pad, occasionally flying an idea by Laughlin, both for her feedback and because hearing the ideas out loud made them seem more "real" to him.

There's no point denying the obvious: it had been more than a month since Orlando, and Hollingsworth was struggling, experiencing the cook's equivalent of writer's block. The meat selections practically tormented him. There might have been four different cuts, but when you got right down to it, they were all *beef*, and making your mark on beef is a distinct challenge. Because beef is such a powerful presence on the plate and the palate, it's often the least creative offering on even the most progressive menus.

Nevertheless, in fits and starts, ideas began to trickle forth. Building on his desire to present something distinctly American at the Bocuse d'Or, something identifiable and straightforward, he began to think of his mother. Hollingsworth often said that he cooked for his mother, tried to make food that, if she were to dine at The French Laundry, she would enjoy eating. His memories of her home cooking are so strong that foie gras at the restaurant is occasionally served atop a slice of Mrs. Hollingsworth's Banana Bread, so identified on the menu and made with her original recipe. This train of thought led him to the oxtail—a tough cut that requires braising or stewing to break down its connective tissues—and it occurred to him that maybe he'd cook it in a way that referenced his mom's beef stew.

It was a start, but the truth was that nothing he thought of or sketched out felt good enough, exciting enough, with enough bells and whistles for a competition. And did he even want those bells and whistles? A tension was emerging between who he was as a cook and what the Bocuse d'Or demanded of its competitors: he did not want his food to look like quintessential competition fare, with what he called "those funny circles." Twenty-eight-years-young, sitting there in his preferred personal-time ensemble of tattered jeans, a T-shirt, and black knit cap, he wasn't interested in cooking *old* food.

As crumpled pages flowed from his pad into the wastebasket, frustration mounted. But he stuck with it, and additional ideas began to come into focus. It dawned on him that he should confit the cod—slowly, gently cooking it in an olive oil bath—because that was the most foolproof way of dealing with the quirk of timing presented by the competition—the notorious lag time between food leaving the window and actually being tasted: "If I were to take a sautéed piece of fish and parade it around for twenty minutes, it's not going to be good," he said. "If I take a confit piece of fish, [it] can be piping hot or it can be ice cold and it is still going to be very good. It puts all the moisture inside of it." That moistness would also provide leeway; the fish could be slightly over- or undercooked and nobody would be the wiser.

He also had a partially formed idea for a garnish: sandwiching something (he wasn't sure what yet) between brioche melba toast rectangles and topping the sandwich-like stack with a rectangular custard and a piece of spring garlic (young, green garlic with a gentle, scallion-like flavor).

And that was where he was with little more than two months to go: a vague notion about riffing on his mother's beef stew, a decision to confit cod (probably), and a brioche-and-custard garnish—the most tenuous of beginnings for three of the eight components he'd need to come up with, then perfect, for his platters.

GAVIN KAYSEN, THREE THOUSAND miles away, monitored what was beginning to feel like snail's-pace progress from his small, sparse office overlooking the Café Boulud kitchen. There were no official systems of reporting established, so information from the West Coast was scarce, but Kaysen had been in touch with Hollingsworth sporadically by phone and e-mail. Having helped inspire Boulud, then Keller, to take on the Bocuse d'Or USA, Kaysen found the notion that not a single recipe had been finalized "nerve-wracking." Perhaps more than anybody, more even than Hollingsworth himself, Kaysen wanted the United States to touch that podium, and wanted to be a part of the effort that got it done. He felt that he understood Hollingsworth's quandary better than the candidate himself: you get picked to go to Lyon, then reality settles in; you realize what you're up against and how well-funded and well-organized the competition is, and that they've been to the event before, and have past medalists consulting them, and you mentally curl up in a fetal position—at least that's what Kaysen figured was going on. He'd done the same thing, but he'd had more time.

The situation wasn't lost on Boulud who, with hopes of jump-starting things, had planned an intensive week for the team in mid-November, reaching out to Joseph Viola, chef-owner of Daniel et Denise restaurant in Lyon and a former organizing committee member (the chefs who serve as technical judges, help parade the platters, and perform other essential tasks) for the Bocuse d'Or. The Bocuse d'Or USA paid Viola an undisclosed consulting fee to fly from France to California and impart his institutional knowledge of the competition to Hollingsworth. A working session was scheduled for Monday, November 17, with Chef Henin arriving that afternoon.

Kaysen had decided to join the group as well. Eager to get out west and light a fire under Hollingsworth, Kaysen arranged a Sunday arrival so the two of them could have a heart-to-heart, man-to-man, chef-to-chef confab before the others arrived. Kaysen also wanted to begin the process of downloading whatever intel he himself had to share, from a competitor's point of view. He was emerging as Team USA's recon guy, the one who had been behind enemy lines and lived to tell the tale, and he wanted to help Hollingsworth and Guest with little tricks such as laying carpet down in the competition kitchen to provide traction on the slick floors or draping a sheet of canvas over the open doorway at the back of the kitchen pod because Kitchen 6, where the team would be competing on Day 2 of the Bocuse d'Or, is right across the corridor from the door to the parking lot that swings open and closed all competition long; Kaysen still remembered well how powdery snow had accumulated in the doorway the day he competed.

Since Hollingsworth hadn't yet determined the food, former candidate Kaysen couldn't help but think about what *he* would do with the given proteins. One notion he had was bleaching the bones on the ribs of the côte de boeuf and making them the centerpiece of the beef platter: a manly celebration of the meat itself that he thought would resonate with other chefs. He had also begun compiling a list of the food that was going to be available from The French Laundry's Garden in January. He read from it: "Lettuces, radicchio, frisée, kale, collards, chard, baby beets, baby carrots, baby turnips, baby radish, green [spring] garlic, baby onions, baby leeks, broccoli, cauliflower, Romanesco (a psychedelic, lime-green summer cauliflower), and Savoy cabbage. Awesome!" He grinned wide as he imagined the possibilities: "You know, Savoy cabbage would be a really fun garnish to do with the beef."

Kaysen had also jotted down ideas for combinations and garnishes: "Cardoons and black truffles are always good with braised beef cheeks and shallot confit or shallot marmalade or a shallot tuile. Celery root, carrot cannelloni, stuffed cabbage. Smoked foie gras or poached foie gras with quince. Apples, celery leaves—one of the two. *Pommes dauphine* or *pommes* croquettes. Foie gras *cromesqui* [a savory croquette that retains heat very well] with port wine gelée or a port wine disk or black pepper tuile. A Lyonnaise-style potato cannelloni made with a *pommes cromesqui* on top of that."

He had just as many ideas for the fish platter: "Cod: Stuffed baby artichokes with confit cod belly wrapped in artichoke with green zucchini. Stencil leaves out of green zucchini for the green. Cod with black truffles is always a great combination. Scallop mousse. Possibly a monkfish liver. Can you poach monkfish liver? In Riesling? *Whatever.* Cardoons are good with shrimp. Shrimp crêpes with cabbage styled like an Alsatian clam chowder."

Kaysen was also taken with the idea of using candy dishes for serving that were produced by Austria's Lobmeyr and obtained in the United States from the design store Moss—individually hand-blown lidded orbs that stood on little stands that The French Laundry and Per Se sometimes used to smoke dishes à la minute: for example, a foie gras composition would be brought to a guest in the orb, the bowl full of freshly applied smoke, and when the lid was removed, the smoke would swirl around the food, dissipating as the diner dug in. At $245 each, these would be an expensive addition to the platters, but Kaysen thought they were worth it. At the moment, he was thinking they should be used to serve foie gras.

As he rattled off the possibilities, Kaysen spontaneously gave voice to the endgame in his mind: "We have got to figure out exactly what it is going to take to have him win," Kaysen said. *"We gotta hit that podium.* That would be huge."

Listening to Kaysen imagine all the possibilities, one could be forgiven for forgetting that he wouldn't actually be competing in 2009. And here's the funny thing about Kaysen: there are guys like him all over the world, chefs for whom the Bocuse d'Or is a sort of idée fixe: they competed once, didn't win, and are now on a mission to succeed, even vicariously. The more extreme cases suit up for a second go at the gold: Rasmus Kofoed of Denmark nabbed the bronze in 2005, then competed again in 2007, winning silver, but had decided against returning again in 2009. But there was one return contestant on the way: Australian candidate Luke Croston had been the commis on the 2003 team, then competed for his country in 2007, coming in twelfth. He would be there again in January 2009. Croston had been hooked on the Bocuse d'Or from his debut as a commis, which he called "a mind-blowing experience." Then twenty years old, he "had never seen anything that big. . . . I wanted to have a go at it myself and . . . see how close I could get to the top of the world," he said. When he placed twelfth, he decided to go for it again, because he was disappointed and felt he could do better. With Serge Vieira advising him, he had stopped working in late summer and begun training about five days a week.

Kaysen's mood swung from excitement to exasperation. Fueled by a personal passion for success at the Bocuse d'Or, Kaysen wanted to be as supportive as possible, but he also didn't want to waste time. For the coming week, Keller's precise, hospitality-minded team had arranged a thoughtful visit for their guests, with no detail left to chance—the schedule indicated where lunch was going to come from and when (for example, "12:30 p.m., Sandwiches from [Bouchon] Bakery"), and group dinners planned each night. Though he imagined one of those dinners might be scrapped in favor of him and Hollingsworth getting in the kitchen and actually *cooking*, Kaysen was okay with them. But when he saw that a tour of the West Coast outpost of The Culinary Institute of America at Greystone, just up Highway 29 from Yountville, had been planned for Tuesday morning, he e-mailed the schedule back with one word added in red next to the field trip: "Why?"

The CIA excursion was promptly canceled.

WITH THOUGHTS OF TOUGH love in mind, Kaysen arrived in Yountville late Sunday morning, November 16. Northern California was summery then, with squint-inducing sunlight, temperatures in the high sixties, and not a trace of humidity. Kaysen ducked into Bouchon for lunch, then met Hollingsworth outside the restaurant and the two of them walked along Washington Street to the Bocuse House, as people had taken to referring to the former home of Edward Keller, where a Marine Corps flag still flew over the porch.

Hollingsworth wasn't thrilled about the coming week. He felt the need to work on his platters and didn't know what to do with all these people around. He ran the question by Keller, who—according to Hollingsworth—told him, "This is your thing, Tim. If you want to meet with these guys for an hour and then you want to leave afterward and go do your own thing, you can do that. This is your deal. You can do whatever you want."

Kaysen was immediately struck, as most visitors were, that the structure that housed Team USA's much publicized training center was, unmistakably, a *house*. Up a few steps from the sidewalk to the porch and through the front door, one entered a living room with wainscoted walls and a built-in entertainment center on the right. To the left was a modest living room outfitted with a brown leather couch, a low-lying coffee table, and behind that was a little office nook with a desk, a computer, and a printer. In a corner were large corrugated cardboard boxes filled with smaller All-

Clad white boxes containing brand-new mixing bowls, pots, and pans—a good indicator of where the team was, or wasn't, in its development.

Just past the living room was the kitchen, with two rolling prep tables in the center of the room, and all that equipment that matched what was to be provided in Lyon organized around its perimeter: a Convotherm combi oven (capable of producing dry heat, steam, and a combination), a Garland salamander (an industrial strength broiler) and electric range, a Delfield refrigerator, undercounter refrigerator, and freezer, a microwave oven, blast chiller, heat lamp—about $100,000 in equipment. But even with all this top-of-the-line machinery, it felt more like a home kitchen than Kaysen had expected, with a skylight in the ceiling and a back door that led out to a small deck. A few details personalized the space even further, like the Mickey Mouse trophy from Orlando that rested on the window ledge, and the round Obama magnet stuck to the side of the freezer, put there by Keller himself. Adina Guest, between homes and taking full advantage of her invitation to live there as a member of the team, also had some personal food items, such as cereal, stored in glass canisters.

The House had been somewhat hurriedly renovated, which led to a few idiosyncrasies: the ventilation system for the stove was positioned several feet away from the cooking surface rather than directly above it, and the area under the sink was not a finished cabinet but rather an open space that housed cleaning supplies and a garbage can behind a drab curtain. (This detail, above all others, nagged at Keller. "It really bothers me," he said. Keller's assistant Molly Ireland said that she knew when she and her colleagues put that curtain up that "it definitely was not French Laundry standard. How did we let that go?" Perfect food might be unattainable, but there clearly was a perfect curtain out there somewhere.)

Hollingsworth and Kaysen—the present and most recent Bocuse d'Or USA candidates—sat down in the living room and got right down to business. They discussed the week on tap and the planning that would have to be done for Lyon. Rather than pushing Hollingsworth as he had anticipated doing, Kaysen adjusted his strategy and took the commiseration route; when Hollingsworth joked that second place in Orlando is the real winner (you get a cash prize and are *done*), Kaysen nodded: "It's a problem. You feel like you won [but are just getting started]."

They talked over the plan for January. Recently, a decision had been made that the team would spend two weeks in Lyon prior to the competition, envisioned as a period of settling in and performing two practices, a few days apart.

"So the second practice and then what else do we do?" asked Hollingsworth.

"That's it. Otherwise we are in Lyon."

"Can we go and eat?"

Kaysen nodded. "Go and eat. It's really more to get your body adjusted to the time change because it's going to take your body about eight days to be fully ready to go and feel comfortable. It's funny: you walk around and all you see is Bocuse d'Or posters." This was a reference to the promotional posters that each team was required to produce; Team USA's poster had already been conceived and designed by Level, a five-person design firm that worked with Keller's restaurants and on his books. The poster depicted Hollingsworth in the colors and style of the iconic Obama "Hope" poster that had become a fixture of the just-concluded campaign, from which the senator from Illinois had emerged victorious.

"It's crazy," Kaysen continued. "You bring posters with you and you drop them off at restaurants. You go out to eat, when you pay your bill you say, 'Oh, by the way, can you put my poster up?' It's a campaign."

Hollingsworth, not exactly an exhibitionist, received this information with a look of something less than enthusiasm.

"Don't worry, I will help you campaign. If you are too shy, I will take care of it. It's fun. We had our posters all over."

Having finished her day at The French Laundry, Adina Guest arrived and the three of them walked across the street to the Garden, completely open to the public, without so much as a picket fence to keep locals and tourists from traipsing among the produce or plucking souvenir vegetables, which just doesn't seem to happen. In the northwest corner of the field was a just-completed hoop house (similar to a greenhouse, but with no heaters), where The French Laundry's Culinary Gardener Tucker Taylor and his team gave ingredients a head start during the winter, keeping them clear of the seasonal rains. Beyond that were the mountains that separate Napa and Santa Rosa. Two flag posts flying an American flag and a Relais & Châteaux flag stood tall in the middle of the field, between the first and second rows of beds.

"When we work lunch, we sometimes sit on that bench over there and write menus," said Hollingsworth.

Kaysen laughed, imagining his urban setting back in Manhattan: "I write mine downstairs in the prep kitchen."

The trio walked along the patches surveying the produce: cabbage, pea tendrils, assorted herbs, petit lettuces, squashes (still the summer varieties), assorted greens, and the last of the tomatoes and peppers for the year. One bed also held a plentitude of tiny *fraises des bois* (alpine strawberries)— Kaysen knelt down, held the stem of a berry in one hand and with the other twisted the fruit off the vine. He popped it into his mouth, its nova of flavor a reminder of a season that was a distant memory in New York.

Kaysen shook his head. "It's November and you are eating fraises des bois . . ."

With the waning sunlight throwing long shadows across the scene and a cool breeze coasting in over the mountains, the members of Team USA seemed more like contented suburbanites in search of a porch and a six-pack than competitors less than three months away from the battle of their lives.

JOSEPH VIOLA WOULD BE right at home on a movie screen: his piercing eyes, stubbly beard, and receding hair slicked neatly back suggest the vaguely familiar, slightly unreadable presence of a veteran character actor— he could be the benevolent college professor or the next Bond villain.

Viola, the chef Boulud had hired to tutor Hollingsworth in all things Bocuse d'Or, arrived at the Bocuse House, rolling garment bag in tow, on Monday morning, November 17, having slept off his transatlantic, transcontinental flight in a San Francisco hotel. Kaysen and Hollingsworth were already there, dressed for work—Hollingsworth in a French Laundry jacket with his name emblazoned on the left breast, black slacks, and black leather clogs; Kaysen in a crisp jacket, freshly ironed by his own hand in his temporary quarters at the Green House, one of the properties owned by Keller and company within walking distance of The French Laundry and the Bocuse House. (Guest was attending a wine seminar by day during this week, so would join the group in the evenings.)

Hollingsworth speaks a modicum of French from some community college courses and from a brief stage at Lucas Carton in Paris, but is far from conversant, so the introductions were stilted, with Viola directing most of his attention to French-fluent Kaysen.

Viola, too, produced a chef's jacket from his bag: it bore the name of his restaurant, Daniel et Denise, with a 2004 MOF symbol on the chest—the symbol carries great meaning in France, shorthand for *Meilleurs Ouvriers de France*, a coveted designation that means one of the "best workers (or craftsmen) of France." It's one of the highest honors a French chef can attain and was the inspiration for the certified master chef program in the United States, though it is much more well known in its home country.

Viola changed into his working clothes, and the trio gathered in the kitchen around the rolling prep tables. Time was short, as Viola would be returning to Europe Tuesday morning, so they got right down to business, breaking out color copies of past prizewinning Bocuse d'Or platters, notebooks, and file folders.

Viola began talking to Kaysen in French. After a few sentences, Kaysen translated for Hollingsworth: "We were talking about the garnish. You should, when you're tasting it, first, close your eyes. Don't look at your garnish. Blindfold Roland, and let Roland taste it. If it's not the explosion that he wants, *then* you worry about the taste. Because everything's about the taste. The presentation is not as important as is the flavor. Then when you start to do the platters, take six of the garnishes [meaning one of each], taste six of them right away, hot. Then wait five minutes, see how they taste. If it has the same exclamation point as when they're hot, you're good. If it doesn't have the same flavor when they're warm or cold—which is what they're going to be—then we have to adjust it."

This confirmed, once again, that the lag time between presentation and plating at the Bocuse d'Or was a real hurdle, that as good as the food had to be, it also had to be good *cold*. Viola suggested using a heating blanket to warm the silver platter before plating the food, so that there would be less time for it to cool off. (Unbeknownst to Hollingsworth, by this time, in Sweden, his old housemate Jonas Lundgren had hit on an even better solution, fitting a battery-powered heating element between the top and bottom panels of his platters, generating just enough warmth to keep the food hot without further cooking it.)

Next, Viola studied photographs of the food Hollingsworth had presented in Orlando, then spoke to Kaysen, who nodded in agreement, explaining that Viola had said how important it was for the visuals of the platter to be perfect, with uniformity of the garnishes.

"Like if you want to do a baby turnip in olive oil," said Kaysen, "all of the tips have to be the exact same way, and the same height." Kaysen pointed to the trimmed green tips of the turnips in the photograph which, while attractively presented, were not in Bocuse d'Or–worthy military formation. "You spend all this time turning a turnip, and doing it perfect and then you have some going here and some going here. Just on the tip, when they look at it across the platter, they all have to be like this—" He touched the stems on the photo in quick succession, saying, "Boom. Boom. Boom." It was fitting that Viola had focused on the turnips, the same ingredient that had exposed the gap between Hollingsworth and his original commis; now they symbolized the learning curve before Hollingsworth himself as he pursued the Bocuse d'Or.

Viola pointed to the society garlic blossoms, the edible flowers that garnished the barigoule bread pudding on Hollingsworth's Orlando platter.

"*Tim-oh-see*," he said, speaking directly to the candidate in broken English, as though addressing a child. "Be careful. Flowers . . ." He shook his head gravely. "No."

Hollingsworth's head recoiled in surprise. Kaysen and Viola conferred.

"A judge will ask himself if the flower's edible," said Kaysen. "If to him it doesn't make sense, he won't eat it."

"Why would he think it wasn't edible?" Hollingsworth asked.

"You have twenty-four different nationalities," said Kaysen. "So, if the guy from Singapore doesn't eat it because it has a flower on it because he doesn't think the flower is edible, then you lose one judge. Know what I mean? That's the hard part. You have to think worldly at that point."

Hollingsworth seemed annoyed. "*Everything* is edible."

"You'd be surprised how many people put things on the platter that aren't edible."

"Really?"

"It's amazing."

Kaysen showed Viola a picture of the artichoke gratin with Hawaiian blue prawns, a garnish that impressed many of the judges in Orlando, so much so that a number of them had made a point of mentioning it to Coach Henin.

Viola spoke to him in French.

"He says that's a very good garnish, but for the finals of the Bocuse d'Or . . . it won't work."

Hollingsworth was beginning to get the picture. "Not good enough," he said.

"Not good enough," confirmed Kaysen. "It needs finesse."

It was an interesting word choice, because like that language about unattainable perfection, there are smaller plaques situated around the kitchens of The French Laundry and Per Se that remind those who work there of crucial elements in their collective success, such as "Sense of Urgency," and "Finesse."

Hollingsworth spoke to Kaysen: "Ask him what the deal is with items on the plate and a vehicle, like a serving vessel." Hollingsworth was thinking about the candy dish *cum* smoke glass that he and Kaysen had been dialoguing about, and which would have to go on a little saucer beside the main plate come serving time.

Viola frowned, conferred with Kaysen.

"He doesn't really like it. All the chefs that have won have never taken the product and put it into something. You can use something as support to give it elevation."

"So it's only one thing?"

"It's only one thing." Kaysen located a color copy of Serge Vieira's meat platters that won the gold in 2005: *Royal Danish Veal Eight Ways à la Georges Roux*. He pointed to a square-shaped potato garnish. "This is nothing but a *pomme fondant*. That's it. But the *cuisson* is perfect. The seasoning is perfect."

Viola again spoke via Kaysen: "The easier the garnish is to lift off, the better off you are."

Something caught Hollingsworth's eye: both Vieira's fish and meat platter had potato preparations on them. At The French Laundry, where major ingredients are never repeated on a menu, this would be verboten. He asked about how such a redundancy would go over with the Bocuse judges.

"It's two different platters," said Kaysen. "The fish platter comes out first. The jury for the meat does not judge the fish platter. They don't make any notes on it. They have nothing to say."

The advice continued, with Viola free-associating and Kaysen interpreting:

› If you get down to the wire and you're running out of time, don't do everything "half-assed"; eliminate, say, a tuile and make what remains "perfect." Kaysen editorialized that you often see chefs hurrying in the final minutes, sacrificing precision.

› You want your food to be complicated, but not "over the top."

› Regarding the best mindset to take into the competition, Viola admonished Hollingsworth to imagine that, "It's not the Bocuse d'Or. It's not a competition. It's not the people screaming. You're cooking for twelve people only. You don't go beyond that. You don't take the stress and all the anxiety that goes beyond that. The second you put your platter down, everybody's going to know you're going to plate, and the music's going to start." Kaysen also warned him that the emcees will be talking about *his* food as he's carving the protein and plating the garnishes. He needed to shut all that out.

› The garnishes aren't judged as highly as the proteins.

› Viola also made a very dramatic show with his hands, holding them in the air like the pans of a scale. "If you have one platter that's here [low] and one platter here [high], you lost. The one platter that's here [low] will not let you win."

In just a few short minutes, Viola had revealed himself to be the very personification of the vagaries of the Bocuse d'Or: he understood the competition in his bones, and while he was trying his best to transmit his knowledge, it was an almost impossible task, full of contradictions (taste is all important . . . but your food better look perfect; keep it simple . . . but not *that* simple) and, of course, delivered in French.

Then the group broke for a lunch from Bouchon Bakery, delivered by Carey Snowden at 12:30 p.m., sharp.

—

AFTER LUNCH, THE CHEFS gathered in the living room and watched Canadian filmmaker Nick Versteeg's documentary *The Bocuse d'Or 2007*, about that year's Canadian team, on the flat-screen television mounted in the wainscoted entertainment center. The documentary follows the Canadian effort, from platter development through competition, and features interviews with other candidates, including Kaysen himself.

Viola and Kaysen, the two guys in the room who had been to the Bocuse d'Or, watched platters float by on the television screen and critiqued them as only insiders could. ("There's no work on that chicken." "Stripes everywhere.") To Hollingsworth, it wasn't just that they were conversing in French, they were speaking an even more foreign language, competition-speak, the patois of the Bocuse d'Or.

At one point, as Hollingsworth checked e-mails on his iPhone, Viola began talking to Kaysen about him as though he weren't there: studying Hollingsworth's face, Viola said, *"C'est bien qu'il soit jeune."* It's good that he's young.

"Il a vraiment une tête d'américain," said Kaysen. And his face is very American. It was a reminder of the shifting times against which the 2009 Bocuse d'Or would play out. President-elect Obama would be inaugurated just one week before the competition began; the days of President George W. Bush, with its unfortunate slaps at Europe in general (for example, Donald Rumsfeld's "Old Europe" dig of 2003) and France in particular (remember Freedom Fries?) were fast being forgiven. The continent that played home to the Bocuse d'Or was becoming more infatuated with an American politician than they had since the days of JFK's Camelot.

As the documentary reached its conclusion, and the audience cheered on the television screen, Kaysen shot up in his chair. "That takes me right back," he said, sounding violated by the force of the flashback.

A moment in the video had brought up another memory as well: the Canadian team was ready right on time, their fish platter in the window, but the Norwegian team before them was ten minutes behind schedule. (Each team has a five-minute timeframe in which to present each platter although, curiously, the Bocuse d'Or technical file—the guidebook provided to candidates that includes the rules and regulations—does not specify, or even indicate, a penalty for going over.) By the time the Canadians' food was served, seventeen minutes after completion, it was downright frigid.

"Ice cold," Kaysen said of the Canadians' platter. "Once their platter sat and it went out it was no good. It was no good at all."

Norway did not medal that year, but it was awarded Best Fish, while Canada went home empty-handed. The episode illustrates a sore point among many longtime Bocuse d'Or observers, who feel that favoritism is showed to France and the home countries of frequent protein-providing sponsors, such as Norway.

Kaysen didn't think that there would be a moment like this at the 2009 competition. "I do believe, knowing Daniel and how he is, I don't think that will happen this year. . . . I don't think our food will sit this year at all . . ." Kaysen couldn't say what exactly he thought Boulud would do, but he firmly believed that the irrepressible chef would have no problem rising from his chair on the competition floor and intervening to ensure fair play.

"He wouldn't just do that for the USA," said Kaysen. "He would do it for any team. If it happened to Singapore, he would say something."

As these conversations unspooled, Hollingsworth came and went. On some occasions, it was to check on something at The French Laundry. On others, it was to go to The French Laundry but not to check on anything; it was because he needed space, a break from all the people around, trying to advise him on how to cook and serve a menu that he hadn't finished devising yet. At one point, Hollingsworth returned as Viola, Kaysen, and Henin (who had just arrived and would be staying in the House's second bedroom) were discussing the schedule. Hearing their anxiety, he averted his gaze and smiled a bemused grin. Though he knew he was in deeper water now, he had changed one of his platters mere days before

Orlando and come back with gold, so the fact that he was a bit behind the assigned schedule didn't concern him.

"*Tout se joue pendant la première heure et demi,*" said Viola. Your first hour and a half is the most important.

"After that, it's a shit show," said Kaysen. "Shit show" is one of Kaysen's favorite expressions. "That first morning was a shit show." "That event was a shit show." That practice, the one we thought would go so well? "Total shit show."

As they spoke, a Thomas Keller Restaurant Group associate, in a button-down blue Oxford shirt and khakis, appeared at the door with a Rosetta Stone box under arm. "I've been instructed to install this on a Macintosh over here," he said.

"Yeah, this would be the place," said Kaysen.

In addition to training for the Bocuse d'Or, Hollingsworth planned to take his French to another level before heading to Lyon. "You do the DVDs," he said, reciting the company's promise, with a touch of skepticism in his voice. "And you are fluent."

Of course, it wasn't quite that simple. Nothing in front of him was.

THAT EVENING, THE GROUP, joined by Adina Guest, headed to dinner at Ken Frank's restaurant La Toque at the Westin Verasa Hotel in Napa. The restaurant is hard to miss, with a giant toque hovering like a foodie mirage above the open-air corridor that runs along its exterior.

In the dining room, after orders were taken, Viola began dispensing his seemingly bottomless pit of Bocuse d'Or wisdom with Henin translating: "Do not overtrain in Lyon. Do it once, and discuss."

Hollingsworth and Guest nodded.

"During the day of the event, your stomach will be upset. You will be nervous. So make sure everything, even salt, is measured." Viola's point was that you can't trust senses that are affected by stress.

In the dim light of the restaurant, Viola, and in turn Henin, assumed an almost spiritual tone, suitable to a séance: "All of us who work around Tim and Adina leave them the room to think about food. We are here to remove any problems and concerns. Starting today, we cannot talk to you about nothing but the platter. Not the hotel, the lodging. You cannot be bothered. Just eat, drink, sleep, dream your platter."

Chef Henin paused before relaying the next sentence from Viola's lips. He tilted his head forward slightly, and looked up, delivering advice that he wholeheartedly agreed with: "And, honestly," he said, "We are late."

Hollingsworth jumped into the abyss left by that proclamation: "Good," he said. "We work well under pressure."

Chef Henin translated for Viola: "Good! Sometimes it's good to have fire in your ass." Henin smirked devilishly: "Well, *he* didn't say *ass*."

Next, Kaysen took a turn translating for Viola: "When the jury tastes your food, it's one bite." Kaysen, who has a penchant for catchphrases and go-to one-liners, editorialized: "It's like I say, you live and die in eight bites."

Over dinner, Viola—with Henin back on translating duty—offered some advice about the realities of the competition world. "In a competition, you need to be smart." Henin, recognizing more counsel he believed in, took a few liberties with the translation, and added: "Not be a goomba, naïve asshole, fuck up something stupid.

"You have to be a little bit slick . . . a lot of these people are sharks. Open cheating is not allowed, but there are tricks—"

"Street smart?" asked Hollingsworth.

This elicited nods from the elders. He got it. But then Hollingsworth jumped in with a joke: "Bring your protein in a wine bottle?"

It was a sly reference to an occasionally alleged aspect of the Bocuse d'Or that you won't find in the press materials, but which are a part of the oral history of the event: the question of whether or not cheating has occurred. The most outlandish drama transpired in 2007, when gold medalist Fabrice Desvignes was accused by representatives of the German and Denmark teams of sneaking in already-prepared ingredients. According to eyewitnesses, two metal containers were delivered to Desvignes' kitchen after the competition began, a violation of the rules. Contest Director Suplisson told *The Times* (of London) that the containers arrived two minutes before cooking commenced due to the snow storm that morning, and contained foie gras and silverware.

Henin told a story about how he once Crazy-Glued some pastry wings to a figure in a competition, probably not a moral offense, but not exactly a textbook maneuver. Sometimes a man's gotta do what a man's gotta do.

After a brief silence, Hollingsworth said, "Integrity is important to us. If we can't win with integrity, then we can't win."

Guest nodded. Though she and Hollingsworth barely know each other, they were in perfect sync on this point.

Integrity was also on Hollingsworth's mind because he was concerned about whether or not it was aboveboard that Viola was even there. Earlier in the day, Viola had revealed that he had just signed on to again serve as an organizing committee member for the Bocuse d'Or, though he had not yet made that commitment when he agreed to counsel Team USA. Was this a conflict of interest?

As Hollingsworth got up to go to the men's room, he said, definitively, "I don't want anybody saying the American team cheated."

A MOCK-UP OF TEAM USA's Bocuse d'Or meat platter—pieces of cardboard held together with clear packing tape—sat on one of the rolling prep tables in the center of the Bocuse House kitchen. It wasn't a gaudy platter. If anything, it was excessively understated: rectangular with a wide lower berth for the main protein, and two narrow tiered shelves at the back for garnishes. The platter had been envisioned by restaurant designer Adam Tihany, whom Boulud had arranged for Hollingsworth to meet with in New York City when the candidate was there to shoot a Bocuse d'Or re-lated *Food & Wine* magazine story in October. The platter would be real-ized by Custom Designers & Silversmiths, a start-up concern spearheaded by Daniel J. Scannell, a certified master chef and member of the United States Culinary Olympic team since 1998, who was the managing partner, along with Richard Rosendale. The two worked in conjunction with third partner, the actual silversmith, Olle Johanson, to bring Tihany's platters to life. Because metal-crafting is painstaking, time-consuming work, the facsimile was all Hollingsworth could use to help plan his presentation; the actual platters would not be available until just before the competition. The showiest flourish was unrepresented on the facsimile: the two elevated tiers would feature a total of twelve illuminated circles on which the smoke glasses would sit, creating a dramatic visual effect.

It was Tuesday morning, and Hollingsworth, Henin, Viola, and Kaysen stood over the platter examining it, trying to imagine it rendered in silver. Viola and Henin shook their heads. Not good enough.

Viola sighed, then launched into one of his pocket lectures, pointing out, with a photograph of the 2005 French fish platter as an example, that the protein is almost *always* elevated, a pedestal effect. Hollingsworth's platters had none of that—the meat platter, represented by the three-tiered cardboard prototype, had some height, but not in the conventional sense, and the main protein would actually be situated *below* the garnishes. And the fish platter would simply be a porcelain rectangle, with no levels at all to speak of. There wasn't even a cardboard version of that one, because no imagination was required to picture it. The understated design was an apt reflection of Hollingsworth's personality, and of The French Laundry aesthetic he had absorbed over the past seven years. But it was not in line with the classic Bocuse d'Or sensibility, and this concerned the elders in the room.

Henin inverted a fluted casserole dish onto the top shelf of the cardboard meat platter to make Viola's point for him. He began riffling through photographs, searching for something specific. "Centerpiece . . ." he said.

"I understand what a centerpiece is," said Hollingsworth, again taking some offense at the presumption of ignorance.

Viola spoke. Henin translated: "By the end of the month, have all the platters conceptualized, would be ideal."

Hollingsworth just smiled, but said nothing.

Viola looked at him, imploringly: "*Tim-oh-see?*"

Hollingsworth's frustration with the crowd of observers bubbled over again: "That's obvious, come on."

Viola spoke, and Henin again translated: "Again, I want to clarify, by the end of the month, have both platters conceptualized."

Hollingsworth didn't even bother replying this time.

Viola also had another point to make, a more abstract one, but a crucial one. He pointed to the Italian platter from 2005: "*Ça n'as pas de vie.*" He waved his hands to animate his words. This does not have life.

Then he pointed to the 2007 French platter. "*Cela a la vie.*" This has life. "*Il a le mouvement.*" It has movement.

And having conveyed all that he could convey in twenty-four hours, Viola changed back into his traveling clothes, took his rolling cart in hand, and left the House.

The next time they saw him would be in Lyon, at the Bocuse d'Or.

AFTER VIOLA DEPARTED, KAYSEN read Hollingsworth an e-mail from Boulud saying that Viola's counsel was no problem, because he had committed to making the trip before he was approached about helping out at the Bocuse d'Or.

Later Henin, Kaysen, and Hollingsworth reviewed the schedule for December. Hollingsworth was off from December 16 to December 19, but Henin was planning to be in Yountville on the twenty-eighth.

"Okay," said Hollingsworth. "I'm working the twenty-eighth, twenty-ninth, thirtieth, thirty-first, and first. Then I'm off the whole month of January."

Henin explained that he couldn't change his schedule to be there the week of the sixteenth. Hollingsworth didn't know what to tell him.

Henin made a theatrically flustered face, and looked at Kaysen, who didn't offer anything. What could *he* do? Henin shrugged, and looked away.

It would be Henin's last stand on the scheduling issue. Having made his case to anybody who would listen, he resigned himself to the situation. "They didn't know [what they were up against]," he said. "You can't blame them. I didn't want to fight it. I said, 'Well, that is what you want to do, that is what you want to do.'"

With nothing more to say on the subject, Henin moved on.

"Since Adina's not here, I can be the commis and peel shallots," he said. He took a paring knife in hand, and got to work.

And so the cooking began, at last.

Hollingsworth was eager to try out the equipment, so he seared some beef cheeks in a sauté pan, basting them with butter. With that melba-custard garnish in mind, he also made an unflavored custard base and cooked it in the oven. And it was a good thing he did: it was faster than he thought it would be, instant validation of the importance of training on the same equipment that would be waiting for him in Lyon.

Meanwhile, Kaysen suited up in an apron and began cooking as well. He turned a potato into ribbons on the turning vegetable slicer, cooked them with a little butter and salt, then transferred them to a mixing bowl with a few thyme sprigs. Then he made a caramelized onion paste with onions, garlic, and water. He laid some ribbons across the width of his station, spooned little blobs of the paste on it, and spread them out. Then he rolled up the potato. He put the potato roll in a pan with some butter and basted it to a dark, amber brown, and transferred it to a paper towel to drain. Then he transferred it to a cutting board, and cut it into one-inch-thick pinwheels.

"What do you think of that?" he asked Hollingsworth.

The candidate nodded politely, but the truth was that he could not have been less interested in what Gavin Kaysen wanted to cook. He understood that his predecessor was trying to rub some sticks together and get a fire started, but Hollingsworth continued to feel strongly that he had to create his own food. He knew that it was taking him a while to get there, but for him, it had to be an organic process that blossomed on its own natural timeframe. Moreover, one and a half days into his allotted Bocuse d'Or time for the week, Hollingsworth felt that he was burning precious hours, that for all of the good intentions behind the visit, a lot of people were going through the motions but not accomplishing anything.

The day didn't get better. When Hollingsworth found himself alone with Coach Henin, he decided to share one of his garnish ideas, that melba-custard–spring garlic stack. Henin, meanwhile, had the côte de boeuf on his mind, and interrupted to ask him what he planned to do with it. The seemingly minor exchange took less than fifteen seconds, but Hollingsworth found the change of subject unsupportive and it put him off.

Combined with his frustration at the passing time and the strangers in his midst, his reaction was extreme; he almost immediately began keeping Henin at arm's length. It was an awkward dynamic: Henin was his own chef's mentor and a man for whom he had a great deal of respect, and so getting off on the wrong foot with him made him uncomfortable, to say the least. (When discussing the tension between them in interviews for this book, Hollingsworth almost always made a point of reinforcing that he bore Henin, the person, not a whit of animosity.)

For his part, Henin was baffled by Hollingsworth's cold shoulder. He speculated that perhaps it was the displaced expression of a young American cook's inferiority complex at being shepherded by an accomplished French chef he barely knew, or perhaps some feeling of inadequacy related to competition.

Neither man discussed his feelings with the other. And the truth was that it hardly mattered since Henin would not return to Yountville in December. In the meantime, the emerging irony was that while Kaysen had made that red-faced proclamation to Eric Brandt in Lyon—that no American team would ever be undersupported again—Timothy Hollingsworth, at least until he had a working draft of his platter to share, might have been happier going it alone.

———

HOLLINGSWORTH HAD TAKEN UP surfing in the past few years, and wanted desperately to hit the beach that Friday to clear his head, but couldn't find the time. Instead, that Friday and Saturday, he tried out one of his possible garnishes at The French Laundry: that brioche with custard, which at this stage in its ideation housed tomato marmalade in its center. Henin had left town early Friday morning, so Hollingsworth was on his own to evaluate, and determined that it needed a little more—he wanted to incorporate spring garlic, which was not available in November, but would be (in Yountville) by the time of the competition in Lyon.

Then Hollingsworth spent a rare Thanksgiving away from his family. Though homesick for his parents and siblings, he embraced the mental break, finding a special sanctuary in the sound of the water splashing against the Maine shore, and sleeping an unheard-of eight or nine hours per night.

He also stole away to Rabelais bookstore, which he had read about in *Saveur* magazine as one of the top ten cookbook destinations in the world. Strolling the stacks, he was able to enjoy the store as he hadn't been able to enjoy very much the past few weeks, with the Bocuse d'Or hovering over him like a storm cloud. Cookbooks were his domain, something he felt an intimacy with, and he took his time browsing, getting reacquainted with books that had helped teach him about food in the first place, long before he was even a commis at The French Laundry.

He looked at book after book, buying up some to take back to Yountville. In particular, he found inspiration in the pages of *At the Crillon and At Home: Recipes by Jean-François Piège*, which had that tightness he so revered. He also looked at a number of books that described, in first person or third, some of the most celebrated Michelin-starred chefs of France, such as Alain Chapel. And he picked up a first edition of the classic that had inspired Keller himself, *Great Chefs of France*, for its photographs of platters, to help him in his continuing quest to get a handle on that style of service and its history.

He also treated himself to a copy of the new work by Andrew Dornenburg and Karen Page, *The Flavor Bible*, which brought back memories for Hollingsworth. When he first moved up from commis to cook at The French Laundry, John Fraser (today the executive chef of Dovetail in New York City) had recommended that he read one of the authors' earlier collaborations, *Culinary Artistry*. The book features extensive lists of ingredients and other foods they get along with. Hollingsworth, who was then starting to participate in those nightly menu meetings, spent his wee hours studying those lists so that he'd look like he knew what he was doing in the meetings when fellow cooks with finely honed palates and improvisational talent turned to him and said, "What do *you* want to run?"

Hollingsworth had had a bumpy adjustment from the rustic style of Zachary Jacques to the ultrafine dining of The French Laundry, but also had a fast, deft pair of hands, and a hunger to learn—French Laundry veterans recall the quiet cook lingering on the margins of the kitchen after his shift to observe or ask to be tasked with further assignments. "He was the commis that stayed late to watch service so we would clear some space on the line so that he could see what was going on," remembers Corey Lee. "He was the commis that, when everyone was done, checked in with everyone to make sure that they didn't need anything."

But for all his motivation, Hollingsworth struggled with the "detail work." He had turned artichokes, blanched tomatoes, butchered fish, but had never been shown "100 percent the proper way to do it." He was also somewhat awed by the overwhelming respect everybody demonstrated for the food, from Keller and Lee to the men and women who shuttled the finished dishes out to the guests.

Sheer determination and raw talent had gotten him through: Hollingsworth would often be the first one on the property, arriving ahead of the official schedule, queasy with nervousness. To this day, when Hollingsworth glides in before sunrise, parking his Toyota 4Runner along Washington Street and walking to the restaurant, the earthy bouquet of dewy grass and wet leaves trigger a Pavlovian sensation of nausea for him.

It was his determination, evidenced even in his stalker-like follow-up after trailing at the restaurant, that drew Keller to him in the first place: "When I think about what it is you look for in somebody, it is not necessarily their talent or their resumé. It is their determination and desire. Somebody who really has a strong desire. People talk about passion all of the time and passion is a great thing, but we all know that passion ebbs and flows. You can't be passionate every day. I look for someone who has desire because for me *it* is always there . . . that was something that I recognized in Timmy early on."

The dedication paid off: Hollingsworth was promoted from commis to cheese, which he worked for seven and a half months, then to garde manger for more than two years, during which time he was dispatched to New York City as part of the team that helped open Per Se. Back in Yountville, he was steadily moved up the line, working every station on his way to sous chef.

Remembrances of those days put Hollingsworth in a more receptive frame of mind, a student's frame of mind, and the shift in perspective produced a change of heart. By the time he returned to the West Coast late Friday night, November 28, he had opened up to the possibility of some conventional competition plating.

"It's hard not to do some [of that]," he said. "I think that's what might win." Hollingsworth's conversion also came from reflecting on the chain of titans that had led to this year's American team—Paul Bocuse, Daniel Boulud, Thomas Keller. You don't mix in that company selfishly, he reckoned, and you don't take for granted the amount of money that had been raised, either. Though the conventional wisdom is that one should—*must,* even—cook from the heart, Hollingsworth was recognizing the inherent dilemma unique to his situation. "I think it's very different from when Gavin went," he said. "I think the pressure was more on himself. Now it's like all these people are doing these things for me, so I want to win *for them* . . . if you step back and look at it, it's like all this support has been raised for me. . . . Maybe I can't do what I want. Maybe I want to compromise a little bit."

He had even found a way to relate this to his day-to-day work: "If you're the chef of a restaurant," he said, "You have to do what the guests want—that's who pays your bills."

Back in Yountville, refreshed from his time away, a set of cookbooks under his arm, and a new peace with the unique demands of cooking for the Bocuse d'Or, his one and only short-term goal was to have something, *anything*, conceptualized. After weeks of agonizing over what would be good enough, and ending up with nothing, he decided that, "I just have to sit down and write this dish." It almost didn't matter what the composition was; he could always change it later.

Hollingsworth also undertook a training regimen called CrossFit, a Web-based program that a member of Laughlin's family had recommended to him over Thanksgiving. The site provides users with a different high-intensity twenty-minute workout each day; for example, do as many push-ups as possible in twenty seconds. Repeat eight times. Then do the same things with sit-ups. One day, the three exercises were lifting a bar over his head, rowing on a machine, and jumping up and off a platform. He enjoyed the workouts, and found them useful, as opposed to Rosetta Stone, which he dropped about this time because its lessons weren't specific enough to what his needs would be in Lyon.

With a new wind at his back, by Tuesday, December 2, Hollingsworth had a rough version of the fish platter conceptualized. The centerpiece, focusing on the one finfish, the cod, would be based on the cod *en persillade* that had been on his list of possibilities for Orlando. He would slice the cod, layer it with a scallop mousse, wrap it in plastic, cook it in a water bath, then paint it with mustard and breadcrumbs, similar to a dish they sometimes served at The French Laundry. He was also leaning toward one of the garnishes that he had considered but that also had not made the cut for Orlando, a fried cod brandade with tomato marmalade.

For the other garnishes, he had ideas, but they were all tainted—if such a thing is possible—by The French Laundry's elegant simplicity. He just couldn't purge his orientation from his system as he conceptualized garnishes such as a ragoût of dried and fresh wax beans, tomato diamonds, and vegetable brunoise. Such bean preparations are referred to at The French Laundry as a "cassoulet," a very loose adaptation of the classic French winter bean stew, and the idea was that it would be scattered about ("a drop here and there") on the individual plates presented to the judges. No doubt those would have been delectable, but they were not intricate enough for competition, and by this point in his crash course, he didn't need anybody else to tell him that.

The custard he'd been imagining was coming into focus as a square or rectangle tinged bright green with spring garlic, which would no longer rest on top but instead would be infused into the custard itself, served on a brioche melba toast with accompanying flavors of tomato compote and caramelized cippoline onion. He was also considering a deep-fried piece of *shirako* (cod sperm . . . yes, you read right), as well as cod roe wrapped in bacon, cooked sous vide, then crisped and finished with a Niçoise olive sauce.

That was his basic fish concept. "Things might change," he said. "It's just on paper now." All he wanted was to have something to work with, a draft he could revise and edit. The custard, for example, could be made with just about anything, and the shirako could be fried or piped out of an ISI gun—a canister fitted with a nozzle and powered by a CO_2 cartridge that aerates wet preparations like whipped cream. What was important was that he had a first draft that he could work over and revise, then worry about plating.

Hollingsworth's goal for the immediate future could not have been more straightforward: Get together with Guest, "find a day and do it after work. Prepare two plates, and we'll eat it."

IRONICALLY, AS HOLLINGSWORTH WAS picking up speed, the team back in New York City was growing ever more anxious. According to Pelka, Boulud so innately trusted Keller, his standards, and his staff that panic hadn't quite set in, but because Hollingsworth had largely gone radio silent, the East Coast contingent had no idea what he was up to. Hollingsworth insists he didn't mean anything by it; there were no formal systems of reporting in place, no instructions on whom to update or when, and so he was going about his preparation on his own schedule and in his own way.

Having reached more or less the same conclusion, on Thursday, December 11, Jennifer Pelka decided to establish a new world order. She sent Hollingsworth the following e-mail, with the subject line Bocuse d'Or USA Training Update:

Hi, Timothy and Adina,

I hope everything is going well out in California! Can you please send on an update to the Board and the rest of the group in regards to your progress in anticipation of the competition? Everyone is eager to hear how the training is going, and we are all certainly at your disposal for help. Ideally, we would like to get a formal update every two weeks until the competition, covering the following:

> Independent training sessions: how often, how are they structured, what have you been focusing on?

> Training sessions with Chef Henin: how often, how are they structured, what have you been focusing on?

> Goals for the next two weeks

> Proteins and garnishes: how far along are you with the decisions? How is menu development? Photos and descriptions to date.

> Timing

> Platters and plating: aside from the MOSS smoker pieces, do you need anything?

> Additional needs before Lyon

> Needs in Lyon

> Day by day schedule in Lyon (Gavin and I are meeting tomorrow about this, and we'll pass on our notes to you thereafter)

Chef Henin, of course, any update notes [from] you would be greatly appreciated as well!

Thanks,

Jennifer

By Friday, December 12, Hollingsworth was having second thoughts about the fish platter. Though the main cod preparation was the same, he had decided that some of his garnishes, while "excellent" from a flavor standpoint, were perhaps too "pedestrian" and it was easy to see his point. Even the name of one garnish, *cassoulet*, suggested adaptable, rustic cooking, not the formal, structured cuisine that impresses competition judges.

He realized that he'd have to return to the drawing board.

On the other hand, it was about this time that he also was gaining some traction on his meat platter, which began with a surge of inspiration not at The French Laundry and not at the Bocuse House, but at home one night in Napa, when he was cooking dinner for Laughlin.

As an accompaniment for steak and salad, he decided to make *pommes dauphinoise*, a classic French dish of scalloped potatoes and cream. Though he hadn't had it in a long time, it was a technique that was seared into his memory, taught to him by former French Laundry chef de cuisine Eric Ziebold: thinly slice potatoes on a mandoline, then bring some heavy cream to a boil and season it with salt, pepper, thyme, and garlic. Add potato slices one at a time, shaking the pan to ensure that each is well coated in cream. As you work, the natural starch in the potatoes thickens the cream even further. Hollingsworth poured the creamy potatoes into a vessel, and baked it until it was nicely golden brown on top, with the cream bubbling up around the sides.

"I hadn't had it in so long," Hollingsworth remembers. "You take a bite of it, and it's *so* good."

Hollingsworth got to thinking: you don't see this dish very often in restaurants, and if you do, it's not usually made all that well. Before long, he'd thought up a Bocuse d'Or–appropriate version: turn the potato on a vegetable slicer, cut uniform rectangles from the ribbons, cook them in cream, and then layer them into some kind of baking vessel. Once baked, the preparation could be unmolded and cut into shapes, even served atop a *pommes Maxim* (thin potato rounds, tossed in clarified butter, and baked together to a crisp in overlapping decorative shapes) to make it easy to lift off a platter. Complementary ingredients could be added; at the moment, he was thinking of punching out cylinders of pommes dauphinoise, wrapping them in carrot for color, and topping them with a poached quail egg and chopped chives. Gee, maybe he was getting the hang of this competition thing after all.

In addition to the pommes dauphinoise, Hollingsworth soon devised a working collection of garnishes for the beef platter. The centerpiece was still a blank, but if all the other components were in place as they turned the corner into the New Year, he wasn't worried about being able to weave the preparation of the final element into his and Guest's game plan.

One of the garnishes he was most excited about made use of that smoke glass Kaysen was so taken with. Convinced that the smoke would be a crowd- and judge-pleasing flourish, he wanted badly to include something like it on his platter. Moreover, he *had* to use the glass or a similar vessel because he was committed to those circular light panels Tihany had incorporated into the platter's design. His first thought was to smoke braised beef cheeks, and accompany them with a brunoise of cabbage, apple, and onion. Another idea he had was to transform one cut of beef, curing the *calotte* (beef cap) from the côte de boeuf into bresaola, or air-dried seasoned beef.

Hollingsworth didn't have much experience with curing, but Devin Knell had been experimenting quite a bit with it during the fall of 2008, and was set up for curing at Ad Hoc. (Hollingsworth had also done some curing himself in the wine room at The French Laundry to good but not great effect.) For the moment, he was planning to cure the calotte with salt, pepper, and sugar, starting at three different times to give him three levels of intensity to choose from, then use the cured meat in a riff on eggs benedict: on a base of fried brioche, he would lay a piece of compressed spinach (made by repeatedly Cryovacing the green with salt and olive oil), wrap the bresaola around that, and top it with a circulator-cooked quail egg that was filling in for the Benedict's poached chicken egg. (Cooking the egg in a circulator would result in a perfectly round orb and make both the yolk and the white seductively runny.) For a finishing touch, he planned to make a truffle hollandaise and pipe it out of an ISI gun, the introduction of air alleviating the vinegary richness, then top the whole thing with sliced truffles.

Centerpiece concepts eluded him, but he had options: if he didn't come up with a better idea, he could always bring the bacon-lined tenderloin from Orlando back for an encore. That left the rest of the côte de boeuf, which demanded a high-impact presentation. It hadn't come to him yet, but if everything else worked, he had little doubt he'd be in good shape.

GRAY SKIES AND A persistent drizzle greeted Yountville on the morning of Tuesday, December 16, but Hollingsworth and Guest didn't mind; they were too excited about the next four days, which they would devote entirely to recipe work.

By eleven o'clock, the two of them were in the Bocuse House kitchen, grinning at each other.

"I'm excited," said Guest.

"Long time coming," said Hollingsworth.

The two of them stood over the rolling prep tables in the center of the kitchen, dressed in their blue aprons, an important symbol of life at The French Laundry. The blue apron, worn by commis and apprentices in French kitchens, is worn by *everybody* during prep time at The French Laundry, a symbol of their willingness to help each other and to always be learning. Hollingsworth and Guest wore the blue aprons in the competition kitchen in Orlando and planned to wear them in Lyon, at least until the time came to plate up. "It means French Laundry," said Guest of the apron. It's a "comfort," said Hollingsworth, "Not as much, but like the American flag is the symbol of our country, the blue apron is the symbol of values."

Hollingsworth showed his commis illustrations of the garnishes he'd been imagining and reimagining, then they broke from their huddle and started gathering ingredients and equipment, getting ready to cook for the rest of the day. What they did *not* do was discuss who would do what. Because they worked together at The French Laundry, they already knew what their division of labor would be: Guest would do all vegetable prep and Silpat work, and Hollingsworth would do all the butchering and the cooking of the proteins, as well as any finishing work that required particular finesse.

One way in which things differed from The French Laundry in this satellite kitchen was the constant presence of music. Hollingsworth doesn't function well in quietude, and so even on this formative day, he put music on the sound system, opting for something relatively low-key: CDs featuring music mixes from Keller's casual restaurant Ad Hoc: "One Step Up" by Bruce Springsteen, "Bye Bye, Blackbird" by Ray Charles, "Wild Horses" by the Rolling Stones, "Could You Be Loved" by Bob Marley. By Hollingsworth's standards, this was easy listening—a mellow way to slide into the long week ahead.

The first order of business was to try that pommes dauphinoise. Guest peeled the potatoes, turned them on the vegetable slicer, par-cooked them in boiling water, drained them, and cut them into squares, arranging them in stacks like wonton wrappers on a sheet pan, which she brought over to Hollingsworth at the stove.

Now the teaching commenced. Hollingsworth poured milk and cream into a large, stainless-steel pan, added salt, pepper, thyme sprigs, and a clove of garlic, and brought it to a simmer. Then he had her taste it, so that she'd know what to look for when she made it—how salty the cream should be, how much the thyme flavor should have infused the liquid before the sprigs were removed and discarded, and so on.

One at a time, Hollingsworth added squares of potato to the mixture. Doing it that way ensured that it never lost its simmer and would continue to thicken. As the potatoes piled up to the top, Hollingsworth added more cream, then agitated them gently with a spatula to help the liquid find its way between the layers of potato.

Hollingsworth then transferred the potatoes to a wide, deep stainless-steel bowl. At the ready, he had a small rectangular pan with deep sides and upward-facing handles. Both of them snapped on latex gloves and as Guest looked on, Hollingsworth put layers of potato into the pan, spooning liquid between the layers. After a few layers, he turned to Guest:

"Got it?"

She nodded and he stepped aside as she stepped in, or "cut in," if you refer back to Keller's original description of The Dance. As usual, Guest worked faster than Hollingsworth, with quick, urgent, compact movements. Although the dishes were still works in progress, Guest treated them as though they were being prepared for competition, working as fast as she could without sacrificing neatness. It was a nod to their accelerated timeline. "I shouldn't start going faster when I am practicing [fully developed dishes] for Lyon," she said. "I need to do it *now*." Just as Hollingsworth was incorporating preparations she knew from The French Laundry into the platters, Guest was treating each visit to the kitchen as a chance to improve her efficiency. She was also under instructions from Hollingsworth to make sure to take on preparations at The French Laundry that resembled her Bocuse d'Or tasks so she could have more opportunities to increase her speed.

Hollingsworth snipped open a sous-vide bag filled with veal stock, and poured the viscous brown liquid into a tall stainless-steel pot. He seasoned three pieces of beef cheek and three pieces of oxtail with salt and pepper then opened up a tin of extra virgin olive oil and heated a few tablespoons in a wide, deep sauté pan. He added the three pieces of beef cheek, searing them well, then transferred them to a paper towel–lined hotel pan. He added diced carrots, leeks, and onion (collectively referred to as a *mirepoix*) to the pan and sautéed them. He transferred the meat and vegetables to the pot with the veal stock, snapped on a pressure-cooker lid, depressed the button in its center to vacuum-seal it, and left it to stew.

"Don't let me forget to take pictures," he said to Guest, remembering Pelka's e-mail from the previous day. "We have to send them to," he paused here for comedic effect, "The Corporation."

Then Hollingsworth left to check on something two doors down Washington Street, at The French Laundry. As soon as he was gone, Guest, who was slicing carrot ribbons on a mandoline, stopped working, walked into the living room, squatted down next to the sound system, and lowered the volume considerably, a benign violation of the chain of command.

BY MID-AFTERNOON, A NUMBER of preparations were ready to be finished and tasted. Hollingsworth removed the pressure-cooker lid from the beef. After the accumulated steam was released, and the meat had been allowed to rest and absorb some of the flavorful cooking liquid, he fished out a piece of beef cheek with a pair of tongs, set it on his cutting board, seasoned it with salt and pepper, cut a piece, tasted it, and grinned like a little kid.

"That's my mom's beef stew," he said.

Apart from this comment, there was virtually no personal chit-chat; what little talk there was was related to the task list.

Moving right along, Hollingsworth heated a sauté pan, added some oil, and seared the three seasoned oxtail pieces to the tawny color of well-done bacon, periodically draining the fat from the pan. He then returned the beef cheeks' cooking liquid to the pressure cooker, added the oxtail, and snapped the lid back into place. The oxtail would fortify the liquid, which would become the basis for the meat platter's sauce. For the moment he did not plan to incorporate the oxtail itself on the platter, for the simple reason that he didn't have an idea for how to use it. It was a risky decision because judges who noticed the absence of the cut might be inclined to penalize him for this end run.

Guest, meanwhile, had baked the potato dauphinoise to a deep golden brown, the cream bubbling up around the edges between the potato and the pan, and had chilled it in the freezer to make it easier to manipulate. She had moved on to making pommes Maxim: punching out one-and-a-quarter-inch circles out of sliced potatoes, tossing them with clarified butter, seasoning them with salt, arranging them in an overlapping circle, and baking them in the oven between two weighted Silpats, which browned and fused them together.

Hollingsworth pulled the potato dauphinoise from the freezer and composed the garnish he had in mind: punching out a cylinder of potato and setting it atop a pommes Maxim, wrapping that in carrot ribbons, topping it with a daisywheel of black truffles, and topping the composition with a hard-boiled quail egg.

Late in the day, Keller himself dropped in to say hello and check in. Seeing the pommes dauphinoise wrapped in carrot, he smiled and said, "That is really French."

Hollingsworth took note of the comment. He knew it meant something, but wasn't sure what, and the chef took off before he could probe him for more feedback.

The team tried a few other preparations that afternoon. Hollingsworth fashioned a light truffle hollandaise, transferred it to an ISI gun, and attempted a version of the smoke garnish with leek puree, a stewed beef cheek cube, and pickled pearl onion. They added smoke with The Smoking Gun, an electric pipe manufactured by PolyScience featuring a carburetor that one lit, and a button that forced the smoke through a long tube.

They covered the bowl for a few minutes, then removed the lid and tasted: the smoke wasn't especially prevalent, so nothing really pulled together the flavors of the beef cheeks and the sweet vegetables, and the puree was too loose.

But Hollingsworth wasn't really focused on the smoke glass. He couldn't get his mind off the pommes dauphinoise. He unwrapped the carrot and topped the potato cylinder with a turned carrot and a pickled pearl-onion layer.

Hollingsworth rested his hands on the table, a pose he lapses into when he's frustrated, when his thinking isn't clear. He couldn't quite put his finger on what was wrong, but he felt adrift, unsure of himself and his decisions.

Guest left him alone and started scrubbing the pans in the sink.

After they cleaned up for the night, Hollingsworth went for a drive to clear his head, then home to Napa. He fulfilled his reporting duties, sending a lengthy e-mail (typed by Laughlin) and several digital photographs of the day's haul to the committee, then he plopped down on the couch and cracked open his sketchpad. He also leafed through those books he'd picked up over Thanksgiving, skimming for inspiration.

But he found himself unmoved. Worse, he was confused. And then it hit him: the food in those books might have been beautiful, but it was only beautiful because it was *different*. "It is not American and not what you would typically do," he thought to himself.

In retrospect he felt he understood what Keller had meant by his comment earlier in the day—"That is really French." He thought that The Chef was trying to tell him: "Tim, you know deep down inside [that this is not you], so why do you go and do something that is not you? Why aren't you being yourself?"

Hollingsworth slammed the books closed, pushed them aside, and broke out his copy of *The Flavor Bible*, the new book by Dornenburg and Page, whose earlier *Culinary Artistry* had gotten him through those menu meetings during his formative years at The French Laundry. He thumbed it to death that night, looking up possible accompaniments for caviar, for cod, for scallops, and for any number of ingredients, both assigned and elective, that he had been grappling with.

He stayed up until three in the morning like that, filling his head with new ideas, sketching them in his notebook, getting ready for the next day, a day in which—if nothing else—he would cook from the heart.

WEDNESDAY, DECEMBER 17 WAS a sunny day in Yountville, with temperatures in the mid-fifties. On his morning e-mail review, Hollingsworth received a note from Kaysen, responding to the update and photographs with a characteristically friendly and supportive missive. But it also contained a question that all but screamed out at him: "Can you explain the garnishes in the pictures for me please . . . what am I looking at?"

What am I looking at?

WHAT AM I LOOKING AT?

For Hollingsworth, the query reinforced the epiphany of the night before: he was drifting too far from the food he wanted to make, veering into the land of nonsensical flourishes. "It's really important that I believe in the food and that I'm comfortable with it," he said, sounding as sure of himself as he had since winning in Orlando. "I can't even tell you how impossible it would be for me to serve the pommes dauphinoise with carrot wrapped around it."

By 11:00 a.m., a sense of déjà vu permeated the Bocuse House as Hollingsworth and Guest were back at it. Once again, he braised beef cheeks, which he sliced and put into a sous-vide bag with maple syrup, then steamed in the oven. The utility of developing and practicing on the Bocuse d'Or equipment was fast becoming apparent: it was taking Hollingsworth some time to get used to the oven. Each time he opened the door to check on the meat, he had to jerk his head back to avoid a face full of hot steam, not the kind of thing you want to have happen when you're being observed on the world stage.

And, as was the case the day before, there was a steady stream of music DJ'd by Hollingsworth, only now it was being piped out of a Bose iPod dock he had brought in and stationed in the kitchen.

As Eminem sang about his daughter, Haley, Hollingsworth butchered a whole cod. Although Guest moved quickly in these sessions, Hollingsworth butchered the cod more slowly than he normally would, using the opportunity to take the fish apart as a chance to imagine the possibilities of what he might do with it. He still didn't have that fish centerpiece finalized, and he hoped—to no avail on this day—that the intimacy of butchering might deliver inspiration.

Guest meanwhile was preparing the potato garnish Hollingsworth was considering for the fish platter, a potato mille-feuille—similar in construct to the dauphinoise, but made by brushing each potato layer with butter, seasoning them with salt, and inserting overlapping strips of bacon every five layers. She moved even faster on this day than she had the day before. Maybe it was because Robert Plant was screeching "Whole Lotta Love" in her ears.

As Mickey Avalon's hardcore rap anthem, "Waiting to Die," shook the kitchen, Guest also retried the pommes dauphinoise; yesterday's were too creamy, the layers slid apart and were hard to punch out. Though this was how Hollingsworth had first made it at home, it wasn't the desired effect for competition. This time, she weighed all the ingredients, even the salt, to track and adjust and be precise. "Otherwise you're just guessing," she said. She also used only cream, with no milk, and omitted the black pepper, which Hollingsworth realized marred the truffle's flavor. (In time, he would also omit the garlic.)

Around 2:00 p.m., Hollingsworth sliced a few wedges from the previous day's dauphinoise and set them aside. He then heated some olive oil in a sauté pan and added some spinach, working it with a silver spoon as it wilted. He sliced some meat from the leftover oxtail from the day before, seasoned it with salt and pepper, and topped it with some grain mustard. This he put between slices of bread, set on a plate, and spooned spinach and potato cake alongside. It wasn't a garnish: it was *lunch* for him and Guest. Even this kitchen had its version of a family meal.

Guest was ready to move on to her Silpat work for the day. Among the garnishes they would be trying was another new one: Hollingsworth had moved on from the custard "stacks" that were part of his first dish conception, but still wanted to include some kind of custard: it was a luxurious and versatile component and one that Guest could make. By now, he envisioned a custard, made unconventionally with eggs but no dairy, and flavored with Champagne vinegar, that would be presented in individual glasses. The custard would be topped with a small amount of intensely flavored shrimp consommé. (He planned to use shrimp consommé in competition but because there was always lobster glace on hand at The French Laundry, that's what he used in this and subsequent practices.) Until he could think of a shrimp-focused garnish, he would add chopped shrimp to the consommé for the sake of using them. A melba topped with sliced scallops and sized to hover high in the glass would complete the composition. In addition to the flavor, Hollingsworth was attracted to the idea of having an inch or so of space between the melba and the custard—his understated way of playing the competition game.

Hollingsworth used French Laundry shorthand to describe the melba toast he had in mind: "Just like the garlic melba, but light." Guest knew that this meant to adapt a melba they used at the restaurant, leaving off the garlic and parmesan. So she set to work, slicing thin mushroom-shaped slices from a loaf of brioche, punching out circles, layering them between Silpats, weighting them, and baking them to the exact desired degree of color and crunch; just thirty seconds too long and they would be overcooked and have a burnt flavor. If they were cooked too little, they might lack the fortitude to support the sliced scallops they had to carry, or to survive the hang time over the steaming hot liquid, which threatened to wilt them.

Over the course of the afternoon, they made several garnishes:

Team USA: Adina Guest and Timothy Hollingsworth
in the Garden across from The French Laundry.
© 2009 by Justin Lewis

Making people happy: Chef Thomas
Keller outside The French Laundry.
© 2005 by Deborah Jones

Four stars forever? Daniel Boulud in
the dining room of Daniel.
Photo by Bill Milne, courtesy Daniel

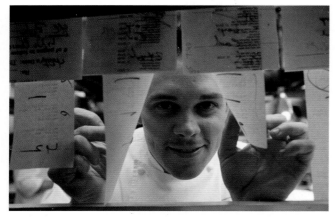

Character in the kitchen: Gavin Kaysen, on the the line at Café Boulud.
© 2009 by Owen Franken

Moment of truth: *(left to right)* Daniel Boulud, Jérôme Bocuse, and Paul Bocuse watch a meat platter go by at Epcot.
Courtesy Nora Carey

Elegant simplicity: Hollingsworth's meat platter from Epcot.
Photo by Will Blunt, courtesy StarChefs.com

Competition style: Richard Rosendale's fish platter from Epcot.
Photo by Will Blunt, courtesy StarChefs.com

The candidate:
Hollingsworth outside
the Bocuse House in
Yountville, California.
©2009 by Justin Lewis

Visiting royalty: Hollingsworth
greets Daniel Boulud, Paul
Bocuse, and Jérôme Bocuse,
January 5, 2009.
© 2009 by Dave Getzschman

Feedback from The Chef:
Keller giving notes,
December 18, 2008.

Paul Bocuse
2009

Officially "The Bocuse House":
Monsieur Paul's signature on the wall in Yountville.

Something to talk about: Coach Roland Henin and Hollingsworth after the second practice.
© 2009 by Dave Getzschman

Game face.
© 2009 by Dave Getzschman

A visit from a friend: Corey Lee offers feedback to Team USA.
© 2009 by Dave Getzschman

Putting it together: Hollingsworth's meat plate takes shape, January 5, 2009.
© 2009 by Dave Getzschman

Inspired by Obama: Team USA's promotional poster. Guest's name was added at Hollingsworth's insistence.
© 2008 by Level

A night to remember: celebrating Inauguration Day at Restaurant Paul Bocuse. (*Left to right:* Kate Laughlin, Hollingsworth, Paul Bocuse, Adina Guest, John Guest, Henin, and Kaysen.)

Your name here? Hollingsworth eyes the past winners' plaques outside Restaurant Paul Bocuse.

Like father, like son: Julien and Marie Boulud entertain Timothy Hollingsworth.

Scouting report: Hollingsworth and Guest size up the competition on Day One.
© 2009 by Owen Franken

Let's Dance: Hollingsworth and Guest in the kitchen, January 28, 2009.
© 2009 by Owen Franken

Judgment day: a platter is paraded before the Bocuse d'Or jury.
© 2009 by Owen Franken

Team USA's fish platter.
© 2009 by Le Fotographe, photo by Etienne Heimermann

"The hardest thing I've ever done":
Hollingsworth portioning his fish platter.
© 2009 by Owen Franken

A face in the crowd: Jennifer
Pelka awaits the results.
© 2009 by Owen Franken

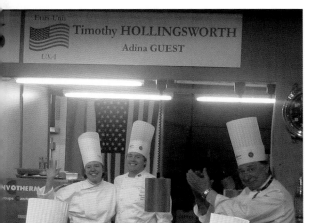

Kitchen's closed:
Guest, Hollingsworth,
and Henin moments after
completing the platters,
January 28, 2009.

Team USA's meat platter.
© 2009 by Le Fotographe,
photo by Etienne Heimermann

Norway's fish platter.
© 2009 by Le Fotographe,
photo by Etienne Heimermann

Philippe Mille's meat plate.
© 2009 by Le Fotographe,
photo by Etienne Heimermann

Dream come true: Norway's Geir
Skeie's promotional photo.
© 2009 by Paal-André Schwital

Victory is
theirs: *(left to
right)* Jonas
Lundgren,
Skeie, and
Mille on the
podium.
© 2009 by Owen
Franken

For the fish platter there were:

> The custard: Hollingsworth sliced a raw scallop into thin rounds and overlapped them in a circular pattern over a brioche melba, then set that in the glass high above the custard, finishing it with a quenelle of Petrossian caviar; and

> The mille-feuille: Once Guest had baked and cooled it, Hollingsworth unmolded it and cut out a rectangle with angled ends, topping the piece with crème fraîche and a quenelle of caviar.

For the meat platter, there were:

> The revised pommes dauphinoise: A rectangle of the potato preparation was set on a rectangular pommes Maxim, the browned top layer trimmed and decorated with chestnut and a salad of shaved celery, green celery leaves, and cutting celery (a microgreen);

> The smoke glass: into the orb that everybody loved went apple puree topped with a tornado-like twirl of bresaola, a brunoise of cabbage, and a chiffonade (long, thin strips) of quick-pickled pearl onion.

> The deconstructed beef stew: a punched-out turnip round (made by pushing a cookie-cutter-like tool through a slice of the vegetable) topped with a cube of stewed beef cheek, then small buttons of punched-out carrots threaded on a thyme sprig and perched horizontally, and pickled pearl onion . . . before tasting that, Hollingsworth put another cube on a paper towel to its left, topped it with broccolini florets and

stem segments and pickled pearl-onion layers. He professed a preference for the look of the second one.

Hollingsworth felt better about this day's work product. In comparison to the carrot-wrapped potato concoction, the one he had just made—with the celery salad and chestnut on top—pleased him both as a chef and as a potential eater. "That looks like something I want to eat," he said. "The other one does not."

Guest agreed with her chef's assessment of the prior day's experiment. "There's just no purpose to it," she said. "Especially the carrot."

Nothing was completely nailed down, and there remained a number of issues unique to the competition: for example, the brioche melba had become soggy after just twelve minutes of resting over the steam of the hot consommé, which wouldn't be a concern in a restaurant, but at the Bocuse d'Or, with that lag time, could prove fatal.

Nonetheless, he was getting warmer. "Once you have one really good thing on a dish it's easy to support those good things. So now it's going to be about going home and defining, finalizing a couple of things, even though they might change."

Despite his growing optimism, once he stopped working, it dawned on Hollingsworth with alarming quickness that he was bone-tired, and the exhaustion spread through him like a cancer on the way back to Napa—his eyelids were at half-mast, at best, and he felt his shoulders slumping. He pulled off the highway and knocked back a coffee from Starbucks, but that didn't do the trick; back home, in his living room, sitting at the table by the front door, trying to hone his concepts, he felt the claws of slumber reaching up though the floor of his apartment, pulling his head down. Fighting for a few more hours of consciousness, he bolted out the front door and sprinted around the block, but it was useless; no amount of stimulation could revive him. He returned to the table, his notebook open before him, but failed to think, his head tumbling forward, then snapping back up in quick bursts of barely deflected sleep.

"Go to bed," implored Laughlin.

"I can't," he said.

"Go. To. Sleep."

"I *can't.*"

"Go to sleep and wake up early."

"Yeah, like that'll happen."

But eventually, Hollingsworth did give in and go to sleep, feeling, for one of the first times in his life, the limits of his stamina, throwing in the towel on a day in which his to-do list exceeded the time he could find, or make, in which to get it done. This was no small matter. Forget the competitors he'd face in Lyon. Forget the judges and the notoriously noisy crowds. He was locked in a struggle with something bigger than all of that, a test of his creative powers and technical skill, his ability to apply all that he knew in an unfamiliar context, his readiness to step forward as a chef in his own right, to emerge from the cocoon of The French Laundry and his role as sous chef, holding forth two platters that announced, "Here, world, this is me. This is who I am and what I stand for."

No wonder he was tired. He was growing, and growth depletes the body and fatigues the mind of a full-grown man just as it does a small child. And there was something else, something he'd been keeping at bay, but that must have been taking its psychic toll as well: the next day, at 6:00 p.m., The Chef, Thomas Keller himself, the most acclaimed culinary figure in the United States, the one Hollingsworth had worked for his entire adult life, would be visiting the Bocuse House to taste his Bocuse d'Or dishes for the first time.

It was enough to make anybody pass out.

CULINARY GARDENER TUCKER TAYLOR'S name doesn't appear on the menu at The French Laundry, but he has a hand in just about every dish served there, especially on the "Tasting of Vegetables" that's offered as an option to the "Chef's Tasting Menu."

On Thursday, December 18, Timothy Hollingsworth parked his SUV in front of the Bocuse House and walked across the street to meet with Taylor for a farm tour. The purpose was to see what was gestating in the hoop house, and might be ready in time for Lyon. He had a look at some fennel and beets, but was most impressed by the turnips—pristine white, with smooth skin and brilliant green leaves. He had an appreciation for the turnips, having taken the time to learn about gardening over his years at The French Laundry, both from Taylor, who occasionally loaned him books on the subject, and from Peter Jacobsen, proprietor of nearby Jacobsen Orchards, which provides produce to a number of Keller's properties. He knew that it was the soil, the unrocky soil, that allowed them to grow into such perfect little orbs. He tasted the turnips raw, and tasted them cooked. He tasted the greens. He found the flavor clean, nutritious even. One of his secret weapons for the Bocuse d'Or, he figured, was the produce grown at The French Laundry—"You can't buy that" was how Hollingsworth described the flavor.

After the farm tour, Hollingsworth and Guest spent the afternoon cooking, getting ready for The Chef's visit later that day. Befitting an emerging theme, the music reflected the mood with a mix of reflective rock, such as "Epiphany" by Staind followed closely by Metallica's "One."

For lunch that day, they had sandwiches from a nearby Pacific Blues. Hollingsworth dunked his onion rings in ranch dressing, which prompted an oddly relevant discussion of flavor combinations encountered in fast-food joints. As a kid, Hollingsworth had liked Maui Zaui pizza from the Round Table chain—a pie topped with ham, bacon, pineapple, tomatoes, and onions that he loved dunking in ranch dressing. He also discovered a bizarre delight one day when he dipped a French fry in a caramel sundae from McDonald's—the hot crunch of the fry, the sweet caramel, the cool ice cream. It might sound like a surprising guilty pleasure for a guy who ended up a sous chef of The French Laundry, but he's managed to apply the central combinations to his sophisticated surroundings: when the waiters at Bouchon ask him what condiment he wants with his fries, he orders crème fraîche. And, though he didn't offer the comparison, the mille-feuille topped with crème fraîche and caviar that he was trying out for his fish platter had much in common with those culinary memories as well. (Hey, if Thomas Keller can make history from a visit to Baskin-Robbins, why couldn't one of his sous chefs look to Round Table Pizza as a muse?)

Aside from lunch, they stopped only to hang out briefly with a surprise visitor, Daniel Humm, executive chef of Eleven Madison Park in New York City, who was in the area to guest chef a holiday event at a Bay Area hotel.

At four fifty-five, the sound of the front door being swung open was audible in the kitchen.

Chef Keller, wearing his chef's jacket and black slacks, entered, slipped off his clogs, and strolled right into the kitchen. His demeanor, as is often the case, was unassuming.

"Hey, how's it going?" he asked.

"Hi, Chef," said Hollingsworth. "It's going well. But we're not quite ready. I heard you were coming later."

"You want me to come back?" said Keller, doing a convincing impression of a man with nothing else going on in his life.

"Yeah."

"Okay, when?"

"You could maybe taste in an hour."

"Okay, fine. I'll come back then."

For the next hour—as The Nationals' CD, *Mansion on the Hill*, washed over the kitchen—Hollingsworth and Guest worked in total silence. As Hollingsworth butchered beef, Guest pulled all the delis (cook-speak for plastic, Tupperware-like containers) from the past few days, all the items and components that had been prepped in anticipation of this evening. Hollingsworth made a custard with clarified butter, eggs, Champagne vinegar, and xanthan gum (a thickener). Then, as he cut pommes dauphinoise and mille-feuille into rectangles, Guest blanched broccolini florets and stalks and turnip rounds, sliced chive slivers, plucked celery leaves,

stripped thyme sprigs of their leaves, and warmed clarified butter for heating vegetables.

As the hour drew to a close, Hollingsworth put tarragon sprigs in the
shellfish bouillon, gave a stir, then discarded them. He then cut the top off
a small lemon, squirted a few drops of juice into the mixture and sniffed.
He shaved the bresaola and prepared the smoke glass; there were already
brunoised pearl onion and Granny Smith apple in the base, which he
topped with the bresaola slices. He added a quail egg yolk to the smoker,
topped it with the lid, added the smoke, then set the timer for three minutes, after which both he and Guest took spoons in hand and tasted.

"More salt?" asked Guest.

Hollingsworth nodded. Yes.

Cooking for The Chef was no small matter. Keller was much more
than an employer to Hollingsworth, who had basically grown up at The
French Laundry. When the two worked side by side, Hollingsworth was
continually awed by his talent and his precision. "You could just sit there
and watch . . . watch him fillet a fish . . . anything he was doing, you wanted
to watch him, because he was always doing it the way that you wanted to do
it. I never saw him do anything wrong. I could never say his station is a little
messy now. I could never say that about him," he said.

Hollingsworth was also among the last generation of cooks to witness Thomas Keller as a daily presence in the kitchen, before The Chef
ascended to his current higher level of being. The young cook would check
the schedule to see when The Chef was working because that was automatically more pressure. "You felt his presence and his pressure and the need
to do your best whenever he was around," said Hollingsworth. We [always]
put pressure upon ourselves . . . but when he is around, he . . . pushes you
to be even better."

Meet Keller today and his placid demeanor makes it difficult to imagine exactly what this must have been like, but front- and back-of-the-house
veterans describe working alongside him as an honor that occasionally re-

quired thick skin. Keller wasn't a constant screamer, the way some chefs can be, in those days, but "if something went wrong, the whole town of Yountville knew it," said Benno.

Keller also had a great deal of respect for Hollingsworth, even when the younger man was a commis. "He has always been the go-to guy," said Keller. "Out of the teams he was always the strongest."

Told of the comment, Hollingsworth was surprised and gratified: "It doesn't shock me but it's not something that I have heard said aloud. I have always tried to be like that. I think that comes from my father, too, because I worked with him a lot as a kid and he was really intense to work for. So if he needed a tool or anything, I was always like, okay, what is he going to need? Okay, he is going to need a crescent wrench or this or that? I wanted to be one step ahead always. . . . That's really carried on from construction . . . to being in the kitchen and wanting to be the person who is one step ahead. I know The Chef is going to ask for this, I am going to get it. Really being able to read someone."

Would he have read The Chef on this day? Would he put something in front of him that excited and pleased him? That made him . . . *happy?*

He'd find out soon enough.

AT 6:03, CHEF KELLER returned to the Bocuse House and again slipped off his clogs. Hollingsworth, who'd been exhibiting his surfer-level aura of carefree nonchalance all day, spun his head around so hard and fast it could have caused whiplash. Something that looked like panic seeped into his eyes and set his jaw on edge. He recovered immediately, looked at Guest, and they both nodded. They were ready.

The first thing the team prepared was the current iteration of the smoker garnish, which Hollingsworth had adjusted overnight: he put some leek puree in the bowl, topped it with a maple-braised beef cheek cube (made by straining and reducing the beef's cooking liquid, adding syrup, then glazing the cubes with the mixture), set a spinach ball on top and a soft-boiled quail egg, then fired some smoke into the glass.

Keller stared at it, curiously, neutrally.

"When are you going to put the smoke in?" he asked.

"When the platter comes back."

Keller's facial muscles tightened, indicating disappointment. "There's something provocative about it smoking on the platter."

"I know. But it takes too long. The food gets too smoky."

Keller nodded. He suggested that maybe another kind of smoke would solve the problem, but he didn't know what that might be. He lifted the lid and the smoke tumbled out, dissipated into the air. Keller tasted.

"Who's going to lift the lid?"

"I'll explain to the maitre d' and he'll have the servers do it."

Keller made a little muffled "mmm" sound and nodded, pondered.

"The puree really absorbs the smoke," said Hollingsworth.

Keller thought for a moment longer, then spoke: "Maybe you could put an isomalt [a sugar substitute] disc so that everything below it doesn't taste like smoke." He hadn't let go of that provocative smoke. "If you lose smoke, you lose drama."

Keller began sketching on a paper towel on the stainless-steel prep table.

"I'd almost look for something . . ." he said as he rendered a rough cross section of the smoker, creating in pencil a mushy mound with a circle perched atop it.

". . . like a puree of apple or something. Bind it. Giving you the ability to top it. Like a panna cotta."

Hollingsworth considered this, but not for long because Keller moved on to the subject of the egg.

"What if we deep-fried the egg?" asked The Chef. "It's still kind of clunky. Is there any way to make it round and deep-fry it? The issue is how to make it stay crunchy forever, but we know that we can do that."

Keller didn't actually know what the method to accomplish this might be, but as his organization had grown, populated by talent he doesn't have to micromanage, he's developed the opinion that no goal is out of reach— he has the time, funding, and resources to solve any riddle.

"I think that would be fun," Keller said.

Keller held up one of the smoke glasses, and it became clear that he'd been mentally multitasking, reconceiving the garnish on a macro level as he'd been discussing the micro.

"I think we need to coat the glass with parsley puree, or maybe coriander," he said. "Liquefy it, put it in the glass, turn it. That would obscure it and you would have the pureed horseradish, apple, beets. As you eat it, you get the parsley off the side, or coriander or whatever. You get the flavor, texture, color, *precision*. I think it would be critical. Precision is critical."

Hollingsworth didn't say much, but he wasn't sure how much of this input he'd be able to use. The pureed green coating the glass was something that would have to be executed to perfection—on fourteen individual glasses (twelve for the judges plus one for the official photographer and one to serve as an example for the servers)—and it went well outside his comfort zone. He was also worried about what an obscuring coat of green would do to the smoke and lights effect he'd fallen in love with. Additionally, he hoped that The Chef wasn't making any judgments about the lack of precision in the bowl. Despite his belief in being precise at all times, in this instance, he wasn't going for precision; he was still stuck on flavors and how to get there. But that was a small matter; because after weeks of realizing, "I can't smoke this; I can't smoke that," and becoming frustrated almost to the point of thinking nothing but a piece of meat could survive a turn in the bowl, the concept of the isomalt barrier was a potentially revolutionary one that gave Hollingsworth room to breathe as he honed the smoker garnish.

As his sous chef turned all this over in his head, Keller shrugged and shifted into his aw-shucks informality: "Okay, I mean, that's just some ideas."

Next up was the pommes dauphinoise. Guest browned a few potato

wedges, presenting them to Hollingsworth on the prep table. Hollingsworth built a stack: pommes Maxim, topped with the pommes dauphinoise, on one end he set a chestnut, on the other a celery salad, then he
drizzled a little chestnut-infused clarified butter over the chestnut.

Keller asked if it would be possible to slice the potato thinner and use
it as a wrapping for other components. He asked Guest for plastic wrap, cut
a narrow sheet and laid it on the table before him. He then cut a thin sheet
of pommes dauphinoise from the pan, set a broccolini spear across the potato, and used the plastic like a sushi mat to roll it up. Then he twisted the
ends of the plastic over and over, squeezing the contents into a cylindrical
shape.

"You can make it as big as you like and put the chestnut in the center,"
he said.

Next Hollingsworth assembled the deconstructed beef stew. Atop a
punched-out circle of turnip, he set a punched-out circle of black truffle, a
stewed beef cheek cube, and a baby beet wedge (inspired by his tour of the
hoop house that morning), and topped them with broccolini florets and
three small punched carrots speared on a stripped thyme sprig—an all-
American composition singing with Northern California produce.

Keller's response was instantaneous: "It's beautiful."

He studied it for a moment. "Why do you put the truffle on the
bottom?"

"It keeps the sauce off the turnip."

"Do you want to do truffle twice?" There it was, that French Laundry
bias against repeating major flavors on the same plate.

"Not necessarily. We're still working that stuff out."

Keller popped the little tower into his mouth.

"Mmmmm. It's really good. I think the flavor of the turnip, carrot, and
beef cheek is exceptional."

"What do you think of the size?"

"Perfect. I wouldn't get any bigger."

Keller continued to taste and think.

"I like it," he said. "It's natural. It's not manipulated. You don't want *everything* to be manipulated."

The comment was a relief to Hollingsworth who not only had a personal preference for simple elegance, but with so little time in which to work, didn't want to create platters with more places to fail than to succeed. Hollingsworth also took great pride in what happened next, or more precisely what *didn't* happen next. As he and Guest prepared the first of the fish garnishes, Keller lowered himself to his knees. He rested his hands on the stainless table and stared at the empty plate that had held the deconstructed beef stew. He tilted his head from side to side, leaned back, thought some more.

But he didn't say a word.

Hollingsworth took the silence to mean that The Chef couldn't come up with a way to improve the garnish, and it was a good feeling.

Keller popped a baby turnip from the table into his mouth and stood up.

"So that's the garnishes for the beef?"

"Yes"

"Is the fillet like we did it before?"

"Yes." (He hadn't actually decided to use the bacon-wrapped tenderloin for sure, but didn't want to worry The Chef with his lack of finality.) "Cod will be en persillade, with scallop mousse. Maybe diced shrimp."

Hollingsworth paused, sighed. "The côte de boeuf, I'm having a hard time with," he said. "Anything beautiful I can think to do, like a showpiece, it won't carve."

Keller nodded, but didn't have an immediate suggestion to share.

Hollingsworth next made the potato garnish for the fish platter: topping a rectangle of mille-feuille with caviar, a crème fraîche quenelle, and chive. The crème fraîche benefited from a subtle employment of molecular gastronomy: Hollingsworth whipped a little gellan gum into it, which kept it from melting on the hot potato.

Keller took a bite. Then another.

"That's excellent," he said. "Where's the bacon from?"

"Hobbs," said Hollingsworth, which was French Laundry shorthand for Hobbs Shore, a Marshall, California charcutier who had just passed away on December 15.

"Are you going to take this bacon with you?" asked Keller.

"Yes."

"Good. The bacon over there is smokier." Hollingsworth had heard this before, one of many references to the multitude of details that would have to be adjusted to on the ground in Lyon.

"Maybe a bacon chip on top," said The Chef. "Something that gives it some crunch." The bacon chip was on Keller's mind because Grant Achatz had just been in town to do a joint cookbook promotion with Keller, and had done a bacon chip as part of his meal. The chip is featured in his *Alinea* book, hanging dramatically from a wire.

Hollingsworth put some scallop carpaccio on a melba. He set this on top of a glass featuring the custard and lobster glace. Keller asked him about the glass. Hollingsworth said he was thinking of using a clear glass.

Keller tasted and made a so-so gesture with his hand.

"The sauce is a little intense," he said, then after a few more seconds, added, "and the shrimp are overcooked. You need to just drop them in."

Because he used to work at The Chef's side at The Laundry, Hollingsworth understood what he meant by "intense." The sauce wasn't burnt-tasting, it was too strong, and the reference to just dropping the shrimp in meant they could go into the broth at the last second and would be cooked by the liquid.

"Can we do anything else with the scallop? Like a mousse?" asked Keller.

Again, Hollingsworth knew what The Chef meant. "He was referring to the scallops being sliced like that. And eating the whole thing when the scallops are kind of sliced so . . . if I were to just puree it and add a little bit of crème fraîche or acid or whatever it is and spread it out; when you eat it you can take as much or as little as you want."

"We've done it raw," said Hollingsworth. "We've done it cooked. I'm thinking about putting something between the scallop and the melba to keep it from breaking down."

"Nuts," said Keller, all but snapping his fingers at the thought. "Toasted, chopped nuts. I'm thinking about ease of eating. How are they going to get all that in their mouth at one time?"

Keller asked what was in the custard and Hollingsworth told him it was clarified butter, eggs, Champagne vinegar, and xanthan gum. He was also thinking of simplifying the custard recipe, using a more conventional and easier-to-make blend of eggs, milk, and cream, flavoring it with agrumato oil, a lemony oil made by pressing lemons and olives together.

"You need something on top of the scallop. Is there anything else?"

"No."

"What about kumquats?" said Keller. "Kumquats are in season. Or just the skin. You can brunoise the skin."

They discussed the bowl. "It's going to be on the fish platter, which is porcelain," said Hollingsworth. "Silver and porcelain might be nice."

"We can have it made," said Keller, who again pulled out his notebook and wrote in it.

Keller and Hollingsworth walked over to the kitchen counter next to the sink and opened *The French Laundry Cookbook* to page 252: a picture of a Roquefort trifle in a funneled glass (like a martini glass minus the stem) that sat in a heavy, steel base. Keller said he would get in touch with Scannell to see if these other pieces could be created in time.

Before he wrapped up his feedback, Keller again mentioned the idea of coating the smoke glass. "Parsley would be too strong," he said. "It could be watercress or coriander." Hollingsworth didn't say anything, but he was leaning toward not following that particular piece of advice. The technique, he felt, didn't suit his strengths and could not be mastered in time.

And that was that. The Chef had dispensed his advice, and the candidate had received it.

Keller shook hands with Hollingsworth and Guest, slipped on his clogs, and disappeared into the December night. Though he had put on a good face during the tasting, he felt that Hollingsworth still had a lot of ground to cover before the competition, both conceptually and in execution. For the chef, it was also a powerful reminder of how quickly things were moving and how little time he'd been able to carve out to help his longtime associate: "Running into the house one day in December and tasting Timmy's garnishes after I have had ten meetings that day is not really productive," Keller commented later. "I think I came up with some good ideas for him but were we able to sit down and drill down into what we wanted to do? No."

Despite this lament, Keller didn't want to impose his vision on Hollingsworth too much; he believed that the sous chef had to make his own decisions, like the chefs de partie in The French Laundry kitchen, so that he could feel comfortable and confident in what he would cook in Lyon.

Inside the house, Hollingsworth wasn't where he wanted to be, even by his own somewhat flexible internal schedule. By night's end, he'd be freely admitting to himself that he wished he had more time, and right then, after the session with Keller, he felt like he could use a few weeks of just brainstorming. But the interaction with The Chef did him good. Though he'd been around him for years, he still felt "shocked" at how supportive he was, but at the same time, he felt more nervous because after weeks of going it on his own, he suddenly had the feeling that he had somebody to report to, which upped the sensation of pressure. Being a cook, this all had the net effect of getting him excited, putting some spring back in his step.

"I am almost ready to go again," he said.

ON FRIDAY, DECEMBER 19, Hollingsworth and Guest deep-cleaned the Bocuse House kitchen and brainstormed. He tried three different adjustments to the beef platter's potato dauphinoise, infusing the cream with chestnut; truffle and chestnut; and chestnut cream. He liked the last variation the best, but found the cream too intense for the potato, and to his eye, the colors marred the pure white hue that Hollingsworth found so lovely. He was leaning toward a black-and-white composition of potato and cream layered with black truffles—three distinct layers of potato with perfect black lines of truffle pressed in between, similar to the mille-feuille he had served in Orlando.

He also devoted some time to thinking about the custard cup garnish, the one that would be served in the little glasses he now had on order, but for which he still needed to secure a silver base. He and Keller had talked about adding kumquat to it and he found himself thinking of a dish they occasionally serve at The French Laundry, a citrus salad, sometimes made with olive, and sometimes with tarragon. Since Guest was jonesing to do a brunoise, he thought about topping the scallop with a brunoised citrus salad, maybe made with blood orange, or with candied citrus zest, julienned, with perhaps some cilantro shoots on top and Niçoise olive on the custard.

For all of the progress he'd made over the past few days, Hollingsworth still didn't know what he was going to do with the central proteins. He didn't have any ideas for the côte de boeuf, and although he'd been telling everybody he knew what the cod would be, he privately felt that that persillade crust was just too damn plain for competition. He might have known what a centerpiece was, but he didn't know what *his* centerpieces would be, and until he did, those garnishes would be conceptually unmoored, like rogue planets with no sun to orbit.

And then out of the blue, during his weekend at The French Laundry, he had a major breakthrough on the cod when he had the idea of enveloping it with a scallop mousse, then sealing it not in breadcrumbs, but with a crust of brilliantly green Sicilian pistachio nut crumbs. He played with the dish Saturday morning, and again Sunday afternoon, both times working at the pass. To make the nuts as fine as possible, he chopped them to a powder, then passed them through a tamis (a strainer-like tool comprising a meshed screen stretched across a frame), pushing them through with a scraper to knock the dust off. He spread the nuts out on his work surface, then set the cod cylinder at one end and gently pushed it along. As it turned, it was transformed, no longer just a mass of white but a beautiful, beguiling green object d'art.

He shared the moment of creation with the kitchen. It's a phenomenon that sometimes occurs at The French Laundry. In a cooking monastery where new dishes—or at least new variations on existing dishes—are conceived and realized daily, there are still moments when something new turns heads. And so, as Hollingsworth put the finishing touches on his centerpiece, turning the cod in that almost glitteringly green pistachio dust, the cooks around him stopped working, craning their heads to get a good look at what he was doing. This wasn't an easy crew to impress, and their attention confirmed for Hollingsworth that he had a winner on his hands.

He was psyched, not only at the outcome, but because he had never, even in all of his cookbooks, seen anybody else confit a piece of fish with a scallop mousse attached to it. All aspects of the moment—the inspiration, the location, and the silent approbation of his colleagues—he took as a confirmation of his belief that working through much of his training was the right thing to do.

"I don't think I would have come up with the cod if I hadn't been in the restaurant," he said. And he felt the same way about the citrus salad. "Working in that kitchen [at the Bocuse House], it's kind of hard to in some ways to be creative. It's nice to kind of step away and be in that same kind of place where you're being creative on a daily basis."

There was still fine tuning to be done: the Sicilian pistachios, not a crunchy nut to begin with, were a bit gummy, so he wanted to cut them with toasted, chopped brioche or regular pistachios. He was also considering a nougatine of pistachios, but worried that might be too crunchy and sweet.

But it didn't matter. He had come up with the elusive centerpiece, and with it one of his two platters was coming into focus. Best of all, he felt that he was balancing on that tightrope between something clean and elegant that he would cook and serve at The French Laundry and something that,

as he understood it, the Bocuse d'Or judges were looking for—one component wrapped in another, then rolled in yet another. "I think the chances of
us being successful with something like this is really, really good," he said.

That night, a member The French Laundry's pastry team was in for
dinner with her parents. They were served discs of cod that all but glit-
tered with a fanciful green dust. They didn't know it, but they were the
first people tasting the prototype of the centerpiece of Team USA's Bocuse
d'Or fish platter.

THE FOLLOWING WEEK, HOLLINGSWORTH received a belated Christmas
present. Still searching for a new way to use the beef fillet, the Fates threw
him a bone when Corey Lee told him to make a potato-and-truffle tart for
a table of VIPs.

There are a number of ways to structure a tart. Lee told Hollingsworth
to make his with a layer of potatoes topped with a layer of truffles. But *tart*
had certain connotations for Hollingsworth and he pictured a round of
flaky pastry topped with overlapping circles of potato and truffle. Lee told
him to go ahead and try it. When Hollingsworth showed him the finished
product, Lee immediately said, "You should do that on your platter."

"Yeah!" said Hollingsworth, imagining punched-out circles of beef
incorporated into the composition. He considered whether he wanted to
introduce a piece of cooked meat to those delicate flavors. "Do you think
it'd be nice with the fillet raw?"

Lee thought for a moment. "Yes," he said.

"Do you think I should sear it?"

"No."

Hollingsworth agreed. His mind was racing. He knew that this was
it: a tart was French, but a *beef* tart came with all kinds of American connotations. He was already using potato on the beef platter, but maybe . . .
maybe . . . what? What could take the place of—

Celeriac! That would be a good alternative. Picturing it in his head—

the white of the celeriac, the rosy red beef, the black truffle—he realized that the color palate was not unlike that of a pepperoni pizza. And if the competition demanded a touch of audacity, then serving the beef raw was his way of doing it.

Before the restaurant closed for the winter respite, he decided that he would add an endive marmalade—a Thomas Keller recipe made with endive, shallots, bacon, onion, and sherry vinegar—to the tart, layering it between the pastry and the "toppings," though he would go easy on the honey, ensuring a balance that any judge, from anywhere, could appreciate.

He still had no idea what to do with the shrimp. But he had solved the riddle of the beef tenderloin with something he believed was true to himself, America, *and* the Bocuse d'Or.

The New Year was looking better and better.

4

Training Season

Time moves slowly, but passes quickly.

—ALICE WALKER, *THE COLOR PURPLE*

T IMOTHY HOLLINGSWORTH WOULDN'T SAY THAT HE THOUGHT HE was dreaming. That's too melodramatic for him. But he couldn't quite believe his eyes when he opened his e-mail early Sunday morning, January 4, and read that Paul Bocuse himself was arriving in Yountville the next day.

Team USA was at T-minus twenty-four days, and counting, until the competition. With The French Laundry closed for the first three weeks of January, Hollingsworth possessed exactly one objective for the next month: do well at the Bocuse d'Or.

On Saturday, he and Guest had performed their first practice, with an encore scheduled for Monday. Daniel Boulud and Jérôme Bocuse would be jetting cross-country for the day, to observe, taste, and offer feedback, and a reporter and photographer from the *Los Angeles Times* were expected as well.

When Hollingsworth powered up his laptop Sunday morning, among the e-mails was one from Jennifer Pelka, which said:

"Hi, everyone. I have just learned from Jérôme that his father wishes to join the group in Yountville. I realize that the group is getting quite large now, but I do hope everyone is comfortable with Chef Bocuse being added to the trip."

Hollingsworth stared at the note, blankly. It didn't compute. *Paul Bocuse is coming here? Tomorrow? To watch us* practice? He wouldn't learn until later that the chef was in the midst of one of his periodic extended visits with son Jérôme in Orlando, so it wasn't like the guy was coming all the way from France. But still.

"Oh, my God," he said, as it sank in.

Laughlin peeked at the message over her boyfriend's shoulder, and burst out laughing. What else could she do? Besides, there was no time for dwelling on it. The sun would rise on Monday soon enough. The best way for Hollingsworth to move forward was with the same plan he'd had before he'd learned that one of the planet's most historic chefs would be present: Get ready.

In retrospect, Saturday's practice had been like losing one's virginity: the main thing had been to get it out of the way. Now improvements could commence. The team hadn't choreographed their routine yet, but Guest took the initiative to give herself the structure she needed, ordering her tasks on a printed grid in neat little fifteen-minute blocks. Such grids are the North Star for culinary competitors, the itinerary to which Roland Henin had referred in his briefing at The French Culinary Institute back in July. They are also exercises in extreme optimism; reducing jobs that require extraordinary coordination, talent, and precision into one or two words. For example, "melbas" meant actually to *make* melba toast: slicing the brioche, punching it out, and baking the pieces to perfection between Silpats.

Hollingsworth, meanwhile, opted to wing it for Practice Number One, operating in the way he first learned to cook, intuitively, relying on his experience to mentally MapQuest the five-hour journey for him. He would get around to regimenting his chores, but he needed to get there the same way he got to his dishes, on his own time and in his own way. On Saturday, he just wanted to *cook*.

The only other person in the Bocuse House that day had been Laughlin, who reprised the role she'd played in the Orlando practices, taking notes as the team called out items they'd need to talk about, or adjust. (At this time, Laughlin was transitioning to a new job with Soutirage, a rare wine merchant based in Northern California, and so had time to devote to helping the team.) Some addressed timing and sequencing, such as "Cook PD [pommes dauphinoise] for less time than 1 hour—check at 35 minutes," "Melbas were 4 minutes at 315 degrees," and "Heat up broccoli last." Some indicated necessary ingredients, equipment, and tools, such as "Paintbrush and olive oil for tart." Some were stand-alone adjustments such as "Freeze beef" [to make it easier to slice for the tart] and "Grind more panko [Japanese breadcrumbs], and grind to a powder." Others were geared to establishing that essential, time-saving efficiency; for example, "Butcher all beef together at once," "Do all meat glue at once (cod and meat)," and "When Vita-Prep is out: horseradish foam, chestnut puree, pistachio puree, prune puree." By the time the day was done, the list would run down the left-hand side of *three* typed pages.

For four hours, Team USA belied the brevity of their preparation, as both Hollingsworth and Guest adroitly fulfilled their responsibilities. But they hit a patch of turbulence at plate-up time. Athletes refer to a *transition game*: switching from one mode that requires a specific set of skills, to another—relocating from the baseline to the net in tennis, or toggling back and forth between offense and defense in basketball. The transition game in the kitchen might be defined as shifting from prep to service, assembling all the individual components you've been amassing, and getting them all out to the diner at the same time, and piping hot. In the Bocuse d'Or kitchen, transitioning meant much more than that: instead of a full brigade, there are just two people charged with putting up close to forty individual pieces (twelve of each garnish plus the centerpiece), each one flawlessly composed and as synchronized on the platter as the North Korean People's Army on a parade march.

The team lost time here, as plating-up became something of a game of Twister. But they finished: on the fish platter there was the cod, the mille-feuille, and the custard cup. (The team also had also prepared a shellfish boudin, or sausage, wrapped in a sushi-like band of Swiss chard. It was lovely, but it was just a placeholder, there to take up practice time and fill up space on the platter. Hollingsworth still didn't know what he was going to do for his final garnish.) The meat platter housed the tart, the deconstructed stew, and the potato dauphinoise topped with the celery salad and chestnut. In the week and a half since Keller's tasting, the smoke glass had also morphed into something Hollingsworth felt good about: in the base of the glass were brunoised blanched Savoy cabbage, green apple, bresaola, pickled red onions, and small croutons that had been sautéed in olive oil and salt. They were topped with an airy cloud of horseradish mousse on which rested a delicate slice of bresaola. Hollingsworth had also figured out what to do with the remaining cut of meat: with the tenderloin riddle solved, he would wrap two cylinders of beef cut from the côte de boeuf in bacon, sear it, then roast it.

There was a *lot* of tweaking to do. Hollingsworth and Guest met at the Bocuse House Sunday afternoon to review these topics as well as the list Laughlin had created, and to determine the changes they needed to make for Monday's practice. Two hours were required to get through it all, but Hollingsworth was feeling good, satisfied that his approach—drawing on techniques familiar to him and Guest from their daily work—was working. If he had created a menu that had required them to master techniques from scratch, the first run-through may not have gone so well. His strategy was ultimately to design the division of labor to max out Guest's schedule, while leaving him free to take on tasks should she fall behind during competition. In sports terms, Hollingworth was not just the team leader but also the ultimate "utility player"—able to step into any position—except that where that phrase connotes mere competence, Hollingsworth could perform any task expertly. It was another application of his French Laundry experience to the Bocuse d'Or; just as he had worked every position in that kitchen, he was able to take on any task in this considerably smaller one.

The battle lines drawn, they were ready to take on their first adversary: time.

ON MONDAY MORNING, TEAM USA had a taste of what the Bocuse d'Or would be like as they prepared to cook publicly for the first time since competing in Orlando. As they readied the kitchen, arranging armfuls of produce and equipment in optimal locations, Kristine Keefer, public relations manager for the Thomas Keller Restaurant Group, looked on along with Betty Hallock of the *Los Angeles Times* and a freelance photographer there to take pictures for her article. After conferring with the photographer, Keefer asked Guest if it would be okay to move a table from the corner of the kitchen so a reflector could be positioned there.

Guest was so in the throes of the chain of command that she wouldn't give an answer, even though the table was outside the practice area. "Ask Chef Tim," she said.

The three Frenchmen arrived minutes before the planned twelve noon start time: Paul Bocuse, nattily attired in a black-and-white checkered blazer and black scarf, along with Daniel Boulud and Jérôme Bocuse. Others had stayed to one side of the imaginary line that marked the perimeter of the training kitchen, but after making his hellos, Boulud marched right in and engaged in some shop talk with Hollingsworth, asking how the equipment had been treating him and how the preparations were going.

As soon as the dialogue stopped, with no fanfare Hollingsworth and

Guest began working. Hollingsworth set about butchering the beef while Guest was out of the blocks with a demonstration of her quick hands and the precision of her technique: one of her first tasks was to peel several Yukon Gold potatoes, which she accomplished by standing the potatoes on end, one at a time, and rotating them with one hand while the other brought her knife down with the persistent ferocity of a wood-chipper, filling the kitchen with a rat-a-tat-tat.

Is there anyplace on Earth where Paul Bocuse *isn't* a celebrity and somebody doesn't want his autograph? In the living room, Keefer handed one of Bocuse's own books to the maestro and asked him to autograph it for Keller, who was out of town that week. She offered a pen, but he raised a hand to freeze her, producing his own from his blazer pocket. The man is so used to signing things that, even at age eighty-two and at the crack of dawn in Orlando, before leaving he had thought to stick his own *plume de choix* in his pocket. Before the day was over, he'd have signed a wall in the living room as well, branding the house that unofficially bore his name.

Friends and fellow employees of the Thomas Keller Restaurant Group dropped in throughout the afternoon, lending the spectacle of the blue apron–clad cooks the air of a sideshow. *Step right up, folks, and see the amazing Chef Timothy and his trusty commis Adina. Marvel at his nerves of steel. Witness the speed of her knife. You will NOT believe your eyes!* Larry Nadeau, maitre d' of The French Laundry, dropped in, as did Jennifer Fukui, director of private events for Keller's Yountville restaurants. In the living room, Hallock interviewed Boulud, who was only too happy to explain the difference between the Bocuse d'Or and other competitions. "The taste is very, very important," he said. This is a point of distinction that Bocuse d'Or's insiders cite with great pride: their contest of choice eschews the outdated conventions of cold-food competitions, all that aspic-drenched stuff meant for the eyes rather than the palate. In the Bocuse d'Or, the chefs do *real* cooking and the judges evaluate primarily on taste. (In truth, though it features cold-food contests, hot food is also a major component of the International Culinary Olympics, but detractors of that event frequently decline to mention this fact.)

Having turned, cut, and cooked those potatoes in seasoned cream, Guest layered the slices into the square vessel in which they'd be baked. Her hands, gloved in latex, moved one square at a time into the mold. Her head was down, but something had occurred that breached even her well-guarded perimeter of attention: Paul Bocuse was standing just a foot away, watching her.

Compelled to say something, she called on the little French she knew to make small talk about the food.

"*Pomme de terre, Chef,*" she said. (Potatoes.)

"*Oui, oui,*" whispered Bocuse, in his gentle, ancient voice. "*C'est pommes dauphinoise, oui?*"

"*Oui.*"

"*Avec oeufs?*" (With eggs?)

"*Non, Chef. Avec crème.*"

"*C'est bon, c'est bon,*" said Bocuse, then added, "*C'est très bon technique.*"

Bocuse shuffled away, leaving Guest atwitter with emotion, concealed beneath a Game Face straining to its breaking point. "Just that little interaction with him meant the world to me," she said.

Like Jonathan Benno before him, Bocuse was blown away. On his way out of the kitchen, he whispered to Boulud: "*Très bonne, la fille.*" The girl is good.

"When you watch somebody work, you can tell if they are good or not," he said later. "The guy is really good, but the girl . . . if he wins, she deserves half the prize."

The East Coast contingent excused themselves to have lunch at Bouchon, taking the car to save Monsieur Paul the walk. As they crossed Washington Street, the depths of Yountville's food culture flowered as the smattering of locals and tourists alike stopped disbelievingly in their tracks; the only thing missing was the screeching brakes of a passing car. The effect was repeated when the trio attempted in vain to surreptitiously enter Bouchon through the back door, but nevertheless turned every head in the joint. Taking in the scene, with its avocado-cream-colored walls and palm

tree exploding like a fountain in the center of the room, its bow-tied waiters and raw bar, Bocuse nodded. "This place is more Paris than Paris," he
said.

As they lunched on a *plat de fruits de mer* (seafood platter), and steak
frites, the three men discussed the hour they had just observed. It was too
early to make any judgments about the food, but the utility of the training
center was already apparent. They also graciously posed for photographs
with Culinary Institute of America students who happened to be dining
there, and the cooks in the kitchen before heading back to the House.

At about a quarter after three, the men returned to find Hollingsworth
and Guest right where they left them, cooking up a storm. Hollingsworth
was multitasking: slicing rectangles of chilled mille-feuille at his station
while whipping horseradish foam (preserved horseradish, nonfat milk,
salt, and Simplesse, a whey protein that helps volumize the foam) in a War-
ing mixer on the counter by the back door. Boulud, uninhibited as ever,
lowered the mixer's speed. Hollingsworth presumed that the chef feared
he was going to overmix the foam, but the truth was that it went into the
mixer hot and had to be cooled off before it would elevate. Not wanting to
correct his guest, the candidate kept mum. So the foam would take a little
longer to happen. That was all right. They had time.

Boulud again walked right into the kitchen and stood inches from
Hollingsworth, crossing his arms.

"How many run-throughs are you going to do in Lyon?"

"Jennifer said two," said Hollingsworth. "But I think one is good for
me. Just to test the proteins." The fish and beef they'd be using in Lyon
were from different pastures and waters than the ones they'd been using in
Yountville. That detail aside, in the midst of just his second practice, Hollingsworth was feeling confident.

"Yeah, yeah. Exactly," said Boulud, although they ultimately decided to
book two sessions, for safety's sake.

Guest pulled brioche melbas from the oven. "Ay, yi, yi," she exclaimed.

"You wanted them less brown?" asked Boulud.

"Little bit, Chef. Thirty seconds makes a difference."

Boulud continued to pace in and out of the kitchen and around the perimeter. He noticed the task list taped to the steel door of the freezer.

"You are fifteen minutes ahead, no?" he asked Hollingsworth.

"Don't pay attention to that," he said. "I haven't looked at it the whole time."

"Because you haven't punched it up yet," said Boulud.

"*Cuisine spontanée*," said Hollingsworth with a shrug as he pulled turnip medallions, beet medallions, and chestnuts, each in its own sous-vide bag, from the circulator.

Periodically, Hollingsworth and Guest called out notes to Laughlin, who had arrived on the scene: "Less salt," said Guest, regarding the chestnut preparation. "One brick for pommes Maxim." "Add to prep time sheet hache [very finely chop] endive marmalade."

Boulud took over the center of the living room and whipped out his cell phone to do business in his instant office. He called his assistant Absil back in New York to adjust his travel plans, then Pelka, to get her going on arranging two days in Lyon.

Corey Lee, in on a day off, and Coach Henin, just arrived in Yountville, walked in shortly before the five-hour mark, and Hollingsworth and Guest began operating with greater urgency. Guest floured mille-feuilles, preparing them for browning, then readied the custards according to a more conventional recipe than the eggs-only version Hollingsworth had first employed back in December: she mixed milk, cream, eggs, and that lemony agrumato oil together, then poured the mixture into glass dishes and set them in a bain-marie (water bath), readying them for steaming in the combi oven. Hollingsworth spread scallop mousse on the melbas and mixed the breadcrumb mixture for the cod in two small pans. Watching all of this, Paul Bocuse gleaned where Hollingsworth was headed. He hadn't tasted anything, but he was already impressed with one aspect of the candidate's strategy: this food did not need to be very hot to taste good.

Hollingsworth put his fish platter together on a sheet of parchment paper draped neatly over a cutting board, the white standing in for the ivory hue of the porcelain on the platter that was being fabricated. The cylinder of olive oil–poached, scallop mousse–encased, pistachio-crusted loin of cod took center stage. (The pistachios didn't coat the cod as uniformly as he'd have liked: a challenge that he'd been wrestling with since conceiving the dish.)

Hollingsworth plated the food: A cross section of the pistachio cod. A slice of the boudin set atop a beet round that was, in turn, pressed into a blob of citrus mousseline, an emulsification based on hollandaise sauce. Dissatisfied with the boudin, once he had plated one portion, he dumped the rest so that as few people as possible would taste it. A wedge of potato mille-feuille topped with a dollop of gelled crème fraîche and a piece of chive. (There would also be a tiny quenelle of caviar, but not in practice.) Alongside the plate was the little "martini glass" with the custard topped with lobster glace (again standing in for shrimp consommé), and the scallop-spread melba with citrus salad on top.

In the kitchen with the team, Boulud and Lee tasted the fish.

"The cod?" asked Boulud.

"It was cooked before," said Hollingsworth.

"You can push it a little more."

"Cook it a little longer?"

"Yeah."

Boulud poked at the center of the roulade-like slices of cod. "Did you dry the pistachios in a food dryer?"

"No."

"Maybe to keep them more green and get them a finer powder."

Hollingsworth disagreed, politely. "I think it works better with the brioche."

As Hollingsworth conferred with Boulud, Corey Lee began washing dishes and pans for him, living that French Laundry ideal even on vacation.

Henin was taking it all in. This was his first hour back at the Bocuse House since November. Much impressed him, but it was far from perfect.

To put the best face forward for the *Los Angeles Times*, Hollingsworth didn't tell anybody, not even his coach, that the boudin was just a placeholder. It would have been useful information, and saved Henin some mental energy, because he was bothered by the boudin. The repetition of the two circular shapes (the cod was also cylindrical) wouldn't win them any points. He stood one cod roulade circle on its side like a tire to give it height and add another dimension to the platter. Meanwhile, Boulud set the "martini glass" bearing the custard and scallop melba on the plate. "I think it's important to incorporate this garnish *inside*," he said, meaning on the plate, not alongside it. It was the same advice Viola had given, which Hollingsworth hadn't heeded. Maybe it was his French Laundry aesthetic holding firm; many dishes at the restaurant are delivered to the table with what the runners call a "follow," a freestanding but complementary component.

Next, Hollingsworth put up his meat platter, working on a new and improved mock-up made of white foam display boards from Daniel Scannell, the certified master chef who was overseeing the realization of the Tihany-designed platters, which had been lined with aluminum foil to approximate silver. The beef tart took center stage, flanked by two cylinders of bacon-wrapped rib-eye. On the tiered shelves behind them were alternating deconstructed beef stews and a mock-up of the smoker. Even on foil, there was a majesty to the composition, a deft mingling of confidence and subtlety that aptly reflected the chef who had conceived them. There was a hush in the room, the same hush that came over the kitchen at The French Laundry when something special went up on the pass. It was the silence of approval.

Paul Bocuse, having changed into his whites for a group photo, shook Hollingsworth's hand. "*Compliment*," he said. Congratulations.

This triggered a round of applause from the spectators, but the celebration didn't last long as the chefs continued conferring. Boulud suggested squeezing some horseradish through cheesecloth into the cream at the last second to make it more pungent; Lee thought the celeriac and tenderloin slices should be thinner and that Hollingsworth should consider returning to the rectangular shape of the rib-eye that had wowed the judges in Orlando because it was an unnatural shape he created by binding two pieces of steak with Activa, the transglutaminase that "glues" proteins together, then using the powder to affix the bacon; Hollingsworth himself thought there was too much marmalade on the tart. As they spoke—and they spoke for a while—Boulud jotted notes in a leather-bound notebook.

Some of the suggestions were purely instinctual: Lee asked Guest to cut a mille-feuille wedge a bit shorter. She did. Everybody nodded: better.

There were also notes that Hollingsworth kept to himself: like the fact that the melbas didn't survive the sitting process well, and that he was beginning to doubt that pureeing the scallops was the best way to treat them. He also chided himself for a rookie mistake: cooking the shrimp sous vide with butter led to the butter breaking when the shrimp were heated again in the boudin. He should have seen that coming, but with so many moveable pieces to shepherd, he hadn't thought that one through. On the meat platter, he was considering incorporating oxtail into the endive marmalade on the tart, in order to actually use the cut on the platter and not just in a sauce. He wouldn't usually combine raw and cooked meat in a single component, but for the sake of incorporating the oxtail, he was almost certain he'd at least try it.

Conspicuously silent was Jérôme Bocuse, who believed that the team had already missed the podium. "For me, referring to what I have seen in the past at the Bocuse d'Or . . . everything was there, but something was not there," he would say later. Bocuse felt that the platters lacked a degree of difficulty and didn't have that three-dimensional quality that judges were conditioned to expect. He also couldn't help but notice that Hollingsworth and Guest, while efficient, were not working in the almost robotic way the top competitors in Lyon would be. It was all about routine to Bocuse, and Hollingsworth's was far from polished. He thought that the intelligence of the food and the team's obvious technical gifts might carry them into the top ten, maybe even the top five, but he doubted they'd be wearing Bocuse d'Or bling come January 28.

He didn't share any of this because, frankly, he didn't believe the gap could be closed. "Twenty days," he said. "What are you going to change?"

Bocuse also felt that the number of advisers contributing opinions was too much of a good thing. "If you got my opinion and then if you got Roland's opinion and then you got Keller's opinion, and Daniel's—at the end of the day, I think you are going to be lost. Daniel's opinion could be the opposite of Thomas's. They might not see the thing in the same way, so who are you going to listen to in the end? . . . For that we had Roland. . . . You cannot have five coaches on a basketball team. You have one coach and you listen to the coach."

Ever the optimist, Boulud, as he gathered his things and prepared to rocket back to San Francisco, took the opposite approach. "I think you're in a very good path here," he said. "It's just a matter of doing it in your sleep. Doing it blind. And don't be afraid. *Bonne chance*."

And with that the three Frenchmen were off, leaving Team USA to finish their preparations in private.

A PALL OF ANTICLIMAX hung over the Bocuse house on Tuesday, January 6. The Bocuses and Daniel Boulud were in the air, somewhere between the coasts, The French Laundry was closed, and it was cold and damp outside. The Bocuse d'Or USA adventure might have begun in summer, but it would end, one way or another, in the harsh chill of winter.

Henin, Hollingsworth, and Guest stood around those rolling carts in the kitchen, comparing notes on Monday's practice. The agenda for the day was to fine-tune some elements of various garnishes, and get reorganized and ready for the next practice, set for Thursday, January 8. It was plain that the platters made great peacemakers: the tension between candidate and coach that had soured their November get-togethers was dissipating. There was now something to discuss, something tangible that had sprung from Hollingsworth's own personality. And so, when Henin asked him if he had been practicing shucking his own scallops, as he'd have to do in Lyon, Hollingsworth didn't mind at all.

"No," he said. "You can't get good ones here."

Henin also asked Hollingsworth if he planned to emerge from the kitchen in Lyon to slice and plate the cod himself, or to avail himself of the option of letting the servers do it.

"Do you think you'll have time?" asked the coach.

Guest, in a rare show of bravado, nodded confidently. "Oh, yeah," she said.

"If you put it together, you know how to take it apart," said Hollingsworth.

The team broke. Adina Guest set up in the kitchen alone and began prepping for the next practice, scheduled for Thursday. As she chopped pistachios, holding the handle of her knife loosely in one hand, while dribbling the blade like a basketball over the nuts with the other, Hollingsworth pulled his cap over his head, tucked his notebook under his arm, and walked over to the offices of the restaurant to meet with his friend Corey Lee.

Lee leveled with Hollingsworth: the flavors and concepts were solid—as he would have expected—but the execution needed work. In French Laundry parlance, they lacked *finesse*. For first time, Lee detected signs that the Bocuse d'Or was affecting Hollingsworth. Gone was the carefree aura the candidate usually exuded. In its place was a heaviness, a tightness of body and spirit. The mounting pressure was squeezing him out of shape, had forced the California smile right off his face.

When Hollingsworth returned to the Bocuse House, Guest had departed to go house hunting and Hollingsworth and Henin stood in the kitchen and discussed the platters. Henin was especially impressed with the beef tart.

"It's a great idea, the carpaccio, or whatever you want to call it. Like a pizza pie. An American pie," said the coach, almost swooning with enthusiasm.

Henin also ribbed Hollingsworth about the ubiquitous music he played when he cooked, suggesting that Hollingsworth turn it up real loud in preparation for Lyon.

"When it's noisy, I can think," said Hollingsworth. "When you're alone in the kitchen and it's quiet, it's spooky. Maybe it's because I grew up with a lot of brothers and sisters."

"We never had this music in the kitchen," said the coach. "You listened to the chef."

The two cooks kept kibitzing while Hollingsworth broke down a mountain of côte de boeuf. Hollingsworth described how he helped out with a dinner at The French Laundry in December, when Chicago restaurant Alinea's Grant Achatz was in town for the joint cookbook promotion with Keller.

There was no doubt about it: Henin and Hollingsworth were engaging in that essential ritual of male-on-male relationship-building—they were bonding.

"How did you pick Adina?" asked Henin.

Hollingsworth told him the story about how he used to think she was European and didn't even know she spoke English. He also shared the one "con" to the numerous "pros" she brought to the table: as talented as Guest was, through no fault of her own, she lacked on-the-line experience. It's a strange downside to a Bocuse d'Or commis drafted from The French Laundry; as a commis, she was world class, but having never worked the hot line, when it came down to service, there were things she had yet to learn.

"In Monday's practice, she almost served a broken sauce," Hollingsworth said, recounting how he showed her how to rescue it by whisking in hot water.

Beneath his convivial exterior, there were things Henin had on his mind. One was a nagging feeling that all of this progress might be a little too late. "This is exactly where we should have been at the week before Thanksgiving where we packed up for the Thanksgiving week," he would say a couple days later. "This is where we should have left it, at this level, and take it from there in early December and have the whole month of December without all the other interference that we are in the process of, unfortunately. Then you imagine where we would be a month later instead of being today. Not that where we are today is wrong, but it is really a month late. Had we been there we would be in better shape.

"We can still make up some of the time even though it is very short." To this end, Henin resolved that he'd do what he could to free up things for the team, managing whatever aspects of the travel he could when they were in Lyon.

"It is good at least to be at this comfort level. Where we are right now, even though it is a month late it is better than it not happening at all. We are going to need that comfort level. That trust. That faith in days and weeks to come."

This was not an optimistic assessment, but "I am not pessimistic either," he said. "I am just saying, look . . . I think it is all in preparations. Same as if you were to become a master chef." This was a reference to the Certified Master Chef exam that he had taken years earlier. The CMC tests all aspects of a chef's culinary knowledge and prowess over the course of several days, and Henin believes that you cannot study for it—you either know your craft or you don't. "It is all what you have done in fifteen to twenty years. You can't make up that time. If you sat on your butt for five hours a day watching TV, you weren't progressing towards the master chef. [The Bocuse d'Or] is the same thing. . . . If you don't do your homework—training, practice, and preparation . . . to the hilt, it will come back and bite you. Whatever portion you didn't do will come back and bite you in the butt. It will. Even if you are a genius. No matter what field it is, swimming or cooking, it will come back and bite you."

Henin also had some concerns about specific items from Hollingsworth's platters, especially the fish. For example, the beet under the boudin had leached some juice into the mousseline on which it sat. Not enough to have been problematic in a restaurant, but point-costly for sure in Lyon. Henin knew that you only needed to cook the beets with a few drops of vinegar to arrest that bleeding, but he didn't bring it up for fear of disrupting the fragile peace with Hollingsworth. "I want to protect this. We can work on the garnish another time as opposed to me coming on strong and saying this garnish sucks and we need to rework it. Because that would take us back to where we were in November and I cannot afford that. . . . He takes it as I am a master chef and I am telling you what to do and you better do it for whatever reason I don't know. He gets on the defensive. I don't want to do that. I am not going to do that because it sets us back too far and it takes too much to come back and I don't want to put him on the defensive. I would rather bite my lips and have bleeding beets. . . ."

The coach didn't share any of this with the candidate that afternoon. Instead, he retired to his room to rest and Hollingsworth turned his attention to the kitchen. The facility appeared clean to the untrained eye, but Hollingsworth knew there were imperfections: streaks on the counter, microscopic detritus in the carpet, grime in the shadowy well of the sink. And so he set about deep-cleaning the room.

For the seven years he'd been working for Keller, cleaning the kitchen had been a part of his daily life. It was the way he decompressed after a night on the line, processed the day, organized his thoughts before sitting down to menu meetings as a cook and then as a sous chef.

He cleaned the same way he cleaned his station at the end of every working day. He scrubbed the counter and the doors of the refrigerators, leaning into the motion, putting the full force of his weight behind the effort. He wiped under canisters and equipment. As he did, he thought about how much work still lay ahead of him. He thought about the previous day, about cooking for Paul Bocuse. All those notes everybody threw at him ricocheted around his head like numbers in a bingo tumbler. He needed to silence them, and this was the way to do it.

Before he knew it, Hollingsworth was lost in his cleaning, almost to the point of dancing. It was a solitary time, and it was clear that he didn't want company. Coach Henin, seeking a dinner companion, periodically emerged from his room, then retreated, not saying a word.

As evening descended on Yountville and cold darkness enveloped the little house, time's merciless march propelling him ever closer to Lyon, Hollingsworth continued to clean. He straightened the stacks of pots and

pans on the utility rack until they were as neat and orderly as the items on a
Bocuse d'Or platter. He thought about the shrimp garnish. He wondered if
there was too much honey in the marmalade, or too much vinegar, or were
they just right?

He vacuumed the carpets, then wrapped the cord tautly around the
cleaner's neck and parked it in the corner.

After three hours, the kitchen looked as spotless and orderly as it had
the day it was first outfitted with the Bocuse d'Or equipment. Hollingsworth stood in front of the freezer and surveyed his handiwork. He still
needed one more garnish for his fish platter. He still had a lot of practice
to do. But he had accomplished something that day, and accomplished it to
perfection.

He was ready for tomorrow.

On Wednesday, January 7, with twenty days until the Bocuse d'Or
began, Hollingsworth and Guest tried some slightly rejiggered items in
the kitchen. Seeking more of a visual punch, he wanted to revisit the rectangular form of the beef with bacon that he had employed in Orlando; a
thinner cylinder of cod with diced preserved Meyer lemon incorporated
to add acidity and sweetness to the scallop mousse; and the scallop tartare
with a smaller melba, that would fit *inside* the glass instead of on top, to
keep judges from picking them up like crackers when the intention was for
them to break them up, so they'd fall into the consommé and custard and
be eaten with the spoon.

When it was all done, with *Masters of Rap*—an eighties-era
compilation—playing in the background, the team, including Coach
Henin, discussed them.

Hollingsworth was still worried that the judges would pick up the melbas, perhaps using their spoon to tip and grip them.

"Maybe mark it in quarters, so as soon as you touch it, it cracks," said

Henin. To illustrate his concept, he set a melba on a cutting board and gently pressed a serrated knife blade into it, perforating it.

Hollingsworth nodded. This was the kind of exchange he was always looking for with his coach. "Like saltine crackers," he said.

Regarding the cod, the entire team found the pistachios a bit gummy, due to the natural oil in the nuts. Hollingsworth wanted to try cutting them with something crispy or drier.

"I still need one more garnish," said Hollingsworth. "I don't like the boudin."

"What happened to the artichoke from Orlando?" asked Henin, referring to the artichoke gratin Hollingsworth served at Epcot. Henin hadn't been a judge there, but others had told him that garnish was a knockout. "Everybody loved that."

"I got bored," said Hollingworth. Henin smiled. He understood.

"You need a big piece of protein," Henin said. They never made a chart, but he was clearly keeping a mental tally of colors and textures and "meaty" was a void.

By way of brainstorming, Henin held up a section of an artichoke heart and stood a shrimp up in it. It was way too old-fashioned for Hollingsworth, but he didn't want to dismiss it out of hand.

"Adina does love turning artichokes," he said. In other words, unlike many previous suggestions from his coach, he'd think this one over.

IN THE MIDDLE OF the night (between Wednesday and Thursday), Hollingsworth and Guest received the following e-mail from Daniel Boulud:

Dear Timothy and Adina,

First I want again to congratulate you on your dedication, talent, and hard work you have been putting into everything in preparation to the Bocuse d'Or in Lyon and you made Monsieur Paul very proud of the American Team!!

I know that it is not an easy task and now we gather as much information and advice about what to expect in Lyon and how well prepared we have to be.

I can say that you have done a fantastic job with both proteins pulling together in time and in harmony. They are two very interesting dishes with a good balanced palate of techniques, textures, taste, seasoning, and look, with delicate flavors. The *cuisson* was overall very satisfying and the full presentation has great potential but remains a work in progress. The counter clock is on and you have exactly 8 days left in the US and about 8 days in France to finalize all the details. Your dishes are very strong and promising and we are looking forward to a great competition in Lyon.

Mr. Paul, Jérôme, and I were very impressed by the almost real replica of the Bocuse d'Or kitchen you will have in Lyon and of course they like the charm of Yountville—TK's father's home is a perfect stage for training. We want to thank Thomas again for making this possible. Thomas, we missed you, but our trip was very spontaneous based on the fact that this was one of the first complete run-throughs. We were all very happy to have been there and Paul is very confident that the team is very strong and has great podium potential. We also are sorry to not have been able to stay that night as we didn't want Paul to stress in the morning to catch our plane. Of course I will have given you these observations in person if I had stayed overnight.

So, now this is my personal observation of my day with you on this run, and believe me I was expecting a full run with still plenty of details to work out. The strongest points overall were that you were very well organized, had a good timing schedule, and worked very well together as a team with Adina. You use original technique for your garnishes and show a lot of good technical skills with your work. You have selected some really great flavor combinations and the seasoning in general was very good. The *cuisson* was basically perfect for the beef and need a little more on the cod but between curing and timing it right it should work well.

Your goal for the next weeks is to refine each preparation to perfection and make sure that you can accomplish what you wish by following your time table rigorously and make it more accurate every full training run. Actually, it will be good to film one full run to be able to take note of your timing. . . . Jennifer will bring a video camera if you think it can help. You did very well for the first 4 hours but the last one was and is the most challenging in the competition, you should build a more detailed timetable for that period. As they're a lot to put together between the 2 platters.

Now that you know what the platter size is and how much has to go on, draw different sketches or if someone can help you with a computer to put everything to scale and make different scenarios of presentation. Don't leave it to your spontaneous feeling because the stress will build so fast and so strong in Lyon that you want to almost robotize your last hour to avoid getting lost.

The use of Roland becomes imperative now to guide you the best way possible without altering your goals, but refine your game plan to a T.

For the dishes 4 most important things to remember is creative technique, taste, presentation, and timing.

As for the cod, there is still a little bit of adjusting to do. I think that the contrast between the scallop and the cod is good, but the cod can be a little firmer. As we talked about, the cod was slightly undercooked. If you need to push the *cuisson* of the cod a little, make sure the mousse stays airy and not gummy.

I think that the contrast between the scallop and the cod is good but you need more flavor. If you want to stay on the citrus theme, it could be interesting to add into the pistachio dust a sharp clean fragrance like fresh grated lime or yuzu zest and maybe a little pinch of powdered sancho pepper—so it will be a little fragrant but with not too much heat. I guess it will blend okay with the pistachio?

To keep the pistachio green, chop it finely with a knife rather than a Robot Coupe to avoid getting the oil to come out too much and then pass it in a fine to medium tamis (so it is fine but not too powdery).

With the pistachio dust, be careful to use a glue that doesn't give any grayish color. I am talking with one of my chefs about something our pastry department uses and Jennifer will try to bring it with her this weekend for you to try. Do you need her to bring super green pistachios??

To make the presentation of the roulade on the platter a little powerful, maybe you want to consider make 2? Or a little longer or fatter one. . . .

I think you should create just a little bit of contrast with a simple design on the roulade. Maybe this décor can be done in advance and brought if it is dry and it takes a long time to make. Another option is to put something between the cod and the scallop mousse to add extra contrast in color and texture. Perhaps this could be a sprinkle of shrimp roe or lobster roe powder?? something with the cod to boost the contrast a little bit.

The hollandaise is very good but is a little rich in egg yolks (maybe it should be a little lighter, more like a mousseline). It also needs a little element of surprise in the flavor, something light and refreshing or maybe a touch more lemon. You need to create a little more sharp layout and artistic presentation.

Let's be sure to know what plate size you will have in Lyon (Jennifer??)

The potato and caviar are very delicious, tasty, perfectly crispy, and delicate on top and it must taste delicious with the real caviar you will be using in Lyon (Jennifer: is Petrossian giving the caviar??). The crème fraîche needs to be a little more than crème fraîche (it is still all in very good harmony, but you need to push it (Touch of chive or dill puree??).

The presentation between the crème fraîche and caviar—you mentioned the possibility of two quenelles next to each other, which I think would be nice and bold. You could do one larger quenelle of caviar in the center and 2 small one each side (a plain and a green?).

For the shrimp roll, the taste and texture are very good and the beets underneath are very tasty. The roll itself needs to be a bit more interesting with the vegetables (carrot brunoise)?? Not sure if I remember the farce composition inside, can you make the shrimp farce a little pinker?

It might be a challenge to find Swiss chard that will be tender and green like yours in France at that time of the year, so in case think of a Plan B if necessary. Also be careful that the beets don't drip any liquid into the platter.

The taste of the custard/consommé is fantastic and the general idea is very good. I worry only that the melba brioche toast might get soggy very fast (maybe you can try it with some very good buttered and press *pain de mie* [a presliced Pullman-like bread] you also want to make sure that the brioche is not sweet). You could also brush or spray a thin film of butter and chill it so it remains crunchy underneath and sealed away from moisture. To make the tartar or spread of scallops, you can maybe try to press it between two pieces of acetate until they are very even, and size them like the toast melba with your cutter. Keep ready until needed then season them on one side add the herbs and fresh zest, then flip it over the toast and peel off the acetate?? This way the carpaccio can be thinner, made faster and at the last minute—instead of having to spread the scallops over—and you won't have to worry about the toast getting soggy. For the grapefruit, you could make a gelée with the juices at 10 or so sheet per liter, a lot of pieces inside. Then roll a boudin in the plastic film and when cold preslice them not too thick so you save time and it's clean.

• • •

Now for the beef, do you think it will require a tiny vessel (plexy or glass for the presentation)?? Like a small shallow half pipe like, closed at each end, and the length of the roast loin or 2 of them smaller for 2 loins?? Let me know and I can have someone in Brooklyn make it with plexy.

The *cuisson* on the beef was beautiful, but we need to do something to add a little more impact. Something that is decorative and tasty, added on top or under the pancetta?? You need to show that you are a great cook and technician. In terms of amplifying flavor, you could consider putting truffle between the beef and the pancetta. Also when you are trimming your beef tenderloin, maximize the size, and when clean trim the shape so you can gradually size it or you could risk to make it too small then is too late.

Once the beef is on the plate, it looks a little lonely and plain. (I see you are using celery do you want to toast a celery root disc between 2 Silpat and make it very crisp and transparent pinch of sugar could help a bit, too). You then make a tiny incision on top of the roast where you will slice it anyway and place those small disks of crisp celery and each slice of tenderloin will get one on top in the plate.

The prune in the oxtail jus is a little too sweet and risky (maybe move the prune with the bresaola—it could go well with the apple and cabbage, and I think the Bresaola needs a little richness on the bottom). The jus could be finished with a black truffle purée with a touch of black trumpets and shallots??

The carpaccio was very good and a beautiful idea. There is great importance to have everything of the same size, and you should really carefully calculate the size and number of slices needs for a 40g truffle and have some back-up options if we can't find the exact truffle you need. Remember you can use the scraps in other preparations, gratin, etc., but those slices with the beef and celery are a lot of work and required careful planning.

The marmalade with the honey was a little too sweet and could dominate the truffle a little too much and could be a little more spicy (could you consider a *frutta di mustarda*) compatible with truffle and celery of course then you will get the sweet and the heat) or keep the way you have it and add couple of drop of homemade English mustard oil??? You don't want the pastry to become too papery and dry—it needs to be flaky pretty flat. May be a *pissaladière* dough with a touch of buckwheat flour and butter instead of olive oil.

For the pommes surprise or pommes maxim, all the garnish has to be very secure so it doesn't move around when you are plating it. Be careful that the chestnuts are braised enough so that they are tender and moist and don't dry up in the jus. The chestnuts may be frozen now unless you have some in CA you want to take with you.

For the braised beef check, the flavor was fantastic. After you are done cooking it, maybe wrap it in plastic film to make it more compact, so when you are trimming it you can cut it into bigger squares or maybe even use a cutter the size and shape of the turnips. You have to be careful it doesn't topple over on the plate, and this will help give it a more secure base for the disc of carrots. They were delicious, but again, they need to be secure as the platter has to travel and the food has to be platted . . . I don't know how much great broccoli rape you will be able to find, so think of an alternative just in case.

The glass with the bresaola is very, very nice, but you have to be careful not to have either too much smoke or not enough. You also have to be sure not to be rushed and overwhelmed at that finishing moment of the platter so my suggestion but I have not try it is for Adina to take the smoke gun just before pick-up and fill two large 1-quart squeeze bottles with a small tip and a cap over with the smoke, keep it enclosed and Adina take the bottles and go with you to dress the beef. Basically you present the platters without the smoke (judge can see the inside which is good), and then right before the plates go out, Adina fills each glass ball with smoke from the bottle. Inject it carefully and keep your cool. You need to do a lot of practices of this to make sure this is working with the timing and the flavor. The flavor of the garnishes is very good. If you take the prune out of the oxtail jus, you could put it on the bottom here for richness. The pieces of apple could be a little bigger so when we crunch on them we know what we are tasting.

That's all for now and so sorry to get to you a little late for your practice tomorrow and last but not least, you have both all our congratulations again and you are on the right track for Lyon.

Good luck with all of the training! We will see you in France soon!

Best regards,

Daniel

THE NEXT FULL RUN-THROUGH took place on Thursday, January 8. In attendance was another journalist, Lisa Abend of *Time* magazine. Hollingsworth had received Boulud's e-mail before the practice, but did not have time to read it closely; he was so far along in his thinking and refinement process that, at the end of the day, he didn't take any specific changes from the chef's lengthy think piece. It was yet another testament to how quickly things were moving; under normal circumstances, this level of feedback from one of the nation's top chefs would be something to mull over at great length, but there just wasn't time.

That day's practice began and, once again, for five hours, Hollingsworth and Guest went through their routine. Though he still opted not to reference his timing sheet, Hollingsworth evidenced more efficiencies in his prep. He butchered and cleaned all the beef at the same time (per his note from the initial practice), and got the pieces to their respective destinations: the beef cheeks and oxtail were in the pot with veal stock and vegetables, the pressure-cooker lid suctioned into place. The tenderloin and côte de boeuf, meanwhile, remained on his station.

He turned his attention to butchering the cod, his hands gliding quickly but delicately as he took the beast apart. The Dance came quickly for him that day, evidenced in almost all of his movements, as when he steadied a section of cod with one hand, using his other to run a knife between skin and flesh with the finesse of a pool hustler. After skinning the other fillet, he put the cod in a stainless-steel bowl, seasoned it with salt and pepper, and set it aside.

He then made the scallop mousse, processing scallops in the Robot Coupe with crème fraîche, salt, and polyphosphate, which would aid the texture of the mousse, allowing the mixture to take on a large quantity of fat without breaking or separating, and to hold water in rather than leaching it. (Hollingsworth likens the effect to that of a hot dog.) He transferred this to a bowl, then used a rubber spatula to fold in diced preserved Meyer lemon.

In perhaps the most complicated maneuver of their routine, Hollingsworth would need to wrap the delicate scallop mousse around the cod. This required a multitude of steps, and each of them demanded extraordinary touch: He transferred the mousse to a Cryovac bag (in which items that will be cooked sous vide are vacuum packed), flattened it out with the back of his knife, snipped a few inches off the top, and sealed it in the Cryovac machine. He transferred the bag to his cutting board and used a rolling pin, then the back of his knife to gently level the mousse as evenly as possible. He set the bag in a sheet pan and poured boiling water over it to cook it, a fog of steam blanketing his work surface.

Next, Hollingsworth sifted Activa through a small strainer to "glue" two pieces of fillet into a rectangle (a reprise of the Orlando presentation), then sifted Activa over the rectangle, lay the overlapping bacon strips on top, Cryovaced it inside a bag, and set it aside.

Preparing for the cod mousse graft, he lay a large swath of plastic wrap on his station. He cut the mousse, which had solidified by the gentle cooking, free of its bag and set it on the plastic. He put the cod on this, sifted Activa over it, cut the mousse again (he had enough mousse for two pieces) and rolled it up using the sheet of plastic as a tool rather than grasping it with his own fingers. Then he wrapped the sausage-like piece in another sheet of plastic, twisting the ends to hold it firmly together. He cut the ends off the cylinder, which would allow the olive oil to permeate the cod and mousse when confited with the plastic, maintaining the cylindrical shape.

He repeated this with the remaining mousse and cod, but the second one was a little off—when Hollingsworth tried to roll up the mousse around the cod, it came up short, not unlike a man trying to button a jacket only to discover that he's gained a few pounds. Hollingsworth calmly unwrapped the bundle, transferred the cod to a clear area of his station, trimmed it, and rolled it again, successfully, then put both cod-mousse setups onto a small steel tray and into a lowboy refrigerator.

The order of steps might seem, to the untrained eye, random, but they were orchestrated to save time in a number of ways: the "beef stew" required an hour, so that was set in motion first, and, of course, consolidating the use of Activa saved Hollingsworth several steps including reaching for it, returning to the refrigerator more than once to store the prepared meat and fish, and needing to clean up the strainer an extra time. Exactly these kinds of efficiencies banked time for a team and could reduce the expenditure of crucial minutes on Game Day.

Meanwhile, Guest was executing an interlocking series of smaller tasks: candying orange peel in successive changes of sugared water while trimming broccolini florets, peeling and slicing celery, cooking chestnuts, and setting just-baked potato mille-feuille into an ice bath to chill it.

Though they barely spoke to one another throughout the first four hours, the final push once again presented complications that led to dia-loguing. They composed the scallop tartare together, making it this time with overlapping scallop rounds instead of a puree, then pieces of grape-fruit and strips of orange rind. It was pretty but it was decidedly *not* uni-form; for example, different melbas had different numbers of grapefruit pieces on them.

When it was over, and the team had put up all their proteins and gar-nishes, altered according to the conversation and experimentation of the past several days, Henin offered his feedback. He had nothing but praise for the beef platter: He was pleased at the balance between artistry and good taste, and liked that the six components all had different shapes. He approved of the three different preparations of the protein (cured, braised, and roasted), and pronounced the sauce, made by infusing reduced beef cooking liquid with prune, "the best I've seen." (One small tinker that he and Hollingsworth agreed on was that the fillet rectangle would be aban-doned in favor of the two cylinders from the previous practices.)

His evaluation of the fish platter was more qualified. "The fish guys are going to feel cheated," he said. "They're going to say, 'Look at those guys [the meat judges] . . .'"

Henin was stuck on the need for a big piece of protein on the fish plate. He took out a pillbox-sized, oval-shaped pastry he had procured from Bouchon Bakery that morning.

"What do you think of something like this?" he said. With his other hand, he dropped a prawn into the bain-marie.

Hollingsworth didn't say anything, just looked at it and considered. Henin mentioned that he felt a lack of urgency in the day's practice, espe-cially during the final hour.

"We're still trying to work out each other's roles," said Hollingsworth.

"Like the beginning, that was picture-perfect," said Henin. He carved out a portion of the pastry, holding it in one hand, then extracted the prawn from the water and held it upside down, its head resting in the newly carved cavity, a slightly different take on the artichoke-shrimp proposition he'd made the day before.

Hollingsworth considered it, but said nothing. Like Henin, he didn't want to threaten the bond that was being established, but the truth was that what the coach was proposing was hopelessly far from anything Hollingsworth would do; it just didn't resonate with him at all. Henin let it go for the moment. No sense in pushing. Things were going too well.

Henin's suggestion assumed that the sponsor-provided shrimp would be of a certain size, but neither he nor Hollingsworth knew how big they'd actually be. Hollingsworth knew the total weight of product he'd be cooking with, but had been unsuccessful trying to ascertain the exact specs. This was especially important with the shrimp, which can vary more in size than the other proteins. At Pelka's request, Carey Snowden had actually gone so far as to try to order the Norwegian seafood and Angus beef from overseas, but they got stuck in customs and were eventually destroyed. (In truth, unbeknownst to the team, full details of the size of *all* proteins were available on the Bocuse d'Or Web site, but were difficult to find, located several "levels" down under a "Themes" tab that had to be double-clicked for its contents to be revealed, a detail that, according to Pelka, was never explained to the team.)

That afternoon, Hollingsworth, still feeling some residual tension between himself and his coach, suggested to Laughlin that they should cook together, and asked her to make the overture. "There had been a couple of hard points and we had a few issues," he said later. "I really wanted to reach out and basically let him know that I *did* appreciate him, and I *do* have a lot of respect for him. It's just that I see things different. It's not that I don't respect his opinion or his history. . . . I felt that he might feel a little bit left out, therefore I wanted to make the extra effort to tie us all together."

Henin would be leaving town for the weekend, but Laughlin set the dinner up for Monday night, three days before the team's departure for France.

———

To help Team USA plan for their departure, Jennifer Pelka arrived in Yountville Saturday morning, January 10, and checked into Petit Logis, a five-room inn tucked behind Bouchon Bakery on Yount Street. When she met up with Hollingsworth, she was caught off guard by his garage-band look—the unshaven face, the ripped jeans, the knit cap. He gave her a tour of The French Laundry, then the Garden, but the sightseeing portion of the day was brief, because Practice Number Four was planned. In addition to Pelka, a number of special guests were expected: Hollingsworth's family—his parents and sisters—as well as two of Laughlin's cousins, close to fifteen people in all. *Step right up, folks . . .*

Though the competition was drawing closer, and practice time was scarce, Hollingsworth was only too happy to talk to his family as he rehearsed, to explain what he was doing at each turn. It was the first time any of them had seen him cook professionally. "They have no idea what I do, or what kind of work goes into what I do. To be able to see it, really was a very special thing for me," he said.

His father's attention was especially gratifying to Hollingsworth. "For him to be there and to watch that and to really be so interested . . . and kind of really show a respect and an interest was really amazing for me. It was very special," he said.

That day, Hollingsworth tried a new shrimp garnish, a shrimp and avocado tart. To make it, he cooked the shrimp sous vide with clarified butter, halved them, and tiled them in long strips, alternating the pieces with slices of avocado, like a long green, pink, and white caterpillar. This he set atop a piece of puff pastry spread with fennel compote, then brushed the shrimp and avocado with a yuzu (a tart Asian citrus) gelée and sprinkled it with a brunoise of red jalapeño. (Though he did not voice it, like many of the dishes to which Hollingsworth is drawn, this one was founded on the flavor profile of a classic of Americana: shrimp cocktail, with the red jalapeño standing in for the cocktail sauce.) On balance, he was happy with it, although he found the yuzu overpowering and the crust crumbly. He and Guest also added a new element to the mille-feuille, topping the individual pieces with quenelles of leek puree made by mounting blanched leeks with crème fraîche.

On Sunday, the team had a planning session largely devoted to all the equipment that would be required in Lyon. Pelka typed a list, divided into three categories: Pack, Ship (that is, FedEx to Boulud's parents' home just outside Lyon), and Purchase There. Hollingsworth and Guest did some fine-tuning, such as reducing the amount of yuzu and changing the pastry for the new tart from a handmade dough to purchased puff pastry. Though most elements in the competition need to be prepared and produced from scratch, Bocuse d'Or rules allow many ready-made items into competition, such as puff pastry and stocks.

That night Pelka, Hollingsworth, Guest, and Laughlin went to dinner at Ubuntu, the Napa vegetarian restaurant with a yoga studio upstairs that the *New York Times'* Frank Bruni had ID'd as the best new restaurant in the United States. It was a relaxed evening that blended planning (for the near future) with enjoying food and wine (here and now).

When the moment was right, Pelka broached a delicate topic: she and the rest of the East Coast contingent were concerned about the modest character of the platter, barely three-dimensional, and with virtually no "old-school" flourishes to trumpet the food.

"If we win for that reason, I don't want to win," Hollingsworth said flatly. After his extended exercise in self-discovery, feeling his way through the conception of his dishes, he had arrived at his own well-defined place. The food was as manipulated as he wanted it to be. If anything, he was considering going more modern by adding some edible flowers to the plate, a personal predilection of his. This was another violation of Viola's advice, but Hollingsworth was feeling real ownership of his platter, and he wanted to remain true to himself.

Pelka persisted. She took the simplicity of the new shrimp tart ("the new tiled shrimp thing" she called it) as an example: such a simple composition would need to be beyond perfect to score; the lines would need to be so well-defined, the color so tantalizingly vivid that even the slightest flaw could prove fatal. Why not hedge their bets with some more razzmatazz?

"What can we do to add more height?" she asked.

Again, Hollingsworth and Guest pushed back. They had performed four practices in eight days and had a swelling sense of command. Didn't Pelka understand: they were on the verge of possibly beating the clock, of giving themselves a chance to actually breathe life into the fairy tale that had been constructed for them? There was no time for new challenges, let alone finding the kind of pieces she was describing. They were getting on an airplane in four days!

"We have a *ton* of time," countered Pelka. If, say, Thomas Keller asked for something, they could get whatever they wanted, whenever they wanted it. As far as she was concerned, it would be the culinary equivalent of a request from the president of the United States. People in the industry didn't say no to Keller, or for that matter to her chef, Boulud.

Hollingsworth relented. The next day, he spent hours on the phone with Daniel Scannell. Scannell agreed to overnight him approximations of vessels—like little footed silver stands to hold the beef cheek stacks; long, half-cylinder vessels in which the pistachio-crusted cod might rest; small rectangular trays on which the bacon-wrapped rib-eye would sit—that could be produced in time to add to the tray, but would not be available until after the team departed for France. If they were lucky, they'd get to practice with them one time, which expanded the potential for the unknown to encroach upon their Bocuse d'Or performance. Culinary competitors don't just rehearse to get the conception and execution of their food down pat; they also fine tune the act of assembling the platters and plating the food so that every single pitfall can be identified and addressed. Throwing additional variables into the equation all but ensured that Team USA would have at least one surprise in Lyon, either in their final practice, or during the contest itself.

The phone call also produced a startling, though not fatal, revelation:

nobody had conveyed to Scannell that the fish platter was supposed to be porcelain, so his company was producing silver trays for both fish and meat. It was yet another sign of how quickly things were moving, as these kinds of details almost never fall through the cracks in the worlds of Boulud and Keller. (The team would likely have ended up with a silver tray anyway because Scannell later pointed out that the time and expense porcelain demands would have made it impossible in the given timeframe.)

Chef Henin returned to Yountville that day, and that evening, the team dinner took place. While Pelka went down the road to Ranch Market Too, an all-purpose grocery, sundries, and wine shop on Washington Street, Guest took to the Garden and procured some greens to accompany the roast chicken and root vegetables the coach would be preparing. There was no salad spinner at the house, so Henin taught her an old-school method for drying greens, instructing her to wrap them in a clean kitchen towel, take them out back on the deck, and swing them around like a mace.

As a gesture of solidarity with Henin, Hollingsworth put Gotan Project on the sound system, a mellow, lyric-free hybrid of tango and electronica. Also out of deference, Hollingsworth offered that he and Guest would function as Henin's sous chefs for the evening, executing his orders and his menu. When the time came to truss the chicken, Hollingsworth mentioned the story in *The French Laundry Cookbook* in which Keller recounts that at twenty-four he didn't know how to truss a chicken, a failing that drove a French chef to fling a knife at him.

Henin confirmed that this was no tall tale: "When Thomas came to me he didn't know how to truss a chicken," he said. It's not easy to imagine Keller not knowing how to perform such a fundamental task, but we all have to start somewhere.

Hollingsworth asked Henin to demonstrate the technique to him.

"Oh, it's really very easy. There's nothing to it," said Henin, as he took his kitchen twine to the bird. It was a fun, relaxed evening and with no discussion of the competition, Hollingsworth felt that he and Henin were connecting over a shared reverence for technique. The two men have more in common than that, though. It had taken a while for them to connect, and the relationship was still far from perfect, but they both have an almost animal attraction to cooking. Both had found their vocation almost by accident, and like Henin, Hollingsworth was known—at least within the Thomas Keller Restaurant Group—as a phenomenal and patient teacher with a rare gift for tailoring his tone and his language to whomever he happens to be instructing at any given time.

Where as Hollingsworth once considered life as an EMT, Henin was supposed to have been an accountant. That's what his father had ordained, and when he grew up in his time in France, that was all there was to it. The problem was, when young Roland started college, he continued to hang out with his gang of friends in the evening, returning home and doing his homework until the wee hours.

His father didn't approve, and when the second year of school began, he put his foot down.

"When you live under my roof, you will do as I say," said the father.

"I said, 'I don't have to live under your roof. That is fine,'" remembers Henin. He moved out. With nowhere to stay, his immediate concern was money. In the newspaper, he found an advertisement for a job as a pastry cook that included room and board. Bingo! He applied for the job, and his timing was lucky: it was the holidays and the shop was doing a brisk business and in need of another set of hands. He was hired immediately and put up in the house the owners kept across the street. "I had a room just below the roof so it was freezing in the winter and boiling in the summer," the chef recalls today.

He planned to stay in college, but soon realized that being an apprentice in a pastry shop excluded going to college. For one thing, he had to begin his day at four o'clock in the morning when he had to start the fire. For another, the apprenticeship came with a conflicting academic requirement: on Thursdays, he went to school (comparable to a community college in the United States) along with apprentices from the local butcher shops and restaurants, to take courses in topics related to his kitchen work, such as sanitation.

That wasn't all he had to do. With its classic French structure, the kitchen at the pastry shop didn't have a dishwasher as you'd find in most American kitchens; all the menial chores were tasked to the apprentice. This kitchen had three apprentices, first-year, second-year, and third-year. As the newbie, Henin had to wash all the pots and pans and scrub the place down at the end of the day. And if he wanted to learn about baking, he had to do it all quickly. He made it his point to do this, and when he finally starting baking, he quickly came to see the work as magical, transforming flour, water, and butter into croissants and brioche. "I was fascinated that I could make these things with my hands. I was not a natural but I was mesmerized by this process. I said, 'Wow, I did that,'" he recalled.

Part of the reason he saw it as "magic" was that nobody took the time to explain the science of it to him. In time, this would become a theme of Henin's kitchen evolution. "I was raised in a straitjacket of classicism," he is fond of saying, summing up the French attitude as: "'Don't ask. It is the way we have been doing it for hundreds of years. . . . You do it and do it and do it and with repetition you become good.' So you become a technician, but you don't understand the *why* of what you are doing."

Henin quit college to devote himself to his new profession. The divide between his old life and his new one was illustrated almost every morning: when he woke up to go across the street and light the fire, his old friends would be coming home from dancing—a perfect evocation of the underreported, unglamorous aspect of a working chef's existence; he's almost always toiling when others are sleeping, or at play.

But Henin also saw the respect that a chef was afforded in France. "This guy was like the king. Even the owner bowed to him," Henin said. "It was the best pastry shop of Nancy. It was right on Main Street. The best reputation. The best clientele. In the afternoon we did *glacier*. We would do the ice cream fresh every day. By the time they opened . . . it was all by hand. Every day we used fresh ice. There was no crystal in the ice cream. It was all fresh. The pastry chef to me was like a god and he had this big aura and everybody kind of agreed with whatever he said. To me that was impressive because I had never met anybody like this."

As the most junior apprentice, Henin was tasked with all the menial work. He'd end the day tired, but if he'd performed well, the chef, whom Henin recalls as a strong man of about forty-five years, would let him sit on a stool and watch him make chocolate, and then to swoop in and clean his marble, all of which—even the cleaning—Henin considered a reward.

After about fifteen months, Henin was feeling burned out by the long, physical hours. He got to talking to one of the restaurant apprentices at his Thursday classes, who told him about a job opening at the Hotel Excelsior. Henin found the idea of switching tempting: "I was finding those hours pretty long. When those guys were in the kitchen they had breaks in the afternoon and they didn't have to start until seven thirty," he said. Henin worked things out with his chef and the academic authorities and switched to the Excelsior, finding it everything he'd dreamed of: "It was a piece of cake in relationship to the pastry shop. You have a better life. It was not as stringent. They had more fun and it was more relaxed. You had a break in the afternoon you could take a nap so if you were out at night you had time to catch up. That is how I switched to the kitchen. That went very good. You had a better group of people. You had more young cooks and more apprentice. We had a dishwasher and a pot washer. You didn't take all the abuse. I was a little bit older and more into it."

Though he never returned to pastry, Henin found it to be the perfect foundation for becoming a chef. "It is more disciplined," he said. "I would recommend that anyone who wants to become a good chef to start in pastry. Not to study the pastry, to learn the discipline that is required. So that later on you can apply it and carry it with you all your life. You are so organized and meticulous sometimes to a fault. But you are a better chef. If you don't get that at the very beginning, that discipline, you never develop it. That is the best time to develop it and it is the only time. Later on you can't. I see some chefs taking the Master Chef and they can't get their act together. They can't get organized and have their priorities. They don't have a system or methodology. In pastry you have to, otherwise you can't make it."

MONDAY NIGHT'S DINNER WAS the last relaxed moment of the week; on Tuesday the team commenced the onerous task of packing for their trip, not just all the personal items required for two weeks overseas, but box upon box of equipment and supplies. The sheer volume of what had to be gotten to Lyon was daunting: among the things the team would be carting along to the airport in suitcases and boxes were plastic wrap, knives, butter warmers, saucepans and lids, towels, Silpats, a pepper grinder, squeeze bottles, circulators, cutting boards, carpets, The French Laundry jackets, and several copies of *The French Laundry Cookbook* to dispense as gifts to those who would be helping them in Lyon (even if they didn't necessarily speak or read English).

Keller had returned to Yountville by then, and Tuesday evening, at the request of The Chef, the team presented a new tasting of their fish dishes. Keller offered suggestions, despite the proximity of the competition: perhaps a small plate should go under the "martini glasses" that housed the custard, and similarly the smoke bowls. The avocados on the shrimp tart should shingle vertically (toward the "guest") rather than left to right, a change Hollingsworth implemented.

Keller also suggested that the caviar for the mille-feuille be presented in a glass tube that would rise up out of the platter, creating the illusion that the caviar was suspended in the air. Once again, Hollingsworth took to the phone, spending a good portion of his Wednesday working his network of sources, including his father and his construction allies, in search of just the right piece. (Ultimately, Daniel Scannell came through with the tube.)

He would later say that spending so much time on the tube, trying to find just the right piece was a mistake, that it took a lot out of him at that point in the game. But, as ever, he did not want to say no to The Chef.

Even measured against the yardstick of a week at The French Laundry, Hollingsworth was exhausted. He was barely sleeping, and the long work hours were taking their toll. He felt "pretty good" about his and Guest's preparation, but the days were falling away and he didn't have a moment to himself, not even for the gym. At least he had enough presence of mind to recognize that the building pressure was contributing to his state of body and mind.

Thursday went by in a shot, as the team (minus Pelka, who had headed back to New York and would rejoin them in Lyon) finished packing and headed to the airport. That afternoon, on the East Coast of the United States, Captain Chesley Sullenberger, his engine kamikazed by a flock of geese, made his splash-landing for the ages on the Hudson River in New York City, saving every soul on board US Airways Flight 1549. The miracle captured the imagination of the world as an instantaneous, Lindbergh-like fame attached to the reclusive aviator, mere days before President-elect Obama, the first African American to ascend to the highest office in the land, was to be inaugurated. It was against this backdrop that Team USA boarded its flight to Lyon, wanting nothing more than to be the next Americans to pull off a historic and improbable triumph.

5

All the Little Screws

You know what the funniest thing about Europe is? It's
the little differences. I mean they got the same shit over
there that they got here, but it's just . . . it's just there it's a
little different.

—VINCENT VEGA (JOHN TRAVOLTA), *PULP FICTION*

TEAM USA GAZED OVER THE TABLE IN DANIEL BOULUD'S PAR-
ents' home: house-cured ham, house-made bread, dry salami,
homemade fig and raspberry preserves, coffee, a bottle of Beaujolais Nou-
veau 2008. The setting felt almost like a restaurant, and in fact had been
a restaurant once, or at least a roadside café, when it was known as Café
Boulud, which the family operated until 1957.

Today, it was the eat-in kitchen of Daniel Boulud's parents, in their modest house on a small, once-working farm in the town of St.-Pierre-de-Chandieu on the outskirts of Lyon. The team had been collected at Lyon's St. Exupéry airport by Boulud's father, Julien, a spry, humble man in his early eighties. They were also met by Adina's stepfather, Dr. John Guest, an acupuncture physician, who had arrived a day earlier and would be joining them for their adventure in Lyon. Slight of build, Dr. Guest boasted an aristocratic and all-but-unidentifiable accent—vaguely European, with a pinch of Great Britain, an amalgam of the various places he had lived in the United States, Europe, and his current home of Toronto, Canada. (In an amazing coincidence, Guest, like Hollingsworth, had taken the last name of her stepfather, although she remains close with her biological father.)

Somehow the team sailed right through customs without a single interrogative challenge to their mountain of luggage. It must have been because it was the Bocuse d'Or season, as young cooks roll into town every other January with similarly massive hauls. The team procured its rental wheels, a Ford sports utility vehicle with three rows of seats and a generous cargo area, and convoyed to the Boulud home, Coach Henin and the Guests in the SUV and M. Boulud transporting Hollingsworth and Laughlin in his petit Peugeot.

The team wound its way along all-but-deserted highways, past rolling hills dotted with the barren trees of January, grassy fields webbed with frost, and a morning fog shimmering in the nascent sunlight. This was real farmland, with livestock around the homesteads and working vehicles, tires caked with hay, sitting idle.

In the car, Dr. Guest asked Henin, who had grown up not too far from Lyon, if he missed France.

"No, no," said Henin, nostalgia, sorrow, and fatigue swirling together in his austere baritone. "The people are too petty, too closed-minded." Gazing out over the hills, he recounted how, years prior, he needed to have a telephone installed for his infirm mother. The transaction would be a piece of cake in the States, but in France, the paperwork took three weeks and the installation of the actual phone took three *months*.

The convoy swept into the Boulud home, a sprawling property bounded on one side by several hangar-sized barns. They were welcomed like old friends by Daniel Boulud's mother, Marie, a diminutive woman also in her early eighties with auburn hair. She dropped their coats on a bed in a guest room, and ushered them across the hall into the eat-in kitchen, where she proceeded to fuss over them, pouring them hot coffee, and gesturing for them to help themselves to the spread.

Coach Henin, Hollingsworth, and Laughlin sat in a pew-like bench by the window, the lace curtains behind them depicting cherries and apples. Over the table, juxtaposed in a two-panel frame, was a photograph of the original Café Boulud, circa 1900, and below it one of a table of fashionably dressed Manhattanites sitting at a table on the sidewalk outside son Daniel's decidedly fancier Café Boulud NYC in 2000.

Having been in transit for close to twenty-four hours, the team ate the way soldiers eat, with unapologetic gusto. Dr. Guest, seated at the head of the table with the Bouluds, punctured the ensuing silence: "You're all too late; I've already adopted them," he said of the hospitable couple.

As ever, Henin acted as translator for the team, relaying their questions and converting the answers:

"Is Daniel their only child?" asked Laughlin.

"No, they have three girls and two boys," Henin told them. Mme. Boulud produced a family photo depicting twelve grandchildren. As she did, M. Boulud tossed in a sweet joke: "I've slept with four women in my life: a young woman, a mother, a grandmother, and a great grandmother."

"What was Daniel like as a boy?" asked Laughlin.

At the question, Mme. Boulud put the back of her hand to her forehead, looked heavenward, and pretended to reel backwards. Everybody sighed dramatically—"Ahhhhh"—as if something great must be coming. "He was very curious, very interested in so many things," she said, via

Henin. "So busy. We'd leave him somewhere, and he didn't realize we were gone. He was always moving."

Everybody savored this image of the pint-sized Daniel, scurrying about these very rooms, busying himself around the property outside.

M. Boulud removed the Café Boulud photographs from the wall and showed them to Adina Guest. He pointed out three men holding pipes in the 1900 picture. It was one of those classic abbreviated conversations between people who have no language in common: "*En les Etats-Unis*, 'no smoking,'" he said pointing to the cigarette-free scene depicted in the Manhattan image. Then, pointing to the pipes in the older sepia-toned photograph, one at a time, he said, "*La pipe, la pipe, la pipe.*"

Guest laughed. M. Boulud sighed. Conversation over.

The Bouluds then provided verbal captions for the food the team was eating, virtually all of which the couple themselves had made: the ham had been aged for twenty-three weeks under M. Boulud's watchful eye; the preserves prepared by Mme. Boulud; the bread, a dingy brown torpedo he referred to as *pain maison* (house bread), made with half white flour and half whole wheat. He bakes nine loaves at a time in his gargantuan outdoor oven, he explained, then freezes them individually. His biggest challenge is knowing a day ahead when he'll want a loaf so he can take it out and give it a chance to revivify.

Determined to dote on her guests to the absolute limit, Mme. Boulud offered little tubs of *fromage blanc*, then a cheese plate of Roquefort, *caprice des dieux* (a double-crème cheese), and Comté. Noting that several of her guests had jam smeared on the plates they were using for cheese, residue from the "first course," she belatedly offered them clean plates. Of her delay, she said, "*Le service est mauvais.*" The service is bad.

Following the meal, the indefatigable M. Boulud offered a guided tour of the property, showing them the tarped swimming pool out back, the mammoth oven and grill with its accoutrements lined up like pool cues along the wall, and sunken tennis court with an Astroturf-like artificial grass surface. Walking back toward the main road, he escorted them in and out of the barns and the little rooms recessed within them, each one a treasure trove of culinary delights—house-cured hams hanging from the ceiling, jars of preserves, onion confit, preserved Swiss chard ribs, reserves of Champagne. One memorable bottle contained a snake suspended in a solution of eau de vie.

"In the old days, this was medicine," he said.

Unexpected and numerous little nooks were scattered about the compound, and M. Boulud clearly delighted in sharing them all. As the team began unloading the rental vehicle—they'd be using the farm as a staging site until Monday, when they would relocate to Paul Bocuse's catering hall—M. Boulud danced out of one of the rooms with a bottle containing a thick, neon-tinged yellow liquid. He poured tastes into small glasses and passed them out: it was a house-made lemon cream fortified with eau de vie, and it was a strong, warming antidote to the morning chill.

The team checked its more delicate cargo. For the most part, everything had survived the trip, although there were casualties: the brioche had got a little bruised, a deli of pistachio cream had ruptured, but the Ziploc bags containing it held firm, and so on. Having assessed their needs, the team packed everything up again and stashed it neatly in one of the rooms.

They left the Bouluds as they were beginning work on an apple galette at the kitchen table, M. Boulud shaving slices on a mandoline, his wife arranging them in circles in a dough-lined tart mold. Just another Saturday at the farm.

Of the morning, Guest said, "It made me appreciate who Daniel was more. . . . Once you meet someone's parents you understand the person . . . amazingly warmhearted people, and then I started seeing those qualities in Daniel."

"That was an amazing experience," said Hollingsworth. "My last time in France was in Paris and it was just working. Parisians say, 'You really need to go to the countryside, you really have to go here or here and experience what it's like.' And that was all those stories combined. It was going to that place in the country and experiencing the living. It was incredible."

The team checked into the Hotel Ibis Lyon Est Bron, a resolutely no-frills traveler's lodge on an industrial stretch of highway about thirty minutes from Lyon proper. Travel plans had kept changing up until the last minute, and by the time the itinerary had been settled on, even über-connected Michel Bouit couldn't procure them enough rooms anywhere closer to civilization. They would crash at the Ibis for one night, then relocate to the Hotel Beaux-Arts in the city center the next morning. It was the kind of decision that rankled Henin: the result of poor planning and a distraction that would diminish the team's mental energy. He was also apprehensive about a plan to move the team *back* to the Ibis eight days later, so that they would wake up closer to the event space during the Bocuse d'Or. An extra half hour of sleep on Game Day was not, in his opinion, worth the hassle and psychic toll of moving again—not even close. (There is an official team hotel, but a number of competitors opt not to stay there.)

That afternoon, without benefit of a nap, Team USA sans Coach Henin drove into Lyon. For all of the money that had been raised for the team, they were still expected to manage an awful lot. First up was a scavenger-hunt-worthy list of items to be located and purchased, including cellular phones, a printer, a power strip, power converters, extension cords, batteries, and hotel pans. So much for Joseph Viola's advice to let the team focus on nothing but their platter. (Another quickly emerging distraction was that, since the team had no driver, Hollingsworth and Henin did almost all of the driving on this and all subsequent days.)

That January afternoon was a dream of spring in Lyon, sunny and temperate, and the city center was mobbed with shoppers and strollers. The recession that had gripped the United States seemed a distant memory as every venue, from cosmetics shops to electronics megastores, was brimming with consumers and shopping bags swung like pendulums at the end of every arm in sight. Adding to the energy of the day were two organized protests—one against overcrowding in the schools, the other contra Israel's actions in Gaza—and Obamamania was in evidence at every newsstand in town, with magazine covers both American and European displaying the imminent president's mug. (The pro-American vibe that week was enhanced by ever-expanding stories about Captain Chesley Sullenberger on both French television and on BBC World News.) The team spent the afternoon roaming the streets in a pleasant delirium—the combined effects of jet lag, sleep deprivation, and the relentlessly unfamiliar details: not just the language, but billboards that rotated every few seconds, street signs shaped like collar stays, and little automated bike rental stations. It was an onslaught of newness and it was intoxicating.

THE NEXT DAY, A dreary, windswept Sunday, following breakfast the team relocated to the Hotel Beaux-Arts, an art deco–styled boutique hotel on Rue du Président Edouard Herriot in the city center, then bee-lined for Halles de Lyon—Paul Bocuse, the famous indoor culinary marketplace. Lined with rows of food booths interspersed with a smattering of restaurants and oyster bars, the market's dropped ceiling rendered it all but impossible to discern just how far back the rows extended. As the team perused *fromageries*, fish shops, and butcher counters, the depth and superiority of the food on offer became increasingly clear. In the United States, a market of this breadth and scope, and the unfailingly artful presentation of the goods, would warrant major magazine coverage. In Lyon, it's just the way things are.

At Cerise et Potiron, a produce shop, Hollingsworth bought a turnip and an avocado, to get a sense of how much he'd have to have sent from Yountville. The team cut the market visit short that day because many of the shops weren't open on Sunday, when Lyon essentially shuts down, and others would be closing early. They drove back to the hotel, then roamed the forsaken streets in search of a *bouchon* (the word means "cork"), a genre of eatery that is most closely if not exclusively associated with Lyon, similar to a bistro, only more stripped down, both in décor and in the scale of the menu. The team had an unremarkable lunch, then marched back to their new hotel, tucked themselves into their infinitely softer quarters, and slept.

———

ON MONDAY MORNING, ROLAND Henin ate in the breakfast room on the second floor of the Beaux-Arts, a mirrored, carpeted space staffed by a solitary waitress clad in frilly French maid uniform, whose main functions were to cheerily intone *"Bonjour!,"* offer *café* to all comers, and to keep the buffet stocked. As hotel breakfasts go, the Hotel Beaux-Arts' was first-rate: a selection of French and alpine cheeses, freshly baked baguettes, scrambled eggs, sliced ham, little foil-topped jars of yogurt, crêpes, and the hazelnut-chocolate spread Nutella, obscenely ubiquitous in Lyon, slathered on breakfast crêpes and available as a filling from *crêperies* and carts around town at all hours.

Henin sat alone at a long table in the dining room, his legal pad resting beside his plate, and wondered where everybody was. Though they hadn't discussed it, he had walked in at eight o'clock, sharp, expecting that they'd follow the protocol established the day before: a group breakfast mixing conversation and planning, after which everybody would briefly return to their room, then congregate in the lobby ready to go.

"If you organize your day that way, even a non-practice day, that will help improve communication," said Henin. "It reinforces the team. You are a family. There is nothing else that exists but the team. Everything else is eliminated but the team. So all the focus is on the team. If you don't have that team spirit, or whatever you want to call that, then you don't have nothing," he said.

And so, Henin finished his meal alone, concerned about losing time and not having a plan.

The plan was *supposed* to be to go to the Boulud family home, sort through the equipment and food that had been shipped there, or stored there by Michel Bouit, and decide what to bring to L'Abbaye de Collonges, Paul Bocuse's catering and special event facility. But Hollingsworth, who had been awake since two o'clock in the morning, watching *The Departed* and then going out for an early breakfast with Laughlin, had thought about it and had decided they should all go to L'Abbaye first in order to introduce themselves to the manager who would be their point person for the week, *then* go to the Boulud compound. He was cross with himself for not automatically thinking of this beforehand; it would have been downright rude to show up with a van full of boxes without first dropping by, making yourself known. Rude by his family's standards, and rude by the etiquette he'd been taught by Keller. He recognized this as a sign that he wasn't firing on all cylinders, that his instincts had been dulled by the travel, the jet lag, the exhaustion, the stress.

There was another bit of news overnight: though the team had been told that two practices had been arranged for them, on Wednesday the twenty-first and Saturday the twenty-fourth, somewhere along the line between Yountville and Lyon communications had broken down. *L'Abbaye* was booked out for a number of events that week, and the *only* available day was Saturday. Hollingsworth absorbed the news painlessly, in part because he and Guest had become so used to cooking on the actual competition equipment in the Bocuse House that he was loathe to cook in *two* unfamiliar kitchens in Lyon.

Henin could not have disagreed more: "Well, yes, it's a big deal because it is going to hurt us," he thought. It was just the latest disappointment for the coach, who was once again confounded by the decisions of his charges. It was fine that they took the weekend to get acclimated, but after two days, it was time to get to *work*. "Everybody carried on into the easy path as opposed to doing our sit-ups," he would say later. "I think right there, after a while, it became like, 'Wait a minute. That is not what we are here for.' Are we here for sitting on our ass and going to restaurants and having a good time? We are here to do a job and that job is to get ready for the battles that we are going to have. But nobody was waking up. Nobody was saying, 'Wait a minute, let's do something about this.'"

Despite his role as coach, Henin kept this opinion to himself. "Who do

I need to voice it to?" he would say later. "Isn't anybody else old enough and mature enough and understanding enough and knowledgeable enough to understand that on their own?"

The difference in attitudes was a fine illustration of the gap between those who are members of competition society, and those who are not. About the cooking life in general, Hollingsworth's and Henin's points of view were actually not that dissimilar. Henin prized total commitment to one's vocation—the level of lifelong devotion that determined whether one would sink or swim in, say, the Certified Master Chef exam—and Hollingsworth had exhibited that total commitment since he first fell in love with his chosen craft about a decade earlier.

But they simply didn't share the same passion for culinary competition. Henin vividly remembers the first time he saw a competition; it was about the same time he first met Keller, way back in 1976, when he visited the International Culinary Olympics in Frankfurt. The event offered spectators the opportunity to purchase food from the competing teams. Waiting in the lunch line, he saw the windows of the kitchen, his view obstructed by the people in front of him so that he could make out the tops of the cooks' white toques. Many of the hats were moving around, but one team's barely moved, which he realized meant they were highly organized, so didn't need to waste time or energy. He later discovered that was the American team, the one that tied with the French. "I was very impressed and I didn't know why," Henin said. "I went to see the cold food. That is when it really started. . . . The following Olympics I competed on my own not really understanding what I was doing. . . . I made a bronze by luck."

Henin went on to compete in other events, and treasured what competition brought to his life. "It's a good thing because you learn a lot," he said. "You get the feedback from the judge. You push yourself to the point that you didn't know that you were able to push or achieve. You learn something all the time. You didn't know you had this in you. You didn't know that you were capable of producing all that stuff. There again it was that amazement when I produced those brioche or croissants."

At the end of the day, Hollingsworth simply didn't feel the same way. He, like his chef, was there because he was asked to be there, not because he had a great *desire* to be there.

It wasn't that he didn't take it seriously. But he felt that his reverence for cooking in general and his experience at The French Laundry in particular were the ultimate preparation. "I've been practicing for this *my whole life*," Hollingsworth said of the situation in Lyon, whereas Henin's opinion was that your whole life doesn't have a damn thing to do with what's waiting for you next week, kid. You think you can hop up on your surfboard and ride that wave that's rolling in from the horizon? Guess again. Because that ain't no point break. It's a *tsunami*.

WHEN TEAM USA FINALLY connected, they discovered that Gavin Kaysen had checked into the hotel. Having slept on his overnight flight, he came bounding down the stairs in a red argyle sweater and a freshly shorn head of hair. En route to the Boulud family farm, Kaysen—there to assist in any way he could over the coming week—shared the news that restaurant Daniel, the cornerstone of Boulud's restaurant empire back in the States, was set to be re-reviewed in the coming Wednesday's *New York Times*. As if there weren't enough going on in the life of Team USA, its chairman's precious four-star rating was on the line.

As a morning drizzle came and went, the team arrived at L'Abbaye, Paul Bocuse's catering space about three miles outside Lyon, a huge hall that accommodates more than five hundred people. The structure is rich with history: it had belonged to his great-grandparents as far back as 1765, was sold, and then reclaimed by Bocuse himself in 1966. It is also festively decorated with the chef's collection of ancient fairground organs, most spectacularly in its main dining room, La Salle du Grand Limonaire, with the "Gaudin," a massive, carnival-like installation of automated musician figurines that come to life when activated. The Gaudin dates back to 1900 and Bocuse had it restored over the course of four years after purchasing the building. In its center today stands a figurine that was *not* part of the original composition: a miniature Bocuse, wielding a conductor's wand—the ultimate illustration of his showmanship.

The team was greeted by Vincent Le Roux, a vibrant and effortlessly charming manager who had spent time working with Jérôme Bocuse at Les Chefs de France in Epcot and so—invaluably—spoke perfect English. At the instruction of Monsieur Paul himself, Le Roux was at the service of the American contingent for the length of their time in Lyon, "twenty-four hours a day," if necessary.

"You see, the American flag, for you," said Le Roux, who seemed to walk on air as he glided by to open the door for them. The team turned to see the Star-Spangled Banner aloft on a flagpole along the roadside, its red, white, and blue snapping against the gray sky. Collectively, the group sighed with humility, buying Le Roux's friendly fib. He didn't have the heart to tell him that the flag, like the one in front of Restaurant Paul Bocuse, was in fact not for them, but a tribute to the veterans and casualties of World War II.

For a staging area, Team USA couldn't have done much better than L'Abbaye, which had an enormous kitchen centered around an island of burners and flattops, with walk-in refrigerators and freezers located just beyond, and plenty of room for storage. Best of all, because it was a catering facility, nobody was working on nonevent days, so on Saturday, the team could go about their business without feeling they were getting in the way of fellow cooks.

After touring the facility, the team filed back into the SUV and followed Le Roux down the road to Restaurant Paul Bocuse, a magnificent structure of red and green that towers over its surroundings. The team got out of their vehicles and looked up to see that over the parking lot, painted on the wall of the building, in classic Lyonnaise mural style, was a portrait of Bocuse himself, pushing open a shuttered window to welcome guests.

The team climbed the stone steps that curved up from the parking lot to the restaurant. Before the glass doors of the main entrance was a walkway, lined with the names of all past Bocuse d'Or medalists arranged on rectangular plaques set right into the ground. Hollywood has the Walk of Fame; Lyon has this. At the near end of the display were a few rows of blank plaques: the one right under 2007 would be replaced soon enough, with the names of the chefs who would triumph just nine days later.

The team was escorted into the restaurant and seated in Salon Fernand Point, one of the main dining rooms, essentially a solarium and also a shrine to the legendary chef for whom Bocuse himself had apprenticed as a young cook, with small, framed photographs of Point decorating the walls. In what would become a running theme of their time in Lyon, double espressos were ordered and *mignardises* (small, sweet treats served with coffee) were presented on tiered silver stands.

The purpose of the visit was to see to the needs of the team, especially the procurement of ingredients for Saturday's practice. To that end, they were joined by the restaurant's chef, Christian Bouvarel, who could not have been more archetypal, with sculpted jet-black hair and mustache, trim build, impeccably starched whites, and the exquisitely erect posture and comportment of a military man, outwardly humorless, with perfect attention to his given mission. He was also a lifer: he had apprenticed for Bocuse at age fourteen, worked elsewhere for a time, and the n returned. That was in 1974.

Before they began going over Hollingsworth's list, Bouvarel had a sidebar with Henin, a serious-seeming debate. Henin reported the chef's thoughts to the team:

"He said that, technically, when they do a competition, one week before the competition they stop everything, they don't mess with anything anymore. Remember what I said, when you're [training] for a marathon, one week before you stop running so that by the time you get to the marathon race, your body wants it so bad. . . . He said one week before if you're not ready, no matter what you do, you won't get any more ready."

Put another way, the chef was actually *discouraging the team from having their practice in Lyon.*

Hollingsworth was unflappable. "Let him know that we need to try their products because we can't get them in America," he said. "Their fish or their meats."

Henin conferred with Bouvarel. "The American meat is younger, it's tender, but it's not mature. It doesn't have the full flavor," he said, via Henin. "The French, or the European meat, is a little bit older, it's more mature, it has more character, more flavor, more taste. It might not be quite as *tender* as the younger one. It's true, he agrees. You are correct. There is a difference in the product. There is no question about it."

With that, Hollingsworth launched into his list, starting with the most basic ingredient he could think of.

"Canola oil. Do you guys have that?"

"*Qu'est-ce que c'est,* 'CA-NO-LAH?' " said Bouvarel. It means, "What is that, canola?" But the chef drew out the pronunciation of *canola* with such disdain that it sounded more like, *Who is this guy, Canola, and who the hell does he think he is?*

Thrown for a loop, Hollingsworth repeated himself: "Canola oil?" No response. "Rapeseed oil?"

Bouvarel squinted and shook his head slowly from side to side. Never heard of it.

"Neutral?" said Hollingsworth. It didn't have to be canola oil, any neutral oil would suffice.

"Vegetable oil?" said Guest.

Henin thought that might work. "*Huile végétale?*" he said.

Bouvarel was a statue of incomprehension.

"Corn oil?" offered Le Roux.

Bouvarel perked up. "*Maïs? L'huile de maïs?*"

Close enough. Hollingsworth wanted it. No problem.

Whew.

"Five pounds of butter," to make clarified butter. Piece of cake. Now they were rolling. He kept going.

"Cream?"

Kaysen, who had been through this kind of thing two years earlier, whispered in Hollingsworth's ear. "Be sure you specify the percentage you want on the cream."

"Percentage?" asked Hollingsworth.

The well-traveled Dr. John Guest interjected: "It's different cream here."

"Heavy cream," said Adina Guest.

"*Very, very* heavy cream," said the good doctor, lest Hollingsworth not understand that the cream was heavy.

Kaysen knew what Hollingsworth wanted, so he euthanized this portion of the conversation before it got out of hand: "*La double est bonne,*" he said.

"Their double cream is like heavy cream," he told Hollingsworth.

It was fast becoming apparent that it wasn't just the proteins; the team also required a crash course in the significant differences between even the most common ingredients in France and what they were used to back home.

"Two liters of crème fraîche," said Hollingsworth, referring to the slightly soured cream he needed for various preparations.

"*Crème fraîche?*" said Bouvarel. Here they went again.

"They have crème fraîche," said Kaysen, baffled by the reply.

"They don't call it crème fraîche?" said Hollingsworth disbelievingly. The chef must have misheard. "Crème fraîche!"

Henin turned to Le Roux, who had worked in both the Orlando and Lyon. "*Crème fraîche en français?*" he asked. How do you say it in French?

"It *is* already a French word," laughed Le Roux, which brought the house down. Everybody was trying their best; it was just a matter of identifying exactly which of the myriad French options the Americans meant when they said *crème fraîche*.

In the intervening minutes, one of Bouvarel's cooks had brought a liter carton of cream out from the kitchen to show it to Hollingsworth.

"Be careful," said Henin. "This one is ultrapasteurized, meaning you don't have to refrigerate it, meaning it may react differently than the one that we use. You'll have to play with it."

"Two liters of milk," said Hollingsworth.

This was surprisingly easy.

"Two liters of nonfat milk? Do you have nonfat milk?"

"Yes," said Le Roux.

"Do you have microgreens? Like *petite* . . ."

Henin did his best here: "*Miniature pour les feuilles de salade?*"

"What type of greens?" said Henin.

"*Petit céleri?*" said Bouvarel.

"No, micro," said Henin. "*C'est la germination.*"

"*De la root ou de la branche?*"

"Do you want the celery stalk, or the leaves?" translated Henin.

"No," said Kaysen, picking up on a miscommunication. "Basically he's saying there's two different kinds of microgreens. One comes from the stalk and one comes from the root."

"One each," said Hollingsworth, hedging his bets, then moved on. "Two navel oranges," he said.

"No problem," said Le Roux.

"Truffles? Has to be large." He made a circle with his fingers. "Like this."

This, too, was doable.

Hollingsworth ran through a list of other necessities: Parchment, foil, plastic wrap. All were manageable. Puff pastry they could have, but it would come in a five-pound block that would need to be sheeted. Brioche was also available, but would be enormous, the size of two Pullman loaves, but better too big than too small. He'd take it.

"Broccolini?"

Henin started trying to explain this, but there was no point. Technically, broccolini is an engineered hybrid between broccoli and Chinese broccoli, but even seasoned culinarians misidentify it as either baby broccoli or broccoli rabe.

"I think we can ask Daniel to bring some," he said.

"Avocado."

"*Oui.*"

"Tarragon?" said Hollingsworth.

"*Estragon?*" translated Henin.

Bouvarel nodded.

After they got through the rest of the produce, Hollingsworth asked if they had the specs for the proteins that would be used in the competition. The team still had not been directed to that essential Web site page, and Hollingsworth didn't want any surprises. Bouvarel thought that the côte de bouef came from the meatier end of the steer, near the shoulder, but wasn't really sure of any details. So Henin and Hollingsworth ordered what they thought made the most sense: scallops in the shells so he could practice shucking, 16/20 shrimp (meaning sixteen to twenty per pound), an average size, and so on.

Henin also asked Bouvarel if his crew could procure a few bricks for the team. The solution they had hit on to keep their platter warm was to heat foil-wrapped bricks in the oven, then use the bricks to heat the metal. This, too, would be done.

After almost ninety minutes, the team was synced up with their hosts. The food they required would be procured. Now all they had to do was get it all to come out the way it did back at *their* Bocuse House, back in Yountville.

TWO MONUMENTAL EVENTS WERE to take place on January 20, 2009: Barack Obama was scheduled to be sworn in as President of the United States at twelve noon Eastern Standard Time, and eight to ten hours later, the anticipated re-review of Daniel would be up on the *New York Times* Web site.

Team USA was transitioning from acclimation mode to preparation mode: they visited the Boulud farm again to sort through a few newly arrived FedEx boxes as well as some boxes Kaysen had left in France two years earlier (Michel Bouit had carted them there during a trip to Lyon in December), picking out what they'd want to transfer to L'Abbaye. They loaded up the van and .drove to the catering hall, where they were met by Chef Serge Cotin, an affable, ruddy-cheeked, middle-aged man with whom Daniel Boulud had worked when they were teenagers, who helped them to stash their things in an out-of-the-way upstairs room until their practice on Saturday.

Needing to print some directions off the Internet, the team was directed up the road to Restaurant Paul Bocuse. What began as a quick errand turned into a visit with royalty as Chef Bocuse invited Hollingsworth, Guest, and Henin to join him for a coffee. Chef Bocuse, out of his whites and clad in a long-sleeved black cashmere sweater and dark slacks, had the air of a benevolent don about him, reinforced by the floor manager stationed to the side of the table functioning as an attendant, lest he or his guests require anything.

Bocuse reminded Hollingsworth and Guest of some key points of the competition (e.g., be ready for the noise), then turned to Chef Henin and spoke in French. Henin broke out in a broad smile and relayed the message to Hollingsworth and Guest: "Monsieur Bocuse would like to invite you and your friends to a dinner tonight in honor of Obama."

Hollingsworth and Guest could scarcely contain their excitement at this invitation. Instead of another meal in another bouchon, they'd be guests of honor at Bocuse's own restaurant, on Inauguration Day. For young American cooks representing their country overseas, it didn't get much better than that. They returned to the city center and Hotel Beaux-Arts where most of them watched the inauguration in their rooms as they gussied up for dinner. For most of the group except Kaysen, it was their first dinner at the restaurant, and so when they returned, they were given a tour of the kitchen, where they stood behind the stoves and were photographed with Chef Bocuse.

Minutes later, in the dining room, they were presented with menus for the evening that—*voilà*—already had the photograph from the kitchen printed on the front, a souvenir before the first course was even served. The old man hadn't lost his touch for the unforgettable flourish.

The meal was, like much of the menu at the restaurant, composed of Paul Bocuse's Greatest Hits—the famous black truffle V.G.E. soup (created in honor of former president Giscard d' Estaing), a beehive of puff pastry towering out of the bowls; rouget crusted with potato "scales" and swimming in an addictively rich white wine and vermouth reduction, finished with cream and decorated with a squiggle of reduced veal jus, *Volaille de Bresse en Vessie "Mère Fillioux,"* a classic of Lyonnaise cuisine, a truffle-stuffed chicken cooked in a pig's bladder (think of it as the original sous vide), which is presented like a veiny balloon at the table, punctured, deflated, carved, and served with rice and vegetables. And all of it followed by a selection of cheese from local celebrity *fromagère*, "Mère Richard" (Renée Richard), and a comprehensive selection of desserts, everything from babas and cakes to ice creams and sorbets, all presented on an array of tables that were carted around with impressive grace.

Throughout the meal, in addition to the food itself, the depths of Bocuse's marketing prowess were on full display—there wasn't a piece of silverware that didn't have the initials PB engraved at the base of their handles, not a plate that didn't have the chef's full moniker spelled out on its rim; even the soup bowl had the name of its contents emblazoned in calligraphic script around its equator.

After a pleasing eternity, the team rose as one, filed back into their SUV and back into Lyon in silence, each ruminating on the experience before it faded into memory. "It was like being able to travel back in time," said Hollingsworth of the evening. "You read about places like Paul Bocuse and Alain Chapel and Pic and Michel Guérard and all these people who are two generations out. You can't really experience what it was like. How was that food? Was it really that good? You don't know. You don't really know. You read about it. Some of the dishes, you're like, wow, that was amazing. To actually be able to travel back in time and experience a three-star Michelin restaurant as close to what it was actually like thirty years ago, forty years ago, that's really, really priceless. . . . The food and the service is so old-school French. It's amazing to have a place still like that. To have that food that you've read about. That soup and the history behind it. Or the fish with the escalloped scales. *Bresse en vessie*. It's amazing."

Later that night, as Team USA slumbered in Lyon, Daniel Boulud, en route back to New York from an inauguration event in Washington, D.C., and stuck in traffic with two of his sous chefs on the New Jersey Turnpike, learned that Daniel had, once again, had a four-star review bestowed upon it by *The New York Times*.

"At restaurants considered much less exclusive," wrote critic Frank Bruni, "you could spend only $30 less on a similar amount of food, and you wouldn't get anything approaching Daniel's bells and whistles. These flourishes make you feel that you've slipped into a monarch's robes, if only for a night, and turn an evening into an event."

As congratulatory text messages and e-mails shook his Blackberry like a maraca, Boulud cranked up Led Zeppelin on the sound system, uncorked some Champagne, and celebrated. After service, the party would continue back at Daniel, and it would not stop until morning, and with good reason: the Bocuse d'Or was one thing, but a review in the *Times*, especially in the current economy, was life and death.

He had survived the most important judgment of all.

AT BREAKFAST WEDNESDAY MORNING, the team met Roger Gural and Isabel Daniels, the candidate and commis who would be competing for the United States at the Mondial du Pain, the bread competition hosted by the Sirha, the gargantuan trade show that was also home to the Bocuse d'Or. (The Sirha also hosts a dessert contest and a cheese competition.) For reasons having nothing to do with the competition, Gural, who bears many resemblances to the actor Steve Buscemi—wide eyes and a nasal accent—was in a bit of discomfort.

"Man, the food here is killing me," he said to the Bocuse d'Or team, referencing the local restaurant diet of protein, fat, and starch. He had a point: unless you were in a position to cook for yourself, the only three sources of green vegetables, if you were lucky, seemed to be *salade Lyonnaise* and certain *soupes du jour* or vegetable side dishes.

In the streets of Lyon, the inauguration was still reverberating. As the team made its way through the Les Halles marketplace that morning, asking purveyors to hang the team poster in their windows, they were welcomed with open arms that made the Bush era seem as ancient as the local architecture. Many vendors gestured the team behind their counters, stuffed them with slices of sausage and cheese, and posed for pictures. When they walked into Brasserie Les Halles around the corner for lunch that afternoon, a lone middle-aged Lyonnaise woman slid down the length of a banquette in the middle of her meal to enable the growing squad to have a seat.

"*Merci beaucoup*," said various members of the team.

"No prollem," came her accented reply.

"Oh, you speak English?" said Coach Henin.

"Yes," she said with a smile, then expanded her answer with an Obama-inspired flourish, "Yes, I can!"

Feeling the effects of the local diet, and still sated from their dinner at Paul Bocuse, many of the team members ordered a salade Lyonnaise. Dr. Guest forewent his menu, handing it to the server and telling her to just bring him whatever dish had the "maximum vegetables."

They ate, they drank some wine, Kaysen pocketed a spoon, and the team left.

When they returned to the hotel, Jennifer Pelka had arrived, bearing, among other crucial items, black Team USA jackets and T-shirts emblazoned with *Je t'aime USA*. These were to be worn at all times to show a united front, she explained, as she distributed them to the group.

That evening at Léon de Lyon, a well-regarded bistro, the team received its first taste of anti-American sentiment when Chef Henin tried to convince the manager to display one of its posters in the window. When Henin teasingly refused to take no for answer, the manager snidely offered to hang it in the bathroom. But things were different later that night when, on their way into a local bar, a Swiss gentlemen heard Pelka and Kaysen speaking English and called out, "Are you two American?"

"Yes," they replied.

The man lifted his smoldering cigarette in the air like a glass of Champagne, nodded regally, and said, "Congratulations."

THE NEXT TWO DAYS were consumed with planning, planning, and more planning. Pelka established the hotel's bar as her office, working on team paperwork, orchestrating events and hotel accommodations for expected VIPs and spectators, and keeping track of the budget. Her constant presence, and that of the other team members and adjuncts who came and went, was met with wildly varying reception by the different staff members of the Beaux-Arts; the women who oversaw the registration desk by day and doubled as barkeeps by night were accommodating, even offering espressos and wine outside the operating hours of the bar. On the other hand, the night man, a bestubbled shaggy dog, could not have been less enchanted, glaring at the team as they came and went. But at least he was consistent: Kaysen remembered him from two years earlier and found that he hadn't changed a bit.

Thursday afternoon, Hollingsworth and Guest met in the salon adjacent to the bar for three hours, a sacred session to which not even Coach Henin was invited. Hollingsworth believed that, because only he and Guest would be in the competition kitchen, they had to spend time alone reviewing their timeline and talking through the specific mental and logistical challenges before them.

Guest found the meeting essential. "That was the single most important thing we did there," she said. "I have to know his mind and he needs to know my mind. And there's no other way of doing that unless you're sitting there alone spilling out your mind. . . . Cooking is not only a technical thing, it's an emotional thing. So I'm getting his emotion of how he wants me to carry out this action, and while I'm talking about a certain doubt or worry I have with this certain technique, he's getting that emotion so he can help me deal with it."

THE WEEK ENDED WITH a bit of melodrama: the team's platters, on the way from Scannell in Rhode Island via FedEx, were held up in customs in Paris, so the team would not be able to practice on them. The larger concern, of course, was whether or not they'd show up in time for the actual competition. Pelka, troubleshooting from her perch at the Beaux-Arts bar, had asked Vincent Le Roux to try to unclog the bureaucracy.

That evening, the team again took over the salon for a lengthy planning meeting that covered all aspects of the remaining days. Everybody was there: Coach Henin, Hollingsworth and Guest, Kaysen and Pelka, and John Guest and Kate Laughlin. Laughlin and Pelka had already spent hours that afternoon working on the menu—the printed list of proteins and garnishes that would be provided to the judges. (It would be inserted into a bound booklet that had been produced by Level, the same design company that created the team poster. The booklet featured a statement by Hollingsworth, photos and portraits of the team, and montages of the Hollingsworth dish sketches, serving pieces, and platter renderings from Tihany's company.) Also, there was another newly arrived member of the growing posse: Allison Wagner, who handles public relations for Thomas Keller Restaurant Group out of the company PR Consulting in New York, was on hand to field media relations concerns. As the team met, she worked at a makeshift desk in the corner, typing and printing.

There was also a potentially ominous sign: Hollingsworth and Kaysen were both drinking bottles of water sudsy with Airborne, a cold-prevention remedy. Hollingsworth had felt a cold coming on for the past twenty-four hours, and was trying to stave it off.

The team discussed the needs for the practice session the next day, as Hollingsworth ran down the long list of items that would need to be executed before practice could commence: slice bresaola, slice bacon, make chestnut puree, make pistachio puree, clean black truffles, make pistachio crumbs. "We could use a lot of help. We have a lot we need to accomplish," he said. "If we could have help from, uh, people who are experienced in the culinary field." This was his polite way of making sure that, in addition to himself and Guest, only Kaysen and Henin would be working with the food.

The to-do list for the day was insanely long: Measure out stocks (veal stock, shrimp base for the foam, the shrimp stock that would be ladled over the custard); determine which smoke (hickory or applewood) to use in the bowls; test the caviar tube, and so on. There was also a growing list of nonkitchen tasks; for example, somebody needed to buy a screw gun for opening and resealing the crates the platters would arrive in. Oh, and they'd need to *make* a surrogate platter out of cardboard and/or Styrofoam for use in the practice. About this last issue, there was some much-needed good news. During the meeting, both Pelka and Laughlin received e-mails informing them that the platters had cleared customs and would arrive at L'Abbaye on Monday.

Forty-five minutes into the meeting, Kaysen's cellular phone rang. He answered it.

"Hello?"

"Gavin!" It was Boulud.

"Hello, Chef."

All other conversation stopped. Kaysen put Boulud on speaker phone and set it in the middle of the table.

"Congratulations, Chef," said Hollingsworth, referring to the four-star review.

"Timothy!" hollered Boulud from New York, quickly establishing an aural presence nearly as vivid as a hologram. "Are you good? Are you comfortable?"

"I'm loose. I'm ready to go."

"Adina, how about you?"

"Yes, Chef. I'm good."

"Don't eat too much *saucisson*, or you gonna get thirsty."

Everybody laughed.

"No charcuterie for twenty-four hours before you go! You have all the equipment, you're fine?"

"Yes, Chef."

"You're going to be able to do a full run tomorrow?"

"Yes, Chef."

"Where are you going for dinner?"

"I think we're ordering pizza," said Gavin. "I don't think we're getting out of this meeting any time soon."

"Okay," said Boulud. "Make sure you tighten up all the little screws so we can fly to the moon!"

Everybody burst out laughing, again.

They disengaged the call and got back to making the list that would guide them in the coming days: when they finished on Saturday, they would have to pack all their boxes in the order they would be unpacked the day of the competition. Because each hand-crafted smoke glass needed to be kept paired with its lid, Laughlin suggested rigging a box with Styrofoam compartments to hold them, but they resolved to keep them in their original boxes and use plastic containers in their stead for the practice.

The meeting went on for nearly three hours. They made lists, debated packing techniques, remembered crucial details. And then they ordered a pizza. It wasn't the best meal they'd have on this trip, but it got the job done.

ON SATURDAY, JANUARY 24, Roland Henin was none too happy. He privately approached Jennifer Pelka and asked her to scale back the size of the group attending what had become the one and only remaining practice session. The team didn't need distractions, he argued; only crucial personnel should be on site. But nobody was disinvited, and as was often the case in this saga, one uncomfortable situation was immediately followed by another: over breakfast, the team learned by e-mail that the silver pieces, the ones that had been agreed upon and ordered from Scannell just before they left California, had been completed at the last possible second and that, to avoid a customs disaster, Scannell would be bringing them with him to France. (He, along with Richard Rosendale, were coming to help the team unload and get set up on Day Two of the Bocuse d'Or, lending their culinary-competition experience to the effort.) Scannell would deliver the pieces to the team personally on Monday at a Bocuse d'Or briefing at the Sirha.

The group convoyed out of town, and pulled into the parking lot of L'Abbaye. Not twenty seconds later, Jérôme Bocuse, just arrived in France, pulled in behind them, looking debonair in his dark coat and jeans.

The team carried the red plastic boxes down from the upstairs holding area. Henin inspected the smokers and proclaimed: "None of them broke! Let's keep our luck going!"

In the kitchen, one of the first orders of business was to fly the American flag, which Pelka produced from a box and draped from a utility rack, holding it in place with silver domes.

The next two hours were spent getting set up for the practice: Guest processed pistachios, measured vinegar, counted eggs into a plastic container, and melted butter. She wasn't performing any knife work, but the urgent, deft movements that she exhibits at her best were seeping into her behavior.

Meanwhile, in the corridor, friends and family were pitching in: Dr. Guest was ironing team jackets and aprons; Laughlin had set up a printer on a wooden table to generate notes and menu drafts, and had a camera around her neck to memorialize the day with photographs.

As the team continued to unpack and set up around the kitchen, Henin appeared to have magically changed into his chef attire: white coat and a blue apron with side towels draped from its strings. He seemed even more towering than usual, a knight suited up in his armor.

The cast of characters from the past few days appeared: Vincent Le Roux, in a suit and tie, and Paul Bocuse, nestled in a heavy winter coat. After the Bocuses left, Le Roux remained to host the team, offering a steady stream of coffees and waters. In the adjacent room, two dishwashers worked, their arms lost in the deep sinks.

Hollingsworth, assuming authority, asked Henin and Kaysen to label containers. As they did, Guest noticed something wrong out of the corner of her eye. She corrected Kaysen on a label. "It's not sugar; it's Simplesse."

Kaysen cocked an eyebrow. Though young, he's a traditionalist, and doesn't use all the newfangled molecular stuff. "How do you spell that?"

"S-I-M-P-L-E-S-S-E."

As 11:00 a.m. approached, Pelka grew concerned that things weren't progressing quickly enough. She knew that Boulud had landed and was visiting his parents. But before long he would be there and he was under the impression that, as in Orlando, the team was going to mimic the timing of the actual Bocuse d'Or, arriving at the crack of dawn and starting at the same time they would on Wednesday. She discretely sidled up to Guest, busy weighing ingredients on a digital scale.

"If you were to guess, how long before you get started?" asked Pelka.

Guest didn't even look up. "An hour and a half to two hours."

Pelka fought to maintain her composure; it was not the answer she was hoping for. Not even close.

Hollingsworth put on his white chef's jacket and his blue apron, engulfed for a moment by the feeling of home, a phantom sensation that he was back in The French Laundry kitchen. He started brushing the black truffles.

Kaysen scanned the kitchen. It'd been a fun week, but now it was all business.

"D-Day," he said to himself.

Hollingsworth noticed Guest's off-the-charts intensity. "How you doing, Adina?"

"Good, Chef."

Clearly joking, he asked, "Ten minutes?"

A slight smile penetrated the Game Face. "No."

"One hour?"

"Maybe."

As all of this unfolded, Coach Henin had receded almost into the background. He leaned in the back doorway, chewing on a toothpick, watching Hollingsworth intently as the candidate began to gain his flow, mixing crème fraîche and gellan in a blender, while periodically coughing into the crook of his arm. Still not 100 percent.

Guest gathered a number of plastic containers on a sheet pan, and walked them into the walk-in freezer, passing under a sign that read *Chambre Froide*.

Off to the side of the room, on a shelf, were eight smoking guns. Newly purchased from a different purveyor than PolyScience, they had arrived, and were still packed, in boxes that bore a photo of Bob Marley on them. He was, by far, the most relaxed person in the room.

KATE LAUGHLIN AND JOHN Guest left to procure some lunchtime sustenance, but Chef Bocuse had other ideas. He returned to L'Abbaye, shuffled into a central passageway highlighted by a gargantuan fireplace, and summoned his dishwashers to move a long wooden table so it was angled under the chandelier. Then he had them light a fire.

As chimney smoke billowed into the hall, a spread was laid out on the table: cheese, sausage, babas, and terrines cut by Bocuse himself. The team filed out of the kitchen and formed a chow line for their second meal compliments of the man who bore the same name as the competition they'd be joining.

"Just to give you a comparison," said Kaysen, as they tucked into lunch. "When I was here [in 2007], our lunch was bread and Uncle Ben's was our sponsor, so I made rice."

As the roar of a passing train shook the air, Kaysen asked, "How do you write a thank-you note for this?"

The group murmured as they ate. Nobody had any idea.

"I know how you can thank him," Kaysen offered, answering his own question. "Win!"

BACK IN THE KITCHEN after lunch, Hollingsworth and Guest reviewed their notes from the various meetings, public and private, over the past several days. Chef Bouvarel dropped by, noticeably more relaxed on a day off, and made the rounds of the kitchen, shaking hands. Hollingsworth presented him with a copy of *The French Laundry Cookbook*. In turn, Bouvarel handed Hollingsworth a yellow jug of sunflower oil. Hollingsworth tasted it; just what he was looking for.

Kate Laughlin brought Hollingsworth a 5-Hour Energy Drink, one of the many items they'd brought along from Yountville, which he knocked back.

Kaysen was doing what he could to help, setting up the circulator tubs: water in one, blended oil (olive and sunflower) in another. Then he took the slab of bacon into another room and returned with two slices, showing them to Hollingsworth and Guest.

Team USA looked them over and said, almost in unison: "A little thinner."

Kaysen left and returned again with two thinner slices and Hollingsworth and Guest noticed that it was a little thinner on one end, not exactly ideal, but it's all they had so they kept moving.

Henin was staring out the window. It had been a long day, and practice hadn't even started yet. On seeing something outside, his eyes widened.

"The Man is here," he said.

"Paul Bocuse?" asked Hollingsworth.

"No! *D* Man."

Chef Serge had seen the same thing: Daniel Boulud had just pulled into the parking lot in his rental car. Cotin came scrambling through the kitchen to get to the phone and call Paul Bocuse. A moment later, Boulud entered in his Team USA jacket, hair perfect, a cube-shaped blue bag slung over his shoulder from which he pulled out broccolini, avocados, and microgreens. After he lined a plastic container with paper towels, he put the microgreens inside to help them survive until competition day.

Boulud walked into the catering hall. Jérôme and Monsieur Paul, now in his whites, walked in. The gang was all there.

Like a father returning from a long business trip, Boulud made up for lost time with the team, asserting his authority the moment he stepped into the kitchen, asking to review the team's five-hour plan, pushing them to get started, and declaring that, "Somebody has to play the role of the commis. The *commis extra*. They need to get used to that."

"Okay, I can do it," said Kaysen, always happy to be Johnny-on-the-spot.

Boulud looked around the room. "And the platters?"

Kaysen delivered the bad news in one quick word: "Monday."

Boulud's jaw set and his eyes widened in horror. You'd have thought he'd just been informed that the *Times* review had been rescinded. "*No!*" he snapped. "It's too late."

"Stuck in customs."

Boulud recovered, immediately, and went into damage control: "Who has his hand on it?"

"Vincent."

That was good enough. Boulud moved right along. He didn't mention the platters again that day.

As Hollingsworth and Guest wrapped up their preparations, Boulud stood in the corner of the kitchen, scanning a list of notes from the January 8 practice.

"How long do you have to set up there?" asked Boulud.

"About an hour," said Kaysen.

"See, that's what I thought," said Boulud. "You were going to come here and get set up in an hour."

In the corner, near the window, Le Roux asked Henin if he wanted some coffee.

"No," replied the coach. "I'm jittery enough as it is."

Kaysen came prancing into the room. "What's going on?"

Hollingsworth told him, "Adina's looking over the list and then we're going to go."

Henin looked at the clock: 3:57. He held up three fingers to Hollingsworth and Guest. Three minutes to start time.

As the minutes ticked by, Henin began doing a drumroll on a Styrofoam fish box.

Hollingsworth leaned over to Guest: "Better to go slow today."

He didn't wait for the coach. "Ready?" he asked Guest.

"Yes."

"Go."

He started a small timer in front of the salamander.

And once again, but for the first time on French soil, they were off.

They did a number of steps by rote now: Hollingsworth butchering his beef; Guest overlapping bacon slices for the tenderloin, then hacking the skin off the potatoes with ferocious speed.

There was a problem right off the bat: Hollingsworth had treated himself to a new knife for the competition, a Japanese Misono slicer, but when he started using it, he realized that it was one inch longer than the one he was used to. This resulted in an on-the-spot period of adjustment.

The room became dead silent as, with the darkness already gathering outside, Henin, Boulud, and Kaysen stood by the window at the back of the kitchen and watched.

Hollingsworth butchered with a focus that surpassed all previous practices: He cut the oxtail crosswise into segments, laying them on a sheet of parchment, then sprinkling them with salt and grinding pepper over them. He erased the fat from the tenderloin and asked Kaysen to take it to the freezer. He seasoned and seared the beef cheeks and oxtail, then put them in the "stew" pot and fixed the pressure-cooker lid in place, then broke down the cod in preparation for the application of the mousse.

For this first (and last) practice, Hollingsworth opened a Styrofoam container of scallops and shucked them, working on the box lid. He told Laughlin, who was back on note-taking duty, that he wanted a different knife, like a butter knife, to perform the task in competition. He moved quickly that day, and even when he talked to Guest or Laughlin, his hands never stopped moving. He set a small stainless-steel bowl in a larger bowl of ice, and transferred the shucked scallops into the bowl.

As Guest began turning potatoes, Henin paced, hands clasped behind his back.

Boulud entered the cooking area and began speaking to Hollingsworth. "You happy with the scallops?"

Hollingsworth nodded. "Yeah," he said. But unlike in Yountville, he gave the chef no more attention than that. He called out the time to Guest. "Thirty-four minutes."

"Thirty-four minutes, Chef."

Henin collected the sacs of roe from the scallops and pureed them with salt, delivering the blend to Hollingsworth.

Hollingsworth made a quenelle of the scallop mousse, quick-cooked it in simmering water, chilled it in an ice bath, and tasted it. He reseasoned the mixture, and set it aside.

Henin approved. "By doing that, the quenelle, you get five points extra from the judges, if they see you. For the testing."

"Yeah?"

"You damn right."

Hollingsworth replied that he had to test the mousse because the ingredients didn't taste quite like the ones back home.

"It's different," he said.

"Yeah, everything's a little different here," said the coach.

Guest meanwhile had started her Silpat work, baking bacon chips in the oven under foil-wrapped bricks.

Hollingsworth went through his usual routine with the mousse, Cryovacing it in a bag, then flattening it with a rolling pin. He spread the pureed roe over one section of the mousse, then set the cod pieces in place, applied the Activa, and rolled two cylinders, one with roe and one without. This would be the one and only time he'd get to test the addition of the roe, but everybody was pushing for it, even the usually demure Jérôme Bocuse, feeling that the addition of some color would benefit the platter, so Hollingsworth was willing to give it a shot.

Then he rolled up the beef and bacon.

They kept going. Guest sliced carrots for the beef cheeks. Hollingsworth peeled the shrimp. Guest cut brunoise of bresaola. Hollingsworth sliced the scallops into rounds. Guest cut the pith from an orange peel, then sliced the peel into strips. In between her tasks, Guest also checked on her Silpat work, monitoring the bacon chips' progress.

By the one-hour mark (5:00 p.m.), Guest was assembling the mille-feuille, but the bacon was falling apart. She informed Hollingsworth.

"Why?"

She showed him the stringy connective tissue.

"Did we not bring good stuff?" he asked.

"I thought it was," she said. "I basically brought all The French Laundry had."

"No more to choose from?"

"No," she said, then added a line that verged on insubordination. "But we can talk about it later."

Hollingsworth, understanding the stress that brought on the comment, didn't bat an eye. "Okay," he said.

After about one and three-quarters hours, Hollingsworth put the pressure cooker in the sink, opened the valve, and let steam pour out; then he moved back to his station, bringing the celeriac and a mandoline and starting to slice the root vegetable.

"All the celery root has holes in it, get two."

"Two, Chef!"

Between the bacon and the celery root, the team was being reminded of one of the fundamental truths of cooking: without good ingredients, you're basically screwed.

IN THE PASSAGEWAY BY the fireplace, Boulud had turned his attention to the judges' packets, the informational booklets that would be handed out to the jury on Wednesday. They'd been written, printed, and bound for days, lacking only the insertion of the final menu. How, he wondered aloud, would the judges have time to read so many pages in the few minutes they had to taste and evaluate each platter? It was a valid—if not obvious—concern, but nothing could be done about it now. One of the few drawbacks to being Daniel Boulud is that you can only devote so much attention to any one of the myriad projects that captures your fancy. Wait until the last minute to focus, and even with all your power and influence, it might be too late, especially with an undertaking as mammoth as the Bocuse d'Or.

Boulud reviewed the menu with Pelka and Laughlin. A French-born chef, reviewing food descriptions composed mostly by Americans was bound to lead to a few disagreements.

"The foam is not a nage," said Boulud. He continued to scan the document. "And *millefeuille* is one word."

"You can do it two ways," said Pelka, who had to look up such things every day as part of her menu work at restaurant Daniel. "Traditionally, it's hyphenated. That's how we did it, right?"

"Yes," said the chef.

Looking over the beef descriptions, Boulud wondered aloud why the team had gone with *rosette* instead of *tart* to describe the beef-truffle-celeriac pie.

"We didn't want to say *tart tart*," said Laughlin, referring to the shrimp and avocado tart on the fish platter.

At almost the exact moment Boulud suggested *galette* as an alternative, Hollingsworth was slicing the fillet for it in the kitchen. He then began assembling the tart . . . er, *galette*. He drew a circle on parchment paper, using a tart mold as a guide. Then he assembled alternating punched out pieces of beef, truffle, and celeriac in a narrowing circular pattern until the circle was filled.

Boulud appeared in the kitchen, his bag over his shoulder, ready to cruise into Lyon and get checked in to the Sofitel, along the Rhône river, the ultra-luxe hotel where all of the Bocuse d'Or powers that be would be based for the week. He'd be back later that evening to taste the food.

For the next hour, the team performed almost wordlessly, executing a passage of steps that they had great comfort with: Guest checking the two potato preparations in the oven, piercing them with a paring knife to discern their level of doneness, then sealing them in plastic bags and chilling them down over ice, while dropping punched turnips and carrots in Cryovac bags, readying them for sous vide cooking.

Christian Bouvarel returned with two young cooks in tow, both wearing hooded sweat jackets. They watched the Americans cook and nodded approvingly. A moment of inadvertent comic relief was provided around 6:30 p.m., when a sleazy-looking guy with a pencil mustache walked in, camera around his neck, telling them he was there for a photo shoot. Bocuse's cooks, showing amazing solidarity with the United States team, pointed to the American flag at the back of the kitchen and told him the team was training and that it was *privée*.

HOLLINGSWORTH ASSEMBLED THE COMPONENTS of the deconstructed beef stew: pinning punched out black truffle and carrots together, and cutting the cheeks into cubes.

Hollingsworth called out the time. "Three-fifteen. What's left?"

Guest: "The yuzu and the melbas."

"You going to make it?"

"I'll push hard, Chef. I think I'll make it."

"Call it out."

"Little job coming up right now is yuzu. Big job is pommes Maxim and melbas and breading dauphinouse."

Hollingsworth was in his element now, helping a young cook with his ability to see the big picture: "You have Gavin the whole time. You can use him the whole time. Have him set up the mise en place for the dauphinoise."

"Yes, Chef."

Hollingsworth wiped down the silver border of his oven with steel wool, then with a towel. The action was a touchstone for him; for a moment, he was back at The French Laundry again. It felt good.

Guest sliced and stacked melbas and diced little croutons to be sautéed and added to the bottom of the smoke glasses. At her instruction, Kaysen set up the breading mise en place for Guest: all-purpose flour in one bowl, whipped eggs in another, panko (Japanese breadcrumbs) in a third. When cut, the rectangles of dauphinoise would be dipped in these ingredients, in that order, after which they would be prepared for frying. (Additionally, they would be flashed in a hot oven just before serving to reheat them.)

Hollingsworth layered avocado shingles and shrimp halves together, the topping for the tart. He was still trying to set Guest at ease. "Three-thirty, Aaaaadiiiinnaa," he said, drawing out her name, almost in the style of a stereotypical surfer dude.

"Three-thirty, Chef."

"How we looking?"

"Okay, Chef," she said unconvincingly.

Henin brought over a parchment-lined sheet tray with twelve Tupperware containers on it; these would stand in for the considerably more elegant smoke glasses that were being kept safe and sound in their boxes.

Guest moved on to making the melbas. She set the punched brioche slices between Silpats, set bricks on them, and went up on her toes, putting all her weight on them. Then she put them in the oven. She was doing well technically, but falling behind her timeline, so Hollingsworth took some jobs off her hands, sautéing the croutons in clarified butter, then turning them out onto a towel-lined tray to drain, and then it was right to the shrimp tart, which he brushed with fennel compote and set aside, and then sautéing rectangles of mille-feuille.

As they rounded the corner into the home stretch, the pace picked up, and communication became more essential:

"I'm going on steam, Chef," she told him, letting him know that she was changing the mode of the combi oven.

Hollingsworth called back, "Steam," as he added the brunoised ingredients to the Tupperware containers. He realized something was missing.

"Shit," he said, then to Guest: "Pickled pearl onions?"

She brought them over on a tray lined with parchment.

"Did you blanch this onion?"

"I did not, Chef."

"You run out of hot water?"

"No."

"Taste it."

She did.

"Taste the heat?"

"That's how we've been doing it."

Somehow a major detail had slipped through the cracks in all their practices because there were two things wrong with the onions: they weren't blanched ahead of time, and the solution wasn't what Hollingsworth called "ripping hot." As a result they were not pickled. They were marinated, or macerated. But there was nothing to be done for the practice, so Hollingsworth added the onion to the cups, then piped in horseradish cream, but ran out before filling each bowl.

"Two pastry bags of horseradish cream," he said to Laughlin, who logged it in her notes as Kaysen handed him the leftover cream in a plastic container and he finished filling the remaining cups with a spoon.

Next up for the smoke bowls was adding the bresaola. Hollingsworth found it hard to separate the refrigerated slices, so he performed a veteran move, nonchalantly sliding the cured meat briefly onto the flattop to warm and loosen it, then he and Kaysen separated it into slices, arranging little tornadoes of bresaola atop the horseradish cream.

Guest readied the custards for the oven, setting the martini glasses in a bain-marie, then covering it in plastic for the steam oven. Meanwhile, Hollingsworth arranged alternating shingles of shrimp and avocado over the fennel compote on the shrimp tart's puff pastry, lifting them with an offset spatula and sliding them onto the pastry sections.

Guest yanked a bag of turnips from boiling water, while Hollingsworth brushed the shrimp tart with yuzu gelée.

Laughlin came in to report on a call she'd made to California. "You can have whatever you want from California. He's leaving Monday morning." This was a reference to Gregory Castells, an old friend of Hollingsworth's and former chef-sommelier at The French Laundry.

"*Anything?*" he said, then the surfer within made a joke: "How about some waves?"

He kept pushing, assembling the shrimp tart on the parchment and trimming one imperfect edge, then asking Laughlin to note that he wanted a Silpat for it in competition because it was a struggle to transfer it from the parchment to the serving tray. He moved on, seasoning the beef cheek cubes, then setting one piece atop each turnip platform.

"How did the cheeks hold up?" asked Kaysen.

"They're soft," said Hollingsworth as Guest assembled the scallop carpaccios.

"Ten minutes, Adina," said Hollingsworth. "You're good, right?"

"Yes, as soon as the custards come out, I'll flash the mille-feuille."

She peeked into the oven, checking on the custards.

"How are they looking?" he asked.

"They're not set yet."

"Turn the oven up."

"Yes, Chef."

Hollingsworth could sense panic in Guest's voice, a frustration and concern that the custards weren't finished. Hollingsworth, the far more experienced cook, knew that this was perfectly normal. Even at The French Laundry, where precision is a religion, custards sometimes took thirty minutes, sometimes they took an hour and a half. There were more factors than usual that affected the timing: How hot was the water when it was added? How many times was the oven door opened to check the custards, allowing heat to escape? And so on.

"You have eight minutes," he said calmly. "You're good."

Paul Bocuse arrived in his whites, Jérôme at his side, and began snapping pictures with a digital camera.

Hollingsworth painted the cod with pistachio cream, then rolled it in the pulverized pistachio, agitating the tray ever so slightly to cause the cylinder to roll without touching it with his fingers, which might mar it. Then he transferred the cod to two small trays and popped them in the oven to warm them through.

Hollingsworth put the scallop-carpaccio melbas atop the consommé-topped agrumato custard. The melbas see-sawed in the glass.

"Melbas need to be one size larger, Adina," he said.

The team had changed course and decided not to create mock-ups of the platters that day, instead using silver trays available at L'Abbaye. Only problem was that the one they were using was much smaller than their competition platter, so they had to cram the components into its confines: the "martini glasses" in an L formation around one corner, the mille-feuille in the opposite corner, and the shrimp and avocado tart between them. Guest pulled the cod cylinders from the oven, and lowered them into the center of the platter. Hollingsworth rested bacon chips against the leek quenelle on top of each mille-feuille. And, at eight minutes past nine o'clock, nearly twelve hours after they'd arrived at L'Abbaye, the fish platter was complete.

The team went right into beef mode, as Hollingsworth inverted the rosette onto the puff pastry, and set the tart on a plate. Heating two stainless-steel pans, he seared the bacon-wrapped beef, turning it as it browned.

Kaysen readied the smokers, putting a pinch of applewood smoke in the carburetor of each smoking gun.

The dauphinoise browned, Hollingsworth piped a dab of chestnut puree on one end, then fixed a chestnut to them. The deconstructed beef stew stacks were assembled.

As he added the celery salad to the dauphinoise, he noticed an imperfection, and called out, "Celery leaves need to be the same size."

Hollingsworth had issues with the beef cheeks, but chalked this up to the fact that, because they hadn't had enough stock to practice with, they had used water. On Wednesday, at the Bocuse d'Or, they'd be using real stock.

Henin grimaced. "They were so beautiful last time. So glossy and shiny."

Guest lifted the plastic lids on the understudy smoke glasses, while Hollingsworth fired the smoke into them . . .

. . . and at nine twenty-eight in the evening, five hours and twenty-nine minutes into their last practice, Team USA was finished, right on time.

WHEN BOULUD RETURNED A few minutes later, everybody tasted. There was no shortage of opinions in the room. Most agreed that the contents of the smoke glass were too salty, which would be remedied by increasing the amount of Granny Smith apple. Everybody also felt that the shrimp tart was missing something; Hollingsworth pointed out that there would be red jalapeño scattered over it on Monday, but that none had been available today.

As for the beef platter, the feeling that the rosette was too sweet, owing to that elusive balance in the oxtail-endive marmalade, led to a brainstorm. Boulud suggested infusing vinegar with the truffle trimmings left over after punching circles. Kaysen had a simpler idea: He squeezed a few drops of lemon juice over the rosette. On tasting it, everybody agreed that it perked up the truffles and nicely offset the flavor of the beef.

"Okay," said Boulud. "Do lemon, do truffle oil, and keep the honey to a thumbnail."

Boulud also suggested to Hollingsworth that rather than spread the raw scallop roe out on the mousse with a spatula, that he should freeze it in a sheet, then lay the sheet over the mousee before rolling it around the cod to help the roe layer maintain its shape. In the chaos of the moment, at the end of a long day, Hollingsworth agreed to do this in competition, even though he had never tried it before.

Laughlin came into the room and Hollingsworth told her that he wanted *a lot* of product from California: turnips, a bunch of celery, broccolini, avocado, leeks, orange, cutting celery, carrots, cabbage, essentially everything except the potatoes.

The team packed up their equipment and supplies and stashed the boxes until Monday, when they'd swing by to do one final inventory, and hopefully to see their platters.

One thing was for sure: the last hour of the Bocuse d'Or would be the hardest for Team USA. As it had in every practice, the transition game proved their biggest obstacle. Hollingsworth felt good about the rehearsal up to then, but what he referred to as the "coming together" continued to be a source of frustration, a riddle that he didn't know how to solve. No matter how they approached it, the final push always disintegrated into an improvised sprint. Hollingsworth knew that he couldn't start the plate-up any earlier, because then the food would be cold. And he couldn't plan extra time because then, again, if all went according to plan, they'd be done early and the food would suffer. To address this as best they could, the team created a separate, smaller timing sheet for the final hour that would be posted in the competition kitchen alongside the task list for the entire five-and-a-half-hour period.

In hindsight, although she found herself a bit rusty, Guest was glad

that Hollingsworth hadn't taken up Pelka on her offer to find them another kitchen for another practice because she had found working in a new
kitchen disorienting.

Coach Henin remained concerned that the team still had yet to complete a full run-through using all the serving pieces. But, ever the optimist,
he continued to hope for the best.

Before they took off for the night, Boulud asked Hollingsworth one
more question, something he'd been meaning to ask since he tasted the
citrus mousseline. "Do you think the egg yolks are stronger here?"

"*Yes!*" said Hollingsworth, emphatically.

Of course they were.

ON SUNDAY, JANUARY 25, with just seventy-two hours remaining before
their day of judgment, Team USA went to brunch.

The first of several events for spectators, guests, and VIPs was planned
for that day, an afternoon meal at Au Colombier, Frédéric Côte's restaurant
on the outskirts of the city. Team USA wasn't exactly energized, having
returned home from practice at well past 11:00 p.m. But it was a command
performance, and just the first of many events planned for them that day.

After brunch, they were to venture to Eurexpo to cheer on Gural and
Daniels as the Mondial du Pain results were announced.

After a week of having Lyon to themselves, there were suddenly all
manner of interested bystanders there to meet and greet Team USA. Alain
Sailhac and his wife Arlene Feltman were there, so too was Owen Franken,
Paris-based *New York Times* photographer (with a striking resemblance and
similar voice to his brother Al, who was in senatorial limbo at the time following a contested election in Minnesota). Writer Bill Buford and his wife
Jessica Green were also on hand with their twin sons.

After the meal, the members of the Bocuse d'Or USA piled into various vehicles and headed to the Eurexpo site. Hollingsworth, piloting the
Team USA SUV, decided to follow Boulud. Before he knew it, he was

treated to a firsthand glimpse of the chef's notorious driving style, as Boulud wove through lanes with abandon. Hollingsworth, matching the chef maneuver for maneuver, found it hilarious.

At Eurexpo, Boulud's car was stopped by a guard, but moments later was waved through. Hollingsworth followed and they parked.

"They said, this is for VIPs," Boulud yelled to Hollingsworth and company as he disembarked his car. "And I said, 'I am as VIP as it gets!'"

Everybody laughed, but not for long as Boulud was suddenly off in the distance, his leather jacket dancing up ahead. Everybody raced to catch up.

Eurexpo was impossibly sprawling and crowded. Boulud kept ahead of his crew, like a celebrity inexplicably trying to shake his own entourage, though he did stop for a moment, having picked up a newspaper off a stack along the way. Turning around, he flashed a story about the Bocuse d'Or, with a profile of him in a sidebar, and beamed: "No matter where you go in the world, it's good to see yourself in the paper."

The team arrived at the Mondial du Pain presentation just in time for the announcements. Team USA did not win, but Daniels nabbed the Best Commis prize.

That afternoon, in Hall 33, home of the Bocuse d'Or, the team met in the media center on the second floor, along with the famed Monsieur Paul himself, and were interviewed by the *New York Times*' Elaine Sciolino, who was blogging from the event. As had been the case from the beginning of this endeavor, there was always time for the media.

ON MONDAY, AT L'ABBAYE, Hollingsworth finally got to see his platters, which had arrived via FedEx in huge, museum piece–worthy crates. They were exactly as he had imagined them and they got him excited for the competition. But their communion was brief, because the team had to get to the Sirha. Two other American teams met with disappointment that day: in Caseus, an international cheese competition, the Yankees placed fourth, while in the World Cup of Pastry event, held in the same hall as the Bocuse d'Or would be in the coming days, the American team's chocolate sculpture *collapsed* just before the judging. Hopefully, these would not be omens for the Bocuse d'Or squad.

After the pastry awards were handed out, in a small meeting room adjacent to the auditorium, there was a briefing meeting for the Bocuse d'Or candidates and judges. Scannell and Rosendale met up with the team here, and Scannell handed the new pieces he had brought over personally. Finally the team was in possession of all the elements of their platters.

The judges drew lots to determine if they would evaluate fish or meat, and the rules were reviewed. (The president of each competing nation's foundation or organization served on the jury, so Keller was among them, and found himself judging fish.) For Hollingsworth, it was an uncomfortable meeting. He found it strange to be sitting there with people he'd be competing with, even his old housemate Lundgren; the old friends sat next to each other, but Hollingsworth felt the Swede had his guard up the whole time. When Hollingsworth tried to trade notes on how much they'd practiced, Lundgren nodded back, but offered nothing. Other teams, Hollingsworth felt, exuded arrogance; in particular, he was put off by the Norwegians, seated near the dais in white jackets with sky blue lettering, who evidenced no desire to talk to anybody else.

That evening, Team USA had dinner at Paul Bocuse, a special meal to welcome them and their spectators. Dinnertime traffic clogged the roads that encircled Lyon so by the time the team got back to Hotel Beaux-Arts, cleaned up, and donned Bocuse-appropriate attire, it was after nine o'clock, and many of the spectators had been waiting for hours. But that was all forgotten at Salon Fernand Point, their virtual home away from home, which had been overtaken by a gargantuan table that extended almost its full length. Keller and his (personal) partner Laura Cunningham (who had been The French Laundry's Director of Operations until 2006) sat alongside Hollingsworth and Laughlin. Alain Sailhac and Arlene Feltman were there, as were the Bocuse d'Or's attorney Joel Buchman and Eleven Madison Park's Daniel Humm, there with his fiancée.

In the midst of a pressure-cooker week, it was a fantastical reprieve, the evening highlighted by toasts from Boulud and Keller, and the meal headlined by *Lièvre à la Royale*, royal hare, rolled out on giraudons and carved tableside by Bocuse himself, up well past his usual bedtime, as was Adina Guest. "I was amazed that I stayed up that late," said the commis. "I really enjoyed the food, the people, the speeches."

The evening was a personal high point for Keller, who called it "an extraordinary, once-in-a-lifetime moment to have. To be sitting in that dining room, in a historic place, with that group of people, telling stories, living stories inside yourself."

For the Francophile chef, who spent the final minutes of the evening taking pictures *of the pictures* that lined the walls, it was a journey to the very heart of his career. "For me, looking at pictures of Fernand Point or Paul Bocuse, remembering when I first heard about that chef, first read the book, how much of an impact that's had on me, being there and watching that food come out, so classic and so true to form, so true to Chef Bocuse, so true to France, the linens starched perfectly, the glasses, the butter, every little detail about that experience was so French and so traditional and so classic and so perfectly executed, you had to be in awe.

"Your life is about those memories," said Keller. "You have to embrace those memories and those moments."

"Why isn't somebody doing this now?" he wondered. "This is a dying art . . . the rouget crusted in potato with a *vin blanc* sauce and a little design in the sauce. You would call that contrived today. If I did that in my restaurant, or Daniel did that in his restaurant, people would say, 'What is that?' But you're there and you eat it and you go, 'My god. Amazing.' The rabbit royal, exquisite."

He added a word he doesn't use often about food: "Perfection."

6

Bye, Bye, Miss American Pie

Listen to those with experience, but also know when to follow your own instincts and desires. You have to pursue your own ideas, do what you feel is right, and give it one hundred percent during the preparation and the big day, so that you have no regrets.

—SERGE VIEIRA, BOCUSE D'OR CHAMPION, 2005

GAVIN KAYSEN, FUELED BY FANTASIES OF VICARIOUS RETRIBUTION, marched through the predawn streets of Lyon on Wednesday morning, January 28. The last time he had been awake at this hour, in this city, was on his own day of judgment. Back in what now seemed like the dark ages of the Bocuse d'Or USA, there were no team jackets like the one he

TIMOTHY

0:00	Oxtail / Cheeks → Roast
0:15	Fillet → Freeze / Rib Rack
0:30	Sauce, Scallops
0:45	Clean / Confit Scallop
1:00	Cod / Scallop / P. Meyer Lemon Mousse
1:15	Shrimp Cook / Roll Cod
1:30	Roll Beef / Celery Root
1:45	Beet Tart x 3
2:00	Hollandaise / Horseradish & Shrimp Foam
2:15	Cod / Cheeks / Scallop Dice
2:30	Start Prune Sauce / Chestnut Redux / Cheek Redux
2:45	Cod / Mille Feuille / Pommes Dauph
3:00	Portion Cheeks
3:15	Portion Potato x 2
3:30	Saute Mille Feuille / Quenelle Leeks
3:45	Assemble Smoke Bowls

ADINA

0:00	Sous vide / Oven / Stock / Water / Fry oil
0:15	Truffles / Cream / Butter → SALT!
0:30	Bacon Chips / Peel Potatoes
0:45	Turn Potatoes
1:00	Mille Feuille & Pommes Dauph → IN OVEN
1:15	Dice Bresaola, Orange Peel
1:30	Chestnuts, Fennel
1:45	Apple, Onion, Turnip, Carrots
2:00	Jalapeños, Grapefruit, CELERY SALAD
2:15	Celery, Cabbage, Broccoli, Leeks
2:30	Shallots, Endive → Marmalade
2:45	Temper Cod & Beef PUFF PASTRY x 2
3:00	Melbas, Croutons
3:15	Fennel Marmalade, Yuzu Gelée
3:30	Hachee, Finish Croutons, Skewer Carrots
3:45	Heat Chestnut Puree

TIMOTHY			ADINA	
4:00	Fire Beef / Shrimp Avo Tart		4:00	Smoke Bowl, Bread Pommes Dauph
4:15	Yuzu Gelée		4:15	Custard, Foam in Bag, JALAPEÑO, CONSOMMEE
4:30	Fire Cod 4:35 / Caviar Platter / 911 PUSH		4:30	Drop cod at 4:35
4:45	Cod Plate!		4:45	ORGANIZE → Linen / Cod Plate
5:00	FISH PLATTER		5:00	FISH PLATTER
0:15	Sear Beef / PLATTER 911		0:15	Fry Pommes Dauph, Glaze Cheek & Chestnut
0:30	Beef Plate		0:30	Heat Turnip, Dauph, Smoke Ready, Beef Plate
0:35	BEEF PLATTER		0:35	BEEF PLATTER

Note: check bain water   Note: check bain water

pulled tautly around him that frigid January morning. There were no industry giants, no half-million dollars in sponsorship funds. There was just
the team. And ironically, on this day, there was just the team again. After all
the money and media that had been stirred up over the past year, it all came
down to the same thing it always came down to: a core group rendezvous-
ing before sunup to head to Eurexpo and cook. At various points in and
around Lyon, similar scenes were playing out as eleven other bands were
coming together for the same purpose.

Day One of the Bocuse d'Or had come and gone the day before, and
Team USA had taken advantage of their spot on the schedule to catch their
breath, sleeping in before heading out to the event site to soak up the atmosphere and watch the platters go by. The setup of Hall 33 was very much
like that of the event in Orlando, writ large: twelve kitchens, twenty-four

judges, plus a table between the fish and meat juries at which Daniel Boulud, Paul Bocuse (or, in his stead for much of the afternoon, Jérôme Bocuse, representing the Bocuse name), and President of the Jury and 2007
Bocuse d'Or champion, Fabrice Desvignes, would sit. The jury area was
flanked by two carving stations at which the food on each platter would be
portioned out onto plates for the judges.

Hollingsworth, Guest, and Laughlin spent most of the afternoon with
Laura Cunningham, seated in the front row of a sponsor box—slightly
closer to the action than the general-admission spectators—getting their
bearings: About three hours before the first platter was set to be marched
out, Vincent Ferniot, a paunchy, mustachioed French television food personality who had served as the French-language emcee of the Bocuse d'Or
for many years, and Angela May, an actress and model making her Bocuse d'Or debut, replacing Jérôme Bocuse as the English-language host,
took the stage. The pair began several hours of commentary, amplified
throughout the auditorium itself where they were visible on a large screen
suspended over the competition kitchens, and transmitted around the
world through streaming video on "Sirha TV," the host event's Web site.
Throughout the late morning and into the afternoon, Ferniot and May
interviewed coaches and sponsors, narrated the action in the kitchens, and
introduced the judges, which included several world-renowned culinary
figures: Anne-Sophie Pic of France, Lea Linster of Luxembourg, Eyvind
Hellstrøm of Norway, Matthias Dahlgren of Sweden, Philippe Rochat
of Switzerland, Juan Mari Arzak of Spain, and of course American's own
Thomas Keller.

Day One of the competition was strangely anticlimactic as the much-
vaunted noise level didn't live up to its legend. Not even close. Hollingsworth and Guest were both encouraged by what they heard—after months
of being warned about the tympanum-traumatizing audience, the reality
was startlingly mild. So, too was the size of Hall 33, routinely described
in the media as hosting thousands of spectators when in reality there were
just about one thousand people in attendance at any given time, including

media who were allowed to roam the area outside the kitchens in the first hours, then banished to a pen between the sponsor boxes and the competition floor when the judges took their seats shortly before the tasting began.

The line-up on Day One included Australia, Brazil, Finland, Mexico, The Netherlands, Sweden, and the United Kingdom. Historically, Day One has *not* produced many medalists, but with Lundgren in the mix, it was not a group to be dismissed. There wasn't much audacity on display that afternoon, no eye-popping surprises, but there were points of interest, as when the Brazilian platter came out with a unique solution to the "keeping the food hot" challenge: a small fire had actual flames licking the beef centerpiece as the platter was paraded before the judges. There was also a moment of heartbreak, when returning candidate Croston of Australia—there with hopes of bettering his twelfth-place finish of two years prior—sliced his cod fillet with its prawn "crocodile" skin (the shrimp that enveloped the fish gave it a croc skin appearance), only to have it go to pieces on him, the flesh all but disintegrating as he brought his knife blade down through it. As most candidates found out that day, the cod had a larger flake than what he was used to. As it turned out, the fish provided was a different variety of cod—skrei, instead of the promised torsk. "It's a little trickier because the fish is soft, especially if it is stuffed," said Odd Ivar Solvold, coach of Norway's Skeie. "We Scandinavians know the fish well—you just need to salt it a bit and be a little more gentle with the heat, but I'm not sure everyone else knows how to work it."

In his first time at the Bocuse d'Or, Thomas Keller found that judging detail came with its own sets of stresses and challenges. Boulud's concerns about the jury not having time to read Team USA's descriptive packet proved well-founded as Keller barely had time to take in each dish, often tasting one team's plates as another team's platter went by, and trying to make written notes at the same time. Before too long he had created his own shorthand system that he later transferred to the official scoring sheets. As for the packets the United States and other teams distributed, he quickly developed the belief that they should be distributed to the judges the night before the competition so they might have a chance to anticipate what each team is preparing and to know what they are going for to guide them in their evaluation and appreciation.

None of the platters seemed especially intimidating until the fish platter emerged from the Swedish kitchen. As it was carried past the jury, bobbing in the handheld frame on the large-screen TV, Hollingsworth saw what might have been a harbinger of doom. The platter, from his old housemate Lundgren, positively reeked of confidence: cross sections of cod poached in its own skin, with lemon-marinated prawns aligned in its center, scallops filled with scallop roe crème, flavored with algae and topped with caviar, little pea custards topped with three perfectly spherical peas. On the edge of the platter was etched, in letters appropriate to the credits of a *Terminator* movie: lundgren SWE 09. *That's my name*, it said. *And don't you forget it.* Thirty minutes later, Lundgren's meat platter made an equally daunting impression: a centerpiece of a ballotine (roll) of grilled fillet of beef stuffed with its own fat and oxtail braised in red wine and veal bouillon. Standing up on their sides were circles of pickled golden beets, filled with foie gras and topped with a graduation cap of four-spice bread. One component was titled "Tastes and Scents of the Forest," featuring porcini mushrooms in an oven-baked onion, set atop a potato pedestal. The platter was clean, perfect, and fanciful, brimming with identifiable flavors rendered in spectacular fashion. Nobody else on Day One would touch Lundgren, and by day's end, it was clear to Hollingsworth that he was the front-runner.

Kaysen, who had been watching the competition intermittently as he roamed around the Bocuse d'Or, catching up with old acquaintances and competitors, had come to the same conclusion. When he connected with Hollingsworth at the end of the day, they were in total sync.

"Jonas's stuff looked good, huh?" said Kaysen.

"Yeah," said Hollingsworth.

"Good for him," said Kaysen. "He deserves it."

———

By Wednesday morning, Kaysen had put Day One out of his mind and his attention was firmly on Team USA. A few nights earlier, he had been relocated to the plush Sofitel because his room at the Beaux-Arts was needed for spectators. It wasn't a long walk to the Hotel Beaux-Arts, and he took it briskly. His sense of purpose was unmistakable, a man on a mission if ever there were one.

His momentum was momentarily stalled, however, when he spied a small passenger van parked across the street from the Beaux-Arts, rather than the passenger bus they were expecting, the same one that had been chauffeuring spectators to brunches and dinner, with its crucial cargo holds underneath for all of the team's food and equipment. Why the transportation company had sent them this van was anybody's guess, but there was no time to place a complaint call, and nothing to be gained. Coach Henin, veteran that he was, was already in the lobby, waiting. Pelka was there, too. On seeing Kaysen, she yelled out, "Hey, GK!" The night man, clearly ready for Team USA to find a new base of operations, shushed her sternly.

Kaysen and Henin barely had to speak to each other. They knew what had to be done and they took off on foot through the darkness, Henin to the municipal garage where the team van was stashed, Kaysen back to the Sofitel and its valet garage. They had to be somewhat anxious about the sheer number of people and amount of equipment they'd need to fit into those two vehicles, but neither man betrayed this, at least to each other: this was go-time. Failure, as they say in the war movies, was not an option.

Hollingsworth, Laughlin at his side, arrived in the lobby, bleary-eyed after just four hours' sleep, having not been able to gain unconsciousness until after midnight. In addition to his nerves, his sleep was marred by revelers in a nearby room who had been partying until about three in the morning, one of whom had passed out in the hallway. Normally, the abbreviated number of z's wouldn't have made an impact on him, but he was tired in both body and mind. "I was excited. I was anxious. I was crazy. It was a little surreal that it was all there, that it was finally happening," he would say later.

When Hollingsworth saw the comically small van awaiting him, he took it in surprising stride. "Of course it's going to happen," he thought. "Of course, something's going to go wrong."

And where was Adina Guest during all of this? The hyperorganized commis was, ironically, scurrying around her hotel room getting her things and her thoughts together as quickly as possible. Although she remembered her father setting the alarm, it hadn't gone off. She woke up at five-twenty, just ten minutes before she was expected downstairs. The panic that set in the moment she awakened gave her the feeling that she couldn't "freshen" herself.

And that was how Team USA began its big day: its candidate exhausted, its commis running late, and its coach and *consiglieri* running through the dark streets of town in search of extra vehicles.

They recovered well. When everybody finally gathered, the team loaded up the boxes that were on hand at the hotel—mostly posters and paraphernalia that Pelka would distribute in the spectator section—and got into the vehicles: Allison Wagner rode with Henin. Kaysen drove his car with Jennifer Pelka riding shotgun. The team itself, including Laughlin and Dr. Guest, piled into the passenger van. Hollingsworth, never exactly a motormouth, said almost nothing. He felt the eyes and minds of the other passengers on him. The scrutiny of even those close to him, such as girl-friend Laughlin, wasn't especially comfortable at that moment. It was just like that drive back in Orlando: headed through daybreak into battle, with little or no sense of exactly how it would play out.

The Team USA convoy navigated the streets of Lyon, winding their way to the Saône, and along its banks toward L'Abbaye. There were very few cars on the road at that hour, and lights along the bridges, little pointil-list pinpoints of yellow, reflected in the still water. The team disembarked at L'Abbaye, and Kaysen took charge of the scene, ordering everybody around, allowing the candidate to keep his thoughts on what *he* had to do when he arrived at the Sirha.

Chef Serge, showing no signs of the hour, was already there, with his blue apron snug around his middle, fulfilling Vincent Le Roux's promise of providing any assistance the team needed, at any hour of the day.

Gavin directed the passengers: "Jen, I want you, Tim, Adina in this car. I want Roland and Allison in the van. You and I are here. I need a parking pass in each car." He was almost a stereotype of authority: Kaysen Crossing the Delaware, and he got the cargo loaded and the crew back in their vehicles and on their way in no time flat.

UNBEKNOWNST TO THE TEAM, that morning's *New York Times,* and its global edition, the *International Herald Tribune,* featured a story by Sciolino describing the first day's action, interspersed with snippets culled from her time with the Team USA and Chef Bocuse on Sunday.

"I hope they will win because we'd really like this competition to cross the Atlantic," Bocuse was quoted as saying. Sciolino went on to quote him as saying that Hollingsworth was, "extraordinary, awesome. . . . He heaped even more praise on Mr. Hollingsworth's 22-year-old 'commis,' or apprentice, Adina Guest," the article continued, "who will work by his side when they compete on Wednesday. 'They don't say 10 words to each other in five and a half hours, but they work together like a fine timepiece,' Mr. Bocuse said. 'The chef is very good, but his assistant, the young woman, is exceptional.'"

There's no telling exactly how this public display of affection from the event's namesake might have affected various constituencies. The likelihood was that most of the competitors didn't see it. But what of the judges, most of whom arrived considerably later in the morning, with plenty of time to scan headlines over their morning coffee and croissants? After the event, Hollingsworth would comment that, "You have to think about it and say are people going to be offended by that. The answer has to be *yes.*"

Asked if Bocuse's wish bothered him, Australian candidate Croston said that he supported whatever attention can be brought to the competition, anywhere in the world. But others took exception. Geir Skeie, the Norwegian candidate, would later remark that, "I think that he should not have those kinds of opinions, or that if he has he should keep them to himself . . . if America . . . won, then people would say it was already decided before the competition. That's no good. It's no good for America, either." Though he declined to name names, Skeie also said that he had heard grousing from other candidates on this front, as well as complaints that Team USA seemed much too intertwined with the Bocuse d'Or inner circle, what with Boulud installed as Honorary President of the Jury and Jérôme Bocuse himself as vice president of the Bocuse d'Or USA.

Skeie's point of view, or something pretty close to it, was shared by none other than Coach Henin, who couldn't escape the uncomfortable feeling that there was, at least on the part of Boulud, "sort of an atmosphere that we were *favorized* in a sense—I am not sure if that is a proper word—but *favorized* by the Bocuse organization. That there was high expectation. I don't want to say a shoe-in, but . . .

"It wasn't spoken, but reading between the lines and feeling the vibes you could almost sense that. It was sort of, 'Oh, we are okay. We are going to do fine. It is in the cards. It's planned.'"

ON SITE BEHIND KITCHEN 6, where the American team would cook that day, Richard Rosendale had already arrived to watch, and he wondered where everybody was. He felt that Hollingsworth was making a tactical error in not getting there earlier. "You want to be the first one there," he said. "You want to have the whites on. The competition starts the minute you walk in the building. Technically the clock hasn't started but the judges begin to create a picture of your level of preparation. . . . You can kind of get to a point where people are rooting for you and they want you to win, just because you have done all the things right. . . . I think that with that needs to be some doses of intensity. There has got to be some passion. You have got to show me you *want* it. They are not just going to give it to you. It's the Bocuse d'Or."

Henin, who had been concerned that the team was about ten minutes behind schedule when they left L'Abbaye was now happy with the arrival time. "Seven eleven, we okay," he practically sang as he cleared the parking lot checkpoint and made his way to the back doors of the competition space. Walking into the hall was like passing through the looking glass . . . into a pressure cooker. Chef-candidates, commis, team support groups, and officials shot past each other in both directions in the corridor that ran behind the twelve competition kitchens, many pushing speed racks or flying a piece of equipment or an ingredient to their designated kitchen. The consultants, the documentaries, the briefings from past competitors: none of them did justice to the current that seemed to be uniting the souls in Hall 33 that morning. There was a palpable sensation of "This Is It," a tension between appreciating the moment and being awed by it. Adding to the swelling intensity was that, in sports terms, the teams were essentially sharing the same locker room—getting their thoughts and their equipment together right alongside their competitors. After all that time training in different countries around the world, they were actually *there*. The moment of judgment was nigh.

The teams arrived more or less in a steady wave from Kitchen 1 to Kitchen 12. Due to the staggered start times, some of those cooks who would begin later opted to arrive at a slightly more civilized hour. Kitchens 1 through 6 showed up first. In Kitchen 5, the Japanese candidate—still wearing a winter jacket over his whites—was operating with a small crew, although there was a television camera set up outside the window, lending urgency to the scene. In Kitchen 4, the Malaysian candidate Farouk Othman was setting up. In Kitchen 3, a show of force was on display: three guys in bullfighter red España jackets assisted the chef and commis in their whites. Denmark's kitchen's curtains were pulled, making it impossible to tell if they were even in there. Behind his kitchen, Number 1, Norway's

Geir Skeie had his platters displayed on a table in the rear corridor, and they were formidable—four five-sided platforms that were visually arresting enough to perhaps win a medal with no food on them. As if flexing their muscles, the Norwegian support staff moved the platters into the kitchen and began polishing them to a sheen, the silver glinting like a knife blade under the lights.

Unlike Hollingsworth, Skeie—who had more than thirty full practice sessions under his belt—had slept great the night before. He had gone to bed at about eleven o'clock and awakened at six in the morning, a solid seven hours, and woke rested and ready, the adrenaline coursing through his body allowing him to forget all about his bum knee.

In the USA kitchen there was a burst of activity. The night prior, Pelka had obtained food for the team and as Guest arranged her station and her ingredients—stocking avocados, red chiles, leeks, and potatoes—she nibbled on whatever was available, a piece of granola bar one moment, a few bites of yogurt the next, a chaser of tomato juice right after that.

"Ah-dee-nah," said Hollingsworth, doing his best to sound casual. "Are you ready?"

"Yes, Chef."

In the back of the kitchen, Kate Laughlin was on smoke-glass detail, unpacking the dishes and ensuring that each orb was situated next to its lid.

As the team did its work, Pelka lay claim to the spectator area across from Kitchen 6, displaying Team USA's poster on the railing and tying duct tape along the length of the aisle on either side of the seating to rope it off. She also put an American flag (on a stick), a whistle, and 2009 sunglasses (the two zeros were the eyes) decorated red, white, and blue on each of the approximately 100 chairs in the section.

On the judging floor, waiters were setting the long tables at which the jury would be seated, laying tablecloths and arranging silverware and bottled water.

Outside the kitchen, Coach Henin was pacing about. As was often the case at moments of import, he seemed especially towering, upright, proud.

At 8:10 a.m., forty minutes before the first kitchen was set to start, Dan Scannell and Richard Rosendale pit-crewed the platters: Scannell opened the top of the beef platter to check the power source on the lights while Rosendale surveyed the outside, wearing white gloves to ensure no fingerprints were transferred to the silver.

The *New York Times*' Sciolino came up to the window to do an impromptu interview with the team. Though Hollingsworth didn't mind, Henin worried that this was a distraction, and as other reporters came up throughout the morning, he made a point of welcoming them with a big smile and trying to *become* the interview subject himself, allowing his charges to keep focus.

For all of the activity on one side of the exhibition hall, all of the kitchens on the other side were either closed (curtains drawn) or dark, with one notable exception: Kitchen 8, the Canadian kitchen, which was awash in activity. David Wong and his crew, all wearing oversized faux hockey jerseys with "Wong 09" on the back, were in full set-up mode. Wong was also the only chef who paid attention to the growing number of passersby, shaking hands and posing for pictures.

"We're going to cook good food for good people," he said earnestly to one bystander.

Hollingsworth slipped out of Kitchen 6 and walked along the back corridor to the two long wooden tables next to Kitchen 1 where proteins and vegetables were being distributed. He didn't have to introduce himself or present any credentials. "They read your jacket, I guess," he said. The attendants handed Hollingsworth his proteins and, surveying them, he realized they were a mixed bag. He was happy with the quality of the beef cheeks ("way cleaner than they are in America" where they have more fat and sinew) and the oxtail, which was clean, with a nice healthy hue and not too much fat. The fillet, however, was a little bigger than optimal, and its "fibers were closer to, not the chateaubriand end, but the tail end. You can almost see the long fibers and shift them back and forth, up the whole thing."

The last protein he took was the one that held the biggest surprise:

the shrimp, the ones he had never obtained the specs for, were about one-quarter the size he expected and were in a frozen loaf. "They were tiny, man! Tiny, tiny. I had never worked with shrimp that small. I was shocked. And they were frozen in a block. They were the exact ones, if you go to the grocery store and you buy shrimp that are frozen in a block of water in one of those cardboard boxes, it was the exact same thing. They were *not* meant to be fresh at all, those were frozen shrimp." (Pity that he had never been directed to that Themes page, which indicated the shrimp were "supplied as both fresh and frozen products with and without shell," and "size 90/120 prawns per kg.")

Back in Kitchen 6, Hollingsworth was introduced to Corentin Del-croix, the commis extra provided by the Institut Paul Bocuse, a young French cook who he estimated was slightly younger than Guest, and who spoke very good English. Hollingsworth briefed him, quickly: "We want you to work over here," he said, pointing to the area just inside the kitchen to the right. "We want you to work clean. I'm going to hand you stuff. I want you to clean it and put it here. Here's the garbage. Do you know where the ice machine is?"

"Yes."

"Do you know how to use a Cryovac machine?"

"Yes."

Hollingsworth, a believer in his ability to judge young cooks almost on sight, liked the guy, had a vibe that he was "a good kid, for sure." There was just one problem, he didn't catch his name.

"Do you remember his name?" he asked Guest.

"No."

Hollingsworth winced. Coming from a place where cooks shake hands on their way in and out of the kitchen every day, this was not the sign of respect he wanted to convey. "It's okay. Let's just call him 'chef.'"

The technical judges—Joseph Viola among them—checked the kitchen, then the lead judge said, "*Bonne chance,*" and slipped out the back and on to the next kitchen. Team USA was cleared for takeoff; all that remained was for the designated organizing committee member to come by ten minutes later and tell them to begin.

Hollingsworth turned to Guest: "This is it. Ready to go?"

"Yes, Chef."

Hollingsworth believed her. To him, she seemed "on," which pleased him—his first goal of the day, keeping day-of panic from settling in, seemed to have been accomplished. His assessment was accurate. "I was just being in the moment," said Guest. "I wasn't thinking, 'Oh, isn't it amazing to be here.' Was just like, 'Okay, what do I need to do next?'"

The mood in the back corridor had the feeling of a wartime farewell; loved ones lingered for as long as possible, then embraced their brave soldiers as if they might never see one another again. Hollingsworth and Laughlin hugged goodbye, then Laughlin headed out to the spectator section. When she got there, and it dawned on her that all of the effort of the past several months had just come to an end, for her anyway, and that now all she could do was watch, she was overcome with emotion and started sobbing.

In the competition area, the committee member appeared in the back doorway of Kitchen 6. *"Bonne chance!"* he said, before heading to the next kitchen.

And they were off . . .

TEAM USA BOCUSE D'OR 2009 MENU

OLIVE OIL POACHED LOIN OF NORWEGIAN COD
Enveloped in Scallop Mousse, Preserved Meyer Lemon and Sicilian Pistachios with Citrus Mousseline and Shrimp Nage

WILD PRAWN AND HAAS AVOCADO TART
Fennel Compote, Chili Peppers and Yuzu Gelée

AGRUMATO CUSTARD WITH SHELLFISH BOUILLON
*Toasted Brioche, Scallop Tartare, Ruby Red
Grapefruit and Candied Orange Zest*

YUKON GOLD POTATO AND BACON MILLE-FEUILLE
*Crème Fraîche–Enriched King Richard Leeks, Hobbs
Bacon Chip and Sacramento Delta Osetra Caviar*

———

ROASTED ABERDEEN ANGUS BEEF RIB-EYE
*Wrapped in Applewood-Smoked Bacon
with Prune-Enriched Oxtail Jus*

ROSETTE OF SCOTCH BEEF FILLET
Périgord Truffles, Celeriac and Oxtail-Endive Marmalade

GLAZED BEEF CHEEKS À L'ÉTOUFFÉE
French Laundry Garden Turnips and Sweet Carrots

CALOTTE BRESAOLA FUMÉ À LA MINUTE
*Granny Smith Apples, Savoy Cabbage
and Horseradish Mousse*

TRUFFLED POMMES DAUPHINOISE
*California Chestnuts, Pickled Red Onion
and Celery Branch Salad*

THE FIRST THING HOLLINGSWORTH did was lay the oxtail on his board and section it; usually he found the sweet spot between the bones and his knife would sail right through, but today, using that new Misono, with its unfamiliar length, he was catching the bone. With his regular knife, he'd have just muscled it through, but that's a bad idea with a new knife, because the thin blade can be easily damaged, so he had to lift it a hair, whittle his way back down, and then go through it. Not exactly an auspicious beginning.

Guest meanwhile, working in the window, began knocking items off her task list. She turned on the sous-vide tanks and the oven, and set two pots on the stove: one with the veal stock, the other with water for blanching. She turned the heat on under both of those. She also readied a pot with fry oil, setting a thermometer in it but not putting it on the stove yet, because all the burners would be required for earlier tasks. Guest handed the overlapping bacon for the rib-eye to Hollingsworth, then made the bacon chips with the presliced bacon. The extra commis wasn't occupied yet, so she asked him to pick tarragon leaves for the scallop tartare composition; just as she might do with a younger commis at The French Laundry, she made sure he knew that she wanted the *perfect* leaves.

Guest next took the potatoes and sliced the skin off of them, turning them with her fingers and bringing her knife down over and over, quick as a wood-chipper: the Adina-Matic was in the house. Hollingsworth, meanwhile, had turned his attention to those pristine beef cheeks. A quick extraction of silverskin from one muscle area and they were ready to go.

Hollingsworth's knife wasn't the only piece of new hardware that would betray the team. Guest, using a brand-new turning vegetable slicer, and picking up speed, sliced the middle finger of her right hand on the blade, nicking it just above the nail. After a moment, a trickle of blood emerged and wouldn't stop. She turned to Hollingsworth. "Chef, I cut my finger," she said.

Hollingsworth kept his cool. "How bad is it? Is it bad?"

"No."

"What do we need? A Band-Aid?"

"Yes."

"Do we have any? Did you bring them."

"No."

Guest was to have brought some first-aid supplies, per a suggestion Henin had made, but had forgotten. Hollingsworth knew this wasn't the time for scolding, and the cost seemed minimal as Guest told him she felt fine and that it wasn't a bad cut; it just wouldn't stop bleeding. Besides, she already seemed frustrated with herself, as was her wont.

"I consciously didn't make a big deal of it so as not to raise her anxiety level," Hollingsworth said.

"Do you need help?"

"No."

That was all either of them had to say. Guest excused herself out the back of the kitchen into the bustling corridor, asking an attendant to send for a bandage. Instead, he sent for the *medic*. In the heat of the moment, Guest's normally referential attitude crumbled. "I don't need a medic, I need a fricking Band-Aid," she said, but nobody heeded her words. Two or three precious minutes later, as Hollingsworth and the commis extra moved about the kitchen without her, the medic hustled over and took several minutes attending to her minor injury that was taking on major proportions of time.

In the kitchen, even though he was using the same make and model of stove he had practiced on, the stock in which the oxtail and beef cheeks were submerged took longer to boil than it had back in Yountville. When he finally found it bubbling, he wasn't sure how long it had been at a simmer. This was one of those moments that make the Bocuse d'Or such a challenge: cooking is almost never the same from day to day. Just as ingredients will vary in quality on the day, you never know what might go down with your equipment. Experience matters at moments like this, and Hollingsworth's told him that it couldn't have been simmering much longer than he'd practiced and that rather than trying in vain to determine the actual time, the best thing was to stick to the plan: one hour with the burner at setting number 3.

This was about the time that Vincent Ferniot and Angela May arrived center stage and kicked off their Day Two coverage, emceeing for the audience and broadcast on Sirha TV. On Day One, the pair had established themselves as something of an odd couple. If you didn't know that Ferniot was actually French, you might think he was doing a cynical impression of a Frenchman, leaning into every accented syllable and mugging shamelessly.

"*Bonjour à vous tous, à la France, et au monde entier,*" Ferniot intoned into the camera.

But at least he was a seasoned broadcast professional, intimately familiar with world cuisine in general and the Bocuse d'Or in particular. May, on the other hand, seemed a bit at sea, and wasn't aided in her efforts by the condescending attitude Ferniot adopted toward her, publicly schooling her on the fine points of the competition, acting a bit like an overbearing father or emotionally abusive boyfriend.

"Good morning, eh-vah-rie-one," said May, overenunciating. "And welcome to the Bocuse d'Or 2009."

Hall 33 hàd only been open to the public for about an hour, but the noise was already significantly greater than the day prior. This was in part because France was competing this day, and the stadium seats across from Kitchen 10, where Philippe Mille had started cooking, were packed almost to the ceiling, pressing up against the windows of the media center, with a few fans waving enormous French flags at the ends of posts. Those not burdened with such weighty props were jumping up and down and shouting encouragement at a chef they could barely see or discern what he was doing.

"They are crazy, I'm telling you," said Ferniot of the French fans, speaking in English. (He freely switched back and forth between the two languages, either to "throw it" to May or to explain a fine point of the proceedings in both languages.) He was allowed to say that; these were his people.

Outside Kitchen 6, a number of the cast of characters from the past few days had reemerged: Bill Buford was on hand in an all-*noir* ensemble, while Owen Franken was snapping pictures for *The New York Times*.

Hollingsworth shut it all out: emcees, the fact that his commis was momentarily off the field of battle, the photographs being taken. He just focused on the work at hand, which was trimming the silverskin from the fillet, putting the meat on a sheet tray and flash freezing it, which would allow him to slice it cleanly and punch out circles for the tart.

In the corridor, Guest, pleaded with the medic: "Sir, I have to go. Can you give me a glove?" The medic handed her a latex glove. She didn't even thank him, just stuck her head in the kitchen and called out to Hollingsworth: "Chef, scissors!"

Hollingsworth handed her a pair of scissors and she cut a finger off the glove, slipped it over the cut, tied it tightly around the knuckle like a tourniquet, and went back to work.

"Is everything fine?" asked Hollingsworth.

"Yes, Chef. I got a Band-Aid."

Hollingsworth kept going; he butchered the rib rack, split it, rounded it, and seasoned it with salt and pepper.

The team was back in business. Next up on Hollingsworth's list was to shuck and clean the scallops, which didn't go as smoothly this time as it had in the practice. Hollingsworth wasn't catching them in the right place with his shucking implement, so they weren't opening as easily for him, and when they did, the fact that some had dirt inside and emitted an unpleasant odor led him to believe that he hadn't wound up with the best specimens. He was keying in to what he realized was going to be a theme of the day: "With everything there's going to be a little problem," he thought.

The commis from the Institut Paul Bocuse asked Hollingsworth if there was anything he could do, and—first checking to be sure the cook knew how to do it—the American asked him to clean the shrimp. The commis set about doing this, working at the station just inside the kitchen door.

Over in Kitchen 1, Geir Skeie was operating in the back area of the kitchen, positioning his commis in the window. Some veterans think this is a wise move for competition because it takes the focus of photographers and spectators off the chef. As Ferniot and May made their way to Norway's kitchen and began a long tour of the windows in ascending order, this conventional wisdom was validated as Skeie could barely be seen on the large-screen television, and he didn't bother to look up or acknowledge the emcees in any way. He wasn't there for publicity; he was there to cook.

As if the noise weren't sufficient, Ferniot and May did what they could to foment even more, like pointing out the noisemakers of choice for the various fans. This sometimes lapsed into derogatory comments as when Ferniot noted the wooden spoons being banged together by chef coat–clad Denmark supporters ("It's not so noisy though. It gives a little click sound. *Click, click, click.*") or when he said, of the pom pom–shaking Spanish fans, "The best noisemaker in España is the voice; they use it pretty well." At this, Spain's candidate, Angel Palacios, busy cutting batons of potato, was caught on camera looking annoyed.

Not everybody had as much support as the European countries; when May introduced Farouk Othman of Malaysia, the first-ever chef from that country to compete at the Bocuse d'Or, the auditorium fell silent. Miraculously, she spotted a lone fan applauding amidst a sea of adversaries. Singapore, which had actually made the podium in 1989, only fared marginally better in the support department with three young men in baseball caps cheering from the nosebleed zone of the bleachers.

Arriving at the United States kitchen, Ferniot and May cajoled the U.S. fan base. Though Pelka and company had commandeered the entire section across from Kitchen 6, the attendance at that relatively early hour was sparse: many expected guests were still breakfasting at their hotels or strolling the endless aisles of the Sirha. May described Hollingsworth's backstory, how he'd begun as a dishwasher and "worked his way up," but he scarcely noticed her, his eyes trained on the cod he was butchering. As Australia's Corton had the day before, Hollingsworth found the fish less than ideal, but he didn't realize that it was a different variety from the one they'd expected; instead he just chalked it up to the fact that some cod are flakier than others.

As Guest composed the mille-feuille and dauphinoise, Hollingsworth put the filleted cod in a bowl with salted ice water to quick-cure it and set a timer for five minutes. But he wasn't really relying on the timer. He was relying on his cook's instincts, the subconscious ability seasoned kitchen professionals have to let their brain keep track of time. The act of setting the timer doubled as setting his *mind* to remember, five minutes later, that time was up. In the meantime, he pureed the sacs containing the scallop roe and added salt to them. Following the revised plan hatched out with Boulud on Saturday night, he spread out the roe on an acetate sheet and set it in the freezer to blast-chill it.

Hollingsworth next turned his attention to the mousse that would envelop the cod: whipping the scallop and crème fraîche mixture in the Robot Coupe, then folding in the preserved Meyer lemon dice. The only problem was that the Cryovac bags provided at the competition were larger than the ones he'd practiced with, and there were no sheet trays large enough to accommodate them. Hollingsworth, whose ability to cook intuitively had served him well since his days at Zachary Jacques, had never measured exactly how wide the sheet would have to be to wrap snugly around the cod, so he had to improvise, poaching one portion of the mousse, then the other, then trimming the whole piece to make it smooth. To allow himself time to figure all of this out, Hollingsworth scrapped making the test quenelle of the mousse he would normally have executed. So much for those extra five points Henin had forecasted at Saturday's practice.

Hollingsworth pulled the acetate sheet holding the pureed roe out of the freezer, the puree having hardened to a frosty, *granité*-like sheet. As he walked it over to his station, it dawned on him that—duh!—he wouldn't be able to roll the frozen sheet; it had no pliability, so would break when turned inward on itself. *Aw, this is stupid*, he thought. *It won't roll. You're kidding me. This sucks. What do I do now?* The few-yards walk suddenly felt like a quarter-mile slog. At his station, he set the tray down to allow the roe to come up to room temperature.

He turned his attention to the rib-eye on his station. For the first time since their first practice, Hollingsworth did not consolidate the Activa steps because the cod was not ready to go. He dusted the beef with the glue, rolled it in bacon and handed it to Guest, who put the pan in the refrigerator.

Hollingsworth kicked himself, hard. If he'd only thought about it properly on Saturday, or in the breathless days since then, he'd have realized that *OF COURSE* a frozen sheet of roe wouldn't roll. You didn't need to be a sous chef at The French Laundry to know that. "But with all the pressure and stuff I didn't really realize it," he said. Profound as it was, Hollingsworth's personal disappointment was self-contained, a fringe benefit to the wordless working method he and Guest had established in their practices. In fact, they were about an hour and twenty minutes in when Hollingsworth spoke to Guest for just the second time since they had begun cooking:

"Do you have the mandoline?"

"Yeah, here."

"You have the punch?"

"Yeah, here."

Hollingsworth pushed the fish aside, cleaned his board, scrubbed it, tossed his dirty towels in the bin, washed the stinky fish smell off his hands, then set his station back up. The act of cleaning, as always, was therapeutic for him, bringing him back to himself, to The French Laundry. With no ability to finish the cod for the moment, he took hold of the celeriac, waved it back and forth on the mandoline to produce slices, then punched out circles while Guest set punched circles of turnips and carrots to cooking in Cryovac bags while also blanching onions, dicing bresaola, brunoising Granny Smith apple, and so on. Though her chef was having a hiccup, Guest was working at her accelerated best. Viewed on the large-screen television overhead, the video seemed to be fast-forwarding as a close-up of her cutting board showed her taking a section of orange mercilessly apart, splaying the peel on the board as her paring knife eliminated the flesh, then shaved off the pith. Just as impressive was Obed Ladrón of Mexico, who cut a green vegetable—perhaps zucchini, but impossible to decipher under the onslaught of his knife blade—into julienne, then the julienne into dice. Watching these two cooks work was a reminder of how impressive it is that more digits aren't sacrificed in the world's kitchens every day.

Meanwhile, the noise in Hall 33 had been steadily mounting to a non-stop, pulsating thunder, lopsided toward the French end of the auditorium, but deafening throughout. The attention paid to the kitchen pods was lopsided as well: seen from a distance, it looked as though Kitchen 10, where Philippe Mille was hoisting an enormous stockpot from stove to sink, was the last kitchen in the hall: a crush of photographers and journalists had gathered to watch him, while just the coach and a single shutterbug were looking in on lonely Kitchen 11.

The excitement and noise in the hall were starting to take their toll, turning things downright nutty: after Vincent Ferniot interviewed representatives of Champagne Thiénot, a sponsor, one of the cameras made its way along the judging tables, a bottle of the bubbly held aloft before it by a techie—what 1980s-era David Letterman would have dubbed a Bottle-Cam shot. Ferniot threw it over to May, who—never having experienced the Bocuse d'Or before—seemed dazed and confused. Like some of the competitors, even having been there for Day One, she was unprepared for the fury of the most impassioned European fans who turn out on Day Two.

"Vincent, I can't hear you," she said straight into the camera, laughing deliriously. "I have now lost track of all time, of all sense of reality. I can't hear anything anymore. I don't even know if there's information to be given at this time. . . ." For a moment, the Bocuse d'Or had turned into Angela May's own personal *Blair Witch Project*. The veteran Ferniot, however, wasn't satisfied with the competing chants and noisemakers that were shaking the foundation of Hall 33 and casually deployed comments designed to whip up even more clamor: "In a way, it's true. It's crazy to be here. Come from the other part of the world, like Japanese, travel all the way around Asia to be here and support their team. It's fantastic." On cue, the Japanese cheering section amped up their volume, jumping in unison and pumping their fists, pouring more vibrations into the pulsating air.

In Kitchen 6, Hollingsworth was starting to be affected by the crowd—even though he preferred his kitchens noisy, this was too much, like Christmastime in Tora Bora. But he fought to maintain his focus as he plowed forward. He pulled the beef tenderloin from the freezer. It didn't feel cold or firm enough, but he tried a few slices anyway. Yep, it needed to harden further. He returned it to the freezer. Off his schedule, he returned to the cod. The puree had softened, but he had quickly come to resent the mousse, which was a struggle to incorporate cleanly into the rolled component. *I can't believe I'm doing this mousse*, he mused, struggling even to hear his own thoughts. "I was frustrated with myself for making a decision that I thought was foolish," he would say later. "Something I'm not entirely comfortable with. Why would I choose to do it this day?" Keller's words from all the way back in November, "This is your thing, Tim," suddenly took on an even deeper meaning. For all the Michelin-blessed consultants he had, the candidate was *the* chef in this little three by six-meter kitchen, and he damn well should have acted like it.

"Is this going to be as pretty as I wanted it to be?" he wondered to himself as he started rolling the mousse around the first cod cylinder. As he saw the roe puree squish out the ends like sauce on a spicy tuna roll, he internally answered his own question: *No*. Again, he berated himself for not going with his gut. "I think without the color it would have looked clean," he would say later. "With the color, it didn't look clean. That's what I believed and I'm sad to say I didn't go with my own belief."

Adding to his self-consciousness was the convention of photographers and reporters who had by then gathered in the window, craning to see around Guest to get a look at him. Hollingsworth rarely minds being watched while he works—he greets visitors to The French Laundry kitchen with an all-American smile and all-the-time-in-the-world attention—but the audible cries of "What's that?" were getting to him because by that point in time he himself wasn't quite sure of the answer himself.

Guest picked up on the photographers' focus, too, and didn't appreciate it. In Orlando she hadn't minded the attention, but it had felt more equal-opportunity to her then. On this day in Lyon, "I had a feeling I was in their way. They were trying to take a picture of Chef Tim. I felt that from them. Not energy that I needed. I ducked and they were snapping pictures of Chef Tim, then I got up and they were like 'Oh, my God.' I could see it in their face or their movements, the fact I was picking up on that meant I wasn't focusing on my stuff which meant that I was a little distracted by the people . . . it didn't bother me that I was in the way, just the energy they were putting out when I was trying to focus it did affect me a little bit. . . ."

Finally, Hollingsworth got the cod cylinders rolled in plastic and transferred them to the refrigerator.

"Adina, don't forget, fifteen minutes before we fire it, we have to pull it out. Actually make it twenty minutes."

There were only two words he expected to hear back, and they were the ones he got: "Yes, Chef." Guest seemed very intense to him at that moment, and he took that as a good thing, the embodiment of all those signs back home at The French Laundry: *Sense of urgency*? Check.

A glance at his task list revealed, to Hollingsworth's surprise, that he was actually *ahead* of his schedule. The only explanation was that although cooking and freezing were taking longer than they were supposed to, his butchering and knife work must have been taking less time than they usually did. Maybe he was dancing a little bit after all. He decided to use the time to help out his right arm.

"How are you looking, Adina?"

"I'm a little behind."

Because of the way the schedule had been designed, this was no problem.

"What do you need? Give me projects. Is the endive made?" This was a reference to the endive marmalade.

"No."

"Okay, give me that."

Based as it was on a longstanding French Laundry staple, Hollingsworth scarcely needed to think before jumping in: he put some honey and Banyuls vinegar (wine vinegar from mostly Grenache grapes) in a small pot, brought them to a simmer, and reduced them, a preparation called a *gastrique*. Then he stirred in the endive and let it simmer. While the marmalade was simmering, Hollingsworth took a few more tasks off of Guest's list, mostly stove work: he blanched the cabbage, broccoli, and leeks, and pickled those pesky pearl onions. Then he moved on to the tart, drawing a circle on parchment paper with his Sharpie and arranging the punched celeriac, truffle, and tenderloin in that narrowing circular pattern. He also processed the ingredients Guest had measured for the hollandaise-like citrus mousseline and the shrimp foam that would sauce the seafood plates. The team was back on track, working in harmony and mowing down the items on their to-do list.

On the competition floor, Ferniot and May brought out the judges, introducing them one by one, just as they had the day before. Paul Bocuse was also introduced, emerging through the curtain that hung between Kitchen 6 and Kitchen 7.

By this time, the journalist pen, which stretched between the sponsor boxes and the judging floor, was packed—photographers and videographers threw elbows vying for position at the front of the pit, while writers with notebooks at the ready were just as eager to be able to lean on the counter for the coming two-hour platter parade.

At the one-hour mark to his fish platter deadline, Hollingsworth was feeling surprisingly good. The cod was a source of concern, but he was otherwise still optimistic. He thought that Guest should have felt the same way, but . . .

"Chef, the custards aren't setting."

Again, Hollingsworth picked up on Guest's anxiety over those custards. He talked to her as calmly as possible: "That's fine, Chef, put them back in the oven. We have time." He also wanted her focused on the work ahead of them, especially the tart: "Adina, the shrimp project is going to be a big project. In twenty minutes we're going to do the shrimp. I'm going to need your help."

At one fifty on the button, Geir Skeie's platter went up in the window of Kitchen Number 1.

As a game show–like anthem underscored his words, Ferniot announced the fish platter to the audience: "*Le premier plat de poisson, le poisson de Norvège.*"

The platter was lifted by two committee members, and it was a formidable piece of work: titled "Norwegian Cod, Scallops and Prawns à la 'Sandefjord,'" it featured loin of cod with lightly smoked scallops and cod belly, green-pea sphere, brandade, Norwegian *Kabaret* (cabaret) with peas, prawns, and onions, a red beet cube with Jerusalem artichokes and black truffles, and potato and leek with quail egg. For sauce, there was a Riesling and horseradish emulsion.

Angela May was moved to praise: "I have to say, this is one of those dishes that, if I were in a restaurant and I saw it walking past me, I would order it in a heartbeat because I eat mostly with my eyes before I eat with my palate."

In the stands, Rich Rosendale was also impressed. "That is going to be hard to beat," he thought.

When plated, the thoughtfulness of Skeie's presentation was undeniable: for example, the Sandefjord—a browned rectangle of cod, a seared scallop, the brandade, and the pea sphere (a glistening Ping Pong ball–sized "pea" no doubt produced via some molecular means)—fit perfectly in a small rectangular indentation, while the beet cube stood on one corner, as though pirouetting at the back of the plate.

And so the clock was ticking. For all of the Day Two competitors, it was only a matter of time. It would all be over, one way or another, soon.

———

TIMOTHY HOLLINGSWORTH CAN'T SAY exactly when his abdominal muscles seized up on him, can't pinpoint the instant when he first perceived the cramp in his gut, a "constant flex" that started in the center and gradually moved around to the side, a sensation unlike anything he had ever experienced in the kitchen, or even at the gym. But it was about one hour before the fish platter was due in the window.

It's a safe bet that the cramp was brought on, in large part, by the shrimp tart. While the puff pastry base remained the same, as did the fennel marmalade, the shrimp themselves, when cooked, were mealy and a bit odorous. To try to mask the unappealing taste, Hollingsworth threw the kitchen sink at them: lobster glace, reduced shrimp stock, *fleur de sel*, Espelette. He then *hacheed* (finely chopped) the shrimp, spread them out, and punched out "shingles" that he would transfer to the pastry with the aid of a spatula. These he would alternate with the avocado shingles, but he was barely started on this project when he wished he had gone with an alternate thought: spreading the shrimp out on the marmalade, then laying avocado on top to neatly mask the disintegrating crustacean. Hollingsworth was used to coming through at moments like these, but today, Keller's kitchen philosophy would be more prescient than it ever had been: There would indeed be no such thing as perfect food. Only the idea of it. The fleeting, oh-so-close idea of it.

Even in the heat of the moment, he was thinking clearly enough to realize that the pain was brought on by stress. "Coming down to the wire, you cannot be late, you have one shot," he said. All those months of exertion, the decision to say "yes" to applying for Orlando, the development of his food, the last-minute arrival of the platters themselves, and the little serving pieces that had just shown up with Scannell on Monday. *Everything.* It was all taking its toll.

To try to relieve the cramp, Hollingsworth stretched out his side, to no avail, then got back to work.

Other platters made their debut, each one named, then described by Ferniot and May, and accompanied by that synthesized music.

Denmark's Jasper Kure sent out a platter featuring, among other compositions, a tartlet with shrimp and dill-glazed peas, and cauliflower with lightly smoked quail eggs, caviar, and radish. The most brazen element might have been the most simple: a turned carrot glazed and sprinkled with fresh herbs. To put something that basic forth in the Bocuse d'Or required immense confidence in technique, precision, and seasoning; it offered no place to hide.

Spain and Malaysia followed, then Japan, one of the countries to which Hollingsworth paid the most respect. Their chef did not disappoint, at least where originality and showmanship were concerned: his platter was headlined by codfish in a shrimp "dress" with fresh wasabi sauce. His written presentation to the judges even came with eating instructions for devouring the garnishes ("left to right"). Those garnishes included turnip braised in soy sauce, stuffed with oysters, sea urchin, and shrimp, and perfumed with yuzu zest; and a scallop croquette scented with algae tea.

"Very unique and very interesting," said Angela May.

Back in Kitchen 6, Guest removed the custards in their martini-glass stands from the oven. She began setting the discs of melba toast she'd just baked inside the rims of the glasses, where they'd be suspended. Hollingsworth stopped her three-quarters of the way through, noticing condensation fogging up the vessels. "Adina," he called out. "You gotta wipe them!"

After the bumpy morning getting to the Sirha and some missteps in the first minutes (his knife adjustment, Guest's injury), it had been smooth sailing for the first few hours. Journalist after journalist commented to Henin that they couldn't believe how little Hollingsworth and Guest spoke to each other.

"They are not talking because they don't have to talk," Henin told them.

But bit by bit, things were beginning to spiral out of control. Kitchen Number 6 had assumed the air of a submarine taking on water and Hollingsworth, the commander, was doing everything he could to keep it afloat and complete his mission. It was an odd moment for reflection, but time stopped for him as a rueful conclusion rippled through his mind. *It really sucks that this was such a fast thing*, he thought. "She was making mistakes that of course she would make because she doesn't work service and that right there is 'service time.'"

If only they'd had more time, he thought. Then he could have positioned Guest at the canapé station at The French Laundry, right next to where he expedited, and she'd have known what he wanted before he knew it himself, and plating according to his standards would have been second nature to her. They'd have been the Astaire and Rogers of the Bocuse d'Or, waltzing their way through the last hour of the competition, instead of staggering toward the finish line. He saw them that way in his mind for a half-second, a different team having a different experience, but then the cacophony of the crowd brought him back.

In the window, Coach Henin was giving verbal updates on the remaining time: "Two minutes," he bellowed.

The shrimp tart, such as it was, was already on the platter, as was the caviar tube. Hollingsworth began arranging matchbox car–sized wedges of potato mille-feuille around the caviar. Once again, his sense of time had abandoned him—he felt like it was taking Guest forever to clean up those custard cups, to get the melbas back inside, and to get them onto the platter, but he also recognized that time might have just been moving slowly for him. When the cups did come over, and he and Guest began setting them around the perimeter of the platter, he noticed that some of the melbas, despite the adjustment in size from the last practice, were not resting perfectly horizontally; some of them seesawed ever so slightly.

I should have designed something a little more simple, he scolded himself. *This is not the best application for something that will be paraded around for twenty minutes.*

There wasn't time to fix those toasts. He knew that. He had recaptured his sense of time and realized that it was dwindling.

Well, that was how the melbas would go out, be seen by the judges, photographed for posterity, and remembered. There wasn't a damn thing he could do about it. After all the preparation, time was finally coming to an end.

Henin turned toward the audience and up at the USA cheering section, bobbing his hands up and down to let them know that they needed to whoop it up, to offer encouragement and help propel the team over the finish line. In the stands, the American contingent—filled out now—hollered their support, some rolling up posters to use them as megaphones, trying to be heard over the still-deafening noise. Gavin Kaysen, a red,white, and blue scarf around his neck, shot a fist into the air and screamed, "Go, Timmy!"

Henin called out: "One minute!"

As it turned out, the coach's reminders were almost superfluous because the emcees had been talking up the fish platter of Japan's Kitchen 5, so Hollingsworth knew his moment was coming up fast.

There was still plenty of work to be done. Having confited the mousse-enveloped cod cylinders, he got ready to coat them, one of the steps that he'd had problems with in practices: he spread the pistachio dust out on a sheet pan, set the cylinders on it, and agitated the pan gingerly to cause the cylinders to turn. *I hope this works, I hope this works, hope this comes out clean, no fingerprints or . . .*

The cylinders lifted out cleanly—evenly coated in green dust. He sighed, reheated them in the oven, and set them on their stands. Set the caviar tower in the shrimp tart. Applied the bacon chips to the mille-feuille. Then he and the commis carefully lifted the platter up into the window.

There wasn't a second to dwell on the imperfections. He and Guest had to prepare the two plates, one for the judges to evaluate and the media to photograph, and one to act as a "how-to" for the servers, guiding them on plating the items from the platter after it made its rounds and was deposited on the carving station.

All of this, however, was just prologue to the last step of the fish stage of the competition: disassembling the platter and reallocating the components to individual plates for the judges. Hollingsworth, who had never participated in a competition before, wasn't ready for the unique plating methodology. Having only worked in restaurants, he was accustomed to always plating from the guest's point of view, and to doing all plates for a given table at one time.

This was different: awaiting him at the carving station were three stacks of four plates each. When the platter finished its rounds and was set down before him like an ER patient, Hollingsworth went to work. The first thing he did was slice the cod and put one slice on each of the three plates that topped their respective stacks. As he prepared to put a piece of mille-feiulle on the plates, he was dealt a devastating surprise: The waiters began turning the plates, so suddenly Hollingsworth was working upside down, which was disorienting to say the least.

"They kept moving plates. You do two plates, one is for the judges to see . . . the second one is for the service staff to know how to plate the dish . . . so I don't understand why I needed to go over there and show them this is where this goes . . . they were waiting for me to tell them where to put it. Nobody was really taking initiative, once I put it on, they would follow. This guy would do this. You have one guy walking behind me. It was utter chaos. The worst part was, you get the fish on all four plates, then they rotate the plate. It kept moving around. I was, like, 'Oh. My. God. This. Is. So. Hard. You have got to be kidding me.' That was the hardest moment of the competition."

Just as soon as he'd begin to get his bearings, the three plates on top of the stacks were whisked away, and he'd start over again, working from the guest's point of view, only to have the plates spun again.

Laughlin, watching from the American section of the bleachers, could hardly look. *He is really struggling*, she thought.

Once again, Hollingsworth was angry with himself. He had noticed something unusual at the carving stations from his observing perch on Day One, but was so interested in the food that he didn't pay sufficient attention to it. "I missed an opportunity to be a little more successful," he would say later. By the time he was done, things were moving so quickly and so confusingly, that he cannot remember what language some waiters were speaking. When one of the servers began walking to the judges with a plate that didn't yet have caviar on it, the commis extra waved her back. "He said, 'That plate needs caviar,' but maybe I just understood it [in French] at that point," Hollingsworth said.

HOLLINGSWORTH RACED BACK INTO Kitchen 6 and looked at his clock. There were about twenty minutes left until the beef platter was due in the window.

"Okay, Adina, where are we?" he called out.

Guest was assembling the deconstructed beef stew stacks. "She struggled a little with that," Hollingsworth would say later, quickly adding, "No more than I was [at that point]."

Hollingsworth gathered himself. As Guest prepared the celery salad for the pommes dauphinoise, he seared the bacon-wrapped beef and transferred it to the oven. Fearful that his own internal alarm clock might fail to go off, he told Henin that he wasn't going to bother setting a timer for the beef, and that instead he wanted the coach to keep him on schedule by giving him a periodic countdown for the final minutes.

He then assembled the beef rosette, brushing it with the lemony truffle oil that had been infusing since Saturday night's practice and transferring it to the center of the platter.

The value of practice—even to a gifted cook—was revealed in these moments: he had the right amount of horseradish cream available because he had realized in Saturday's run-through that he needed two bags' worth. But he had never practiced with the little stands that had just been delivered to him on Monday. He put the pommes dauphinoise rectangles on the stands, then set the stands on C-folds (folded paper towels) on a sheet tray, before heating the pommes dauphinoise through in the oven. This was standard operating procedure back home at The French Laundry, where the cooks never put anything directly on a piece of metal. But when he removed the tray from the oven, he got the surprise of his life: the rubber coating on the bottom, there to keep the stands from sliding around or scratching the surface on which they were set, *had melted onto the C-folds.*

"Adina, they all stuck!" he said. "I have to spend time doing this."

Guest responded with a deadly serious, "Yes, Chef."

And so, Hollingsworth spent the next several minutes peeling paper from the bottoms of the stands. To do this, he had to remove the potato dauphinoise from the stands, pick away at the paper, and then replace the dauphinoise. He quickly abandoned the idea of perfection, as he had had to abandon so much that day, leaving bits of paper fused to the very bottom of the stands if he was reasonably sure they would be out of view of the jury. It was a nerve-wracking exercise, and frustrating as well, because the time it consumed made the whole incident pointless: he might as well have not bothered heating the stands at all because by the time he was done peeling paper, the potato had cooled down. The tension compounded the difficulty of his next task: setting the little stands—the steel still hot from the oven—with the potato dauphinoise on top, between the delicate smoke glasses on the platter. He tried using a towel to protect his fingers, but the towel only got in the way, so he decided to go unprotected. He managed to land several rectangles without incident, but eventually the law of averages took hold and he toppled one of the smoke glasses. It didn't break, but desperately wanting to continue his forward movement, he assembled a new one using extra ingredients and one of the spare glasses.

They were down to the wire, inside that five-minute window between "time" and "too late." Hemorrhaging minutes as they were, Hollingsworth decided not to add the smoke to the smoke glasses until the carving station; they'd lose drama, but perhaps save their bacon by getting done before time was up.

On the dais, Jérôme Bocuse was unable to conceal his concern, and he cheated a few steps away from the table to peer in at Kitchen 6, situated over his right shoulder. "Normally, in that five minutes, you see that everything is almost done and ready to go and they were still scrambling," he said. He thought back to his impressions back in Yountville earlier in the month: "That reflects again on the routine."

Not wanting to distract Hollingsworth, Henin decided that he'd issue reminders by holding up pieces of paper with the remaining time on it. But Hollingsworth, never one to be distracted by noise, expected the coach to just scream out, "Okay, Tim, pull the beef." As a result, Henin had to wave his signs to get the candidate's attention. Those guys, they just never clicked.

Hollingsworth removed the bacon-wrapped beef from the oven and put the cylinders on the platter. Guest arranged the deconstructed beef stew stacks around them, and they lifted the platter up into the window, thinking they were perhaps late, but just making their allotted timeframe. The platter kept the team's secrets well: with the exception of the absent smoke, it looked every bit as spectacular as it ever had.

After the platter had made the rounds, and the time came to plate, Hollingsworth made an adjustment based on his experience on the fish platter, taking command of the carving station and arranging his plates around the platter. This time, things went easier, but even as the plates were whisked away to the judges, Hollingsworth knew that he had come up short. Minutes later, in the kitchen, with the curtains pulled shut, Hollingsworth was immediately overcome with a feeling of profound disappointment, in himself, and the job that he and his team did.

"I know we didn't win," he said to Guest.

He and Guest broke down their kitchen and cleaned it, the cramp in his side lingering for a good fifteen minutes into the process. Once done, he walked along the corridor behind kitchens 7 through 12, past the reception and meeting rooms, and past the sentry posted at his velvet rope and stanchions, where Laughlin was waiting for him.

"That was the hardest thing I ever did," he said to her.

Hollingsworth then returned to the holding area, where the wait was excruciating—there was still about an hour to go before all of the platters had been served and the other kitchens cleaned, and then of course there was the tabulating of the scores.

Other countries had joined the fray: the Czech Republic, Canada, and Singapore, which bought the event to Kitchen 10 and France.

Out on stage, Ferniot and May didn't even try to conceal their obvious excitement, and that of the audience. ("We better do it, before we have a riot," said May of the rabid French fans.) When the fish platter was finally marched out, it did not disappoint: the centerpiece was cod fillet with Biarritz flavors, a tribute to the seaside town in southwest France where Mille and his commis had practiced in order to escape the intense media scrutiny that always attaches to the French candidate. The cod's topping comprised many ingredients closely associated with Biarritz cuisine such as Espelette pepper, chorizo, piquillo peppers, and Bayonne ham. Garnishes included a tender shrimp dome and tawny crisps (shrimp arranged in a circle over a rounded brown pastry cup) with golden eggs, a delicate tart of scallops on a bed of baby spinach with a layer of caviar beads, and a cone of leeks and sea-flavored baby squid topped with urchin roe. Minutes later, for the beef platter, there were wood-grilled beef steak layered with foie gras and encased in a flaky pastry, braised beef cheeks with a carrot topiary, beef tenderloin with tiny garden vegetables, a miniature shrub of tender leeks, and the showstopper: oxtail and caramelized celery combined and formed into an enormous charcoal-colored "Black Diamond."

When the competition was finally over and the judges found their way backstage, Keller patted Hollingsworth and Guest on the back and said, "Good job. I'm proud of you guys." But he couldn't help but ask about the smoke bowls.

"Chef, I didn't think we had time," said the candidate. This was actually one of the things he was ultimately least disappointed in because, "In the long run, I think it probably tasted a lot better." That said, Hollingsworth will forever wonder whether or not he would have earned some more points had those glasses contained smoke when they were first paraded—

would the drama of the visuals have predisposed more judges to love his food?

As Hollingsworth and Guest hung out backstage, strangers—including many judges—came up to him and offered encouragement in a multitude of languages. All the positive vibes conspired to almost make him believe that he had a shot, but not really, "not in my heart." Hollingsworth didn't even think about what place he deserved. By that point, he just wanted to do well enough to not be embarrassed.

Just as his spirits were lifting, however, he was met with some criticism. Judge René Redzepi of Denmark came up and told Hollingsworth that he didn't understand that the rosette was not supposed to be warm, and judge Lea Linster reinforced this by telling him that both the rosette and the smoke bowl garnish confused her. "Where I'm from, you would say it a different way on the menu, you would say it's meant to clean your palate or something," she told him.

Hollingsworth received this with a mix of shock and disbelief. "To me that is crazy," he thought. "There's freaking raw meat on it." For all of the time and debate that had gone into the menu writing, had the failure to state an intended temperature cost Team USA?

FINALLY, AT ABOUT A quarter past six, the pomp of the awards ceremony commenced. Hall 33 was by then packed quite beyond its capacity; the media pit was a zoo, and the stairway that led to the media center was crawling with spectators watching the action from outside the hall itself.

Three circular podiums had been hauled out on stage, the winners' circle, or *circles*. After all the necessary introductions, the various teams emerged from the wings, along with their presidents, with each group hoisting its flag. Some teams exuded confidence in the moment, like Skeie, who held his aloft as though charging into battle. Hollingsworth, on the other hand, held the Stars and Stripes at his side.

In the audience, Pelka and Laughlin held hands, their seriousness undercut by Pelka's attire: the 2009 red, white, and blue sunglasses and a flag draped cape-like over her shoulders. Desperate for information, she made eye contact with Jérôme Bocuse. She assumed that Paul Bocuse knew who the winner was, and that one would think that if he knew then Jérôme would find out.

This led her to wonder about who knew what down there on the stage. Daniel Boulud would not make eye contact with her—was he hiding something? Keller seemed impassive, maybe blue. "I don't think Thomas knows," she thought. "Or he knows and it's not what he wants."

When she finally locked eyes with Jérôme Bocuse, he nodded in her direction. She shrugged and he looked away. When he looked back, she surreptitiously held up one finger. First place?

He shook his head, "No," and looked down.

"Oh, man," she thought, believing that first place had been within reach. She held up two fingers.

At this, Bocuse nodded slightly, which she took to mean "Yes."

"Oh, my God," she said to Laughlin. "Jérôme just told me that we came in second."

"Do you really think so?" said Laughlin. "Second is amazing."

After consolation prizes were handed out for Best Promotional Poster (Brazil) and Best Promotion (Czech Republic), it was time for the award for Best Fish, which was presented to Jasper Kure of Denmark. He accepted his little goldfish statue with obvious disappointment, which was even more evident when it was announced moments later that he had also won Best Meat and had to hold up a little cow and pose for pictures with *those* sponsors. A ripple of confusion went through the media section—had there been a rule change? How could one country win both those prizes and not take the gold? (The answer is that those awards are for the best fish and meat outside the top three finishers.)

Then came the top prizes. When it was announced that France won the bronze, the first time it had failed to win gold or silver, anything seemed possible.

"Holy shit," thought Pelka. "We won." She squeezed Laughlin's hand even tighter.

There was just one thing: on the dais, Hollingsworth and Guest looked scared to her, almost miserable, which pretty much summed up Hollingsworth's feeling at the moment, standing up there for an extended time, sure that he hadn't placed.

Pelka's feeling was magnified when Jonas Lundgren won the silver and took up his place on the podium. By the time Paul Bocuse emerged to read out the name of the winner of the Bocuse d'Or, nobody knew what to expect. But as it turned out, it would be an anticlimactic resolution as a familiar victor was announced: Norway!

Pelka let go of Laughlin's hand and almost instantly began sobbing into her cape, but as Skeie and his commis dashed up to the highest pedestal, attaining his lifelong ambition, it was difficult to begrudge him his victory. He had wanted this since the age of twelve, and had devoted much of the past two years to attaining it. As confetti rained down on him and the Norwegian national anthem began to play, he held the trophy aloft and howled.

Later, when the score sheets were distributed, Hollingsworth would learn his fate: a sixth place finish, the same as Hartmut Handke had pulled off in 2003. Where the three top medalists had earned scores of 1,020, 994, and 993, Hollingsworth had amassed 911 points. For all of the problems in the kitchen, he wound up in rarefied air, among the half-dozen who had crossed the 900-point threshold: the remaining eighteen candidates scored between 669 (South Korea) and 891 (Iceland).

When Pelka reunited with Jérôme Bocuse in the competition area, he informed her that *nobody*, not even Paul Bocuse, knew the results before they were announced; he had merely been telling her what his best *guess* was with his head shakes and nods.

In their own way, others had a more painful ending: Jasper Kure, who placed fourth, missed the podium by an excruciating seven points, even though he had the top meat score of any team, including the medalists. France, meanwhile, had been one minute late with its fish platter, earning a twelve-point penalty, which ended up making the difference between second and third place. There are those, Gavin Kaysen among them, who believe that Mille was crucified for the sins of the past, for other times—like the one depicted in the 2007 documentary—when late finishers were *not* punished for much more severe infractions. Asked for comment, Mille refused to complain. "I have to respect the rules," was all he said of the matter.

As for Luke Croston of Australia, who had come back to the Bocuse d'Or to better his twelfth place finish of 2007 . . . he once again came in twelfth, perhaps due to that disintegrating cod; he would never know exactly.

For his part, Roland Henin was at peace with the outcome for Team USA: "Even if we were to do a bronze, it would have been somewhat pushed," he said later. "It would have been fabricated. It would have been almost unfair and just unreal and I was in a sense—I don't want to say *happy*— I was *fine* with the fact that we didn't do a bronze, simply because we didn't deserve a bronze. We got what we deserved, and I want to be clear about that. We got what we deserved. We were not at the bronze level. Period. Had we had a bronze I would have definitely lost faith in the judging process."

Similarly, Laughlin, while sad for her boyfriend, was, "a little bit relieved. Just in that I thought if the U.S. team can come in here, and if Tim can come in with limited practice and exposure to this type of competition and get on the podium, then what does that say for the whole Bocuse d'Or organization? I had never really questioned the integrity . . . but we had kind of formed this bond with Paul Bocuse and his staff. . . . I was almost relieved that at the end of the day that it just comes down to these numbers. . . . The general feeling was not relief, of course, but sadness for Tim because I know he would feel that he disappointed people and that was what was hardest for me, that he would feel that he let people down."

She wasn't far off: Hollingsworth felt stung by the already-nagging feeling that he knew he had been capable of doing better. For a guy who had been raised by his father to abhor shoddy workmanship, who had spent seven years questing for perfection on a daily basis, who relentlessly pushed himself to do his best and to bring out the best in those around him, and who was the go-to guy at The French Laundry, the realization that he didn't fulfill his potential was a bitter pill to swallow.

There was another argument to be made, and it was an obvious one with a much less punitive message: with just three and a half months to do *everything*, with just five full practices under their belt, while still basically working their regular jobs, Hollingsworth and Guest had matched the best-ever result by an American team headed up by a veteran competitor who had trained more than a year. They had come in eight spots higher than Kaysen, who had logged more than fifty practice runs. Kaysen insisted that the sixth-place finish, while short of the podium, was a resounding validation of Hollingsworth's talent. "It's technique. He knows how to season. He knows how to cook," said Kaysen. "All of the other stuff is the fluff that gets you on the podium. That is the foundation of the competition. The competition was built for that."

But that logic only went so far with Hollingsworth, who knew he was being evaluated by a different yardstick: "Everybody thinks you had three months off, paid," he said, referring to media coverage of the team's preparation. "Therefore it's like, yeah, you can kind of feel that way, but you can't because that's not what other people think."

Keller, who had the prescience, way back at The French Culinary Institute briefing the prior July, to indicate that he didn't necessarily expect a win for the USA in 2009, again took the long view, putting the result in perspective: "What happens to a chef that wins or loses a cooking competition?" he reflected at a later date. "It doesn't really define who that chef is or who that chef is going to become. I think it's a moment, an experience in each one of our lives that we could appreciate and enjoy. Because we were *chosen* for this. We were *asked* to do this and we agreed to do this. We do that for the experience of it and you try to do the best you can. Is it ultimately going to define who I am or who Timmy is or [who Geir Skeie] is? No.

"We are defined every day by what we do and *re*defined every day by what we do. It is a day-to-day thing. Cooking is a day-to-day thing and it is a commitment that you make. So if you win the Bocuse d'Or yesterday, that was yesterday. What are you going to do *today*? It's not a piece of art that lasts forever. You could paint a piece of art, it becomes a masterpiece, and you may never paint another masterpiece as long as you live but at least that masterpiece is still there and it lasts forever. Food is not like that . . . you win the whatever—Bocuse d'Or, James Beard, whatever accolades you win—once you win it, it's over. You won it for the work that you did the day before.

"So what are you going to do tomorrow?" he asked.

THE NEXT MORNING, DANIEL Boulud drove to his parents' home. Jennifer Pelka was in the car with him. On his cellular phone was Georgette Farkas, his publicity director back in New York, asking for direction on how to spin the U.S. result.

"You can't jump into the pool and compete with Michael Phelps," Boulud told her. He and Keller and Jérôme Bocuse, they had all taken this on with little time and long odds against them, that was the spin.

Once he was done with the call, he continued to drive along the highways, the same ones he'd navigated as a young cook. He squinted into the sunlight.

"Disappointment in life can be motivating," he said. "When I opened my first restaurant that was Restaurant Daniel on Seventy-sixth Street, it was after I spent six years at Le Cirque and I was twice four-star review. I was expecting maybe my first restaurant to get three stars because I wasn't trying to be fancy or anything, but very good. The review was two stars and the staff was devastated. For me, I felt, you know, this is not going to knock me off my horse. *We gonna show them the best fucking two-star they have ever seen if that is going to be the verdict.* And eight months later, we had four stars again. So in a way I think that it is a motivation. I think this should not knock us off."

He continued: "What I think is that Timothy did an amazing job," he said. "And I tell you in my own notes of tasting the food and taking notes on the food I really felt that the people who were on the podium weren't the one that impressed me most with taste. When you have twelve different judges and all of them are judging very unevenly how can you just guess right?"

"But, Chef, what do we have to do better?" asked Pelka.

"We have to have time to train!" Boulud shouted. "The Norwegian [chef] had a year to think about his dish and a year and a half to train! . . . It is a very hard game to play and I think we played very well."

Hollingsworth helped pack up boxes that morning at L'Abbaye, then retreated with Laughlin, declining to go out to dinner with the group that night. He turned twenty-nine that Friday, January 30, and commemorated the milestone with dinner at Restaurant Pic. Still very much pushed out of shape by the past several months, Hollingsworth had to skip dessert. He just didn't have the appetite for celebration. Not yet. He needed some time.

That Sunday, he and Laughlin boarded a flight back to New York, and then on to San Francisco. They arrived late in the evening, with seven bags in tow, heavy bags stuffed with extra French Laundry cookbooks, kitchen equipment, their clothes, and so on. It was the first time in weeks that they were not on a schedule, not having people around telling them where to be or what to do.

They also didn't have any transportation. The competition was over, the committee was on to the next one, and nobody had thought to provide a courtesy car for the returning candidate. And so, Timothy Hollingsworth, who had found instant fame, been profiled in the pages of *The New York Times* and *Food & Wine*, boarded a bus back to Napa. Once there, he and Laughlin called on some friends to give them a ride home. They didn't go out. It was late. The trip had been hard.

And, besides, he had to be at work in the morning.

Epilogue

ADINA GUEST HAS FLASHBACKS.

During her mornings at The French Laundry, she will be cutting vegetables and find that, although it's quiet around her, "I am freaking out in my brain because I am having flashbacks of all the noise and how it felt to be there. . . . I am looking around me and I am like, 'These people have no idea how it is.' I am looking around at the other commis and even the morning sous chef and it's like, 'You have no idea what it's like to cook in front of five thousand people that are screaming your ears deaf and you have to concentrate,' and I am, like, 'Damn, Adina.' I can't believe that I have been through that."

Guest had learned what countless commis and candidates had before her—Bocuse d'Or memories, like wines, cheeses, and certain meats, intensify with age. Despite the occasional bouts of culinary post-traumatic stress, she feels grateful for the experience, which she says left her feeling like more of an adult. She says that she may even try to become the American candidate at some future date.

If there was a big winner on Team USA in 2009, it was Gavin Kaysen and, by extension, the Bocuse d'Or USA itself. Kaysen had successfully turned Boulud and Keller on to his professional idée fixe: Boulud resolved to reprise his role as chairman, and Keller—again at the request of Paul Bocuse—would be back as president and had offered up the Bocuse House for training. Jérôme Bocuse, too, would remain in place as vice president. The Bocuse d'Or USA had also been transformed into the Bocuse d'Or USA *Foundation*, with a scholarship component. Nora Carey, formerly director of the Epcot International Food & Wine Festival, came on board as executive director, and Jennifer Pelka, while still working for Dinex, would spend much of her time as Director of Competition and Events for the Foundation.

"This year *was* a Cinderella story because we went from nothing to something," said Kaysen, whose dream had come true: future candidates would have an organization to support them in every possible way. Nearly two years from the 2011 Bocuse d'Or, the new foundation was already on the march, soliciting sponsors, identifying potential candidates to be encouraged, and bringing relationships to bear in upping the Bocuse d'Or's profile in the United States. For example, a planned episode of *Top Chef* scheduled to air in November 2009, featuring Boulud, Keller, Jérôme Bocuse, Hollingsworth, Kaysen, and Pelka as guest judges, would offer a unique prize to the winner of its elimination challenge: a role as a finalist in the next Bocuse d'Or USA trials.

Keller wasn't sure if he'd be back for a third time, in 2013, but he wanted to help create an entity that could continue to grow and thrive on its own without him. It was similar to his goal for his restaurants. Keller often speaks of his desire to leave a legacy, to create such strong foundations in his restaurants that they can live on and continue to evolve after his time, and this had become his personal goal for the Bocuse d'Or USA Foundation as well.

At the very least, with adequate time to focus and to weave the Bocuse d'Or into his and Boulud's calendars for the next two years, Keller was certain of one thing: "We will be much more prepared in 2011 than 2009."

As for Hollingsworth and Henin, they had not spoken to each other in the months since Lyon. But on Thursday, May 7, 2009, Hollingsworth learned that the coach would be passing through Yountville, and sought him out. With the competition behind them, the two men greeted each other with a warm handshake outside Bouchon Bakery. The sun was shining on them again, as it had been when they began this adventure.

Henin congratulated Hollingsworth on his news: in early April, it had been announced that Chef de Cuisine Corey Lee would be leaving The French Laundry to open his own restaurant, and that Hollingsworth would be taking over as chef de cuisine of one of the best restaurants in the United States. It was *his* ultimate moment of judgment as a restaurant chef, the culmination of his career to date. Not bad for a former dishwasher who got hired "by accident," as Keller likes to say.

The two men may not have become intimates during their time together, but they would be forever linked in American culinary history, perhaps more for what surrounded them that May afternoon than for the Bocuse d'Or. In many ways, Keller's success, manifested in his restaurants and other properties around town, began with Henin, though the mentor refused to take credit for it.

"Thomas doesn't have to do that [thank me all the time] and of course he has done it a lot more than really is necessary," Henin said later. "I am happy that I was instrumental, but a lot of it came from him, too. I didn't create it from something that didn't exist. He is like going in a garden and growing something. If the soil is not good, no matter how much work you put into it, you're going to be limited in your harvest. But if the soil is really good then your harvest is going to be so much better . . . maybe I was instrumental in putting him in the right direction, or to help him see the light, but I think that the basic foundations, the basic stocks, the basic earth, the quality of the earth was there. I didn't create that. I just helped. I was just an instrument in the development."

Hollingsworth would be the next link in the chain, the conduit from Henin to Keller to all those cooks and commis the new chef de cuisine would help develop over the coming years.

Inevitably, the Bocuse d'Or crept into the conversation, as Henin reminded the candidate of the original schedule he had created, and how it would have included serving food to invited guests so the team could have practiced serving from the platters. What might that have meant in the end, the coach mused aloud.

"It was a great experience," said Hollingsworth, disengaging from the past as they shook hands and said goodbye. "It changed my life."

He wasn't just being polite. Hollingsworth still rides himself harder than anybody else for his performance. His colleagues at The Thomas Keller Restaurant Group profess nothing but pride in him and Guest, and for a time the Bocuse d'Or USA Web site homepage welcomed visitors with a congratulatory message for the 2009 Team. But Hollingsworth maintains profound disappointment in his result, a regret that he believes "will never go away." (So deep is the wound that, as of May 2009, he had not visited the Bocuse d'Or Web site to view the official photographs of his platters, nor had he featured cod on any of his menus at The French Laundry since the competition.)

Nevertheless, with the distance of a few months, Hollingsworth had come to appreciate his competition experience more than he could have imagined when he reluctantly embarked upon it. Of the conversation with Henin, he later confirmed his assertion that the Bocuse d'Or "changed my life socially, professionally, intellectually." As was the case with preparing for the team trials in Orlando, he found the opportunity to spend months fine-tuning a group of recipes—rather than serving them for a day, then moving on—invaluable to his development, not to mention the time overseas and the national and international attention.

For all of the disappointment the coach had suffered throughout the process, this revelation put a smile on his face. "He said, 'I am a better cook,'" said Henin. "He has a different view, a different understanding of things. . . . That by itself is already worth every pain or every sweat or blood or whatever you want to call that."

The next day, Henin spoke to the graduating class of The Culinary Institute of America at Greystone, about ten miles up Highway 29 from Yountville in St. Helena. He began the way he often did, a humble expression of gratitude for the introduction and some kind words about the host institution. His address built to a comparison of a cook's career to a seven-course meal. "You have just completed the hors d'oeuvre course," he said. "You have had just a taste of what a chef is about, and of course you are hungry for more."

He went on: the fish course was the beginning of a career, and it was a delicate one. If it went well, his audience would move on to the next phase, "the main course . . . now you will be really cooking. . . . You will have to make choices about the kind of chef you want to be and the kind of life you want to lead." After that would come the salad and cheese courses, which for Henin meant serving as a mentor to other chefs. "Whatever path you are on," he said. "You will be the legacy you will leave to others."

Adopting a wistful tone, Henin continued. "Some day you will wake up, you will look around, you will realize that it is time for dessert, the sweet time." This would mean different things to different people; they might lecture, coach, give speeches, write a book, all the while reflecting on how they might have tweaked things along the way.

"If you've done things the right way," Henin promised. "You will realize it has been the kind of meal you always dreamed of.

"Then, finally, you pour yourself a small glass of the perfect fine *digestif*," he concluded. "Raising your glass in a toast, to all those who have helped you along the way . . . all those people who have been a part of your success."

As heartfelt as all of this was, the most profound passage of Henin's remarks preceded this coda, when he told a story, a humorous parable, about two young students on the verge of graduating from The Culinary Institute many years ago—whether it is true or not is anybody's guess, and doesn't really matter. The tale began the weekend before the final exams, when the two young men in question decided to get a head start on their celebration, partying up the road at Johnson & Wales.

"Suffice it to say, they had a good time and, as you can imagine, didn't make it back in time to the CIA." said Henin, milking the melodrama.

Trembling, the two students went to their chef-instructor, telling him they had left campus to *study* for the exam, and on the way home got a flat tire. "They were impoverished culinary students and had no spare, and had to wait a long time for someone to come to their rescue," Henin continued, his voice dripping with sarcasm.

"The instructor, being such a nice and understanding person, thought about it and agreed that, yes, they could make up the final exam the following day."

Relieved, the students went back to their dorm and crammed for the test. When they showed up the next morning, the instructor put them in separate rooms and gave each of them a copy of the exam. The first question, worth five points, asked them to name four mother sauces, the ones that provide the foundation for just about any Western sauce you'd ever want to make—a layup if ever there were one.

"*'Cool!'*" exclaimed Henin, imitating the students, his voice shooting up about three octaves. " 'This is going to be easy, a piece of cake.' They answered the question and turned the page." Henin abruptly shifted to a solemn, almost funereal tone. "They were, however, unprepared for what they saw on the next page.

" 'For ninety-five points,' " Henin continued, taking a long pause before slaying his momentary pupils with the punch line: " *'Which tire?'* "

It had been half a century since he had wandered into that little pastry shop in Tarare, France, more than thirty years since he had flung that Frisbee at a young cook on the beach of Narragansett, Rhode Island. But even though Roland Henin was an older man now, well past the canapés and the main courses, he wasn't done with his dessert just yet, wasn't quite ready to sip his *digestif*.

There was still plenty he could teach everybody.

NOTES AND REFERENCES

3   "Chefs who can step into": Edward, G. Leonard, *American Culinary Federation's Guide to Culinary Competitions: Cooking to Win!*, John Wiley & Sons, Inc., 2006, page 1.

6   "Ten thousand people died": According to the National World War II Museum, there were about 10,000 Allied *casualties* on D-Day; of those, about 2,500 were American fatalities.

10   "a food competition without French participation": Paul Levy, "Culinary 'Olympics': Eating Takes 2d Place," *The New York Times*, November 5, 1980, page C3.

16   So while many European countries: Florence Fabricant, "Tilting at the Bocuse d'Or," *The New York Times*, May 28, 2009.

77   "You have to pursue": *Gourmet Challenge*. Glénat, 2005, page 125.

124   The most outlandish drama: Charles Bremner and Marie Tourres, "We were whipped by cheat chef, say the losing cooks." *The Times* (London), February 20, 2007.

183   "Dear Timothy and Adina": Author's Note: This letter has been edited to correct *some* grammar, spelling, and punctuation.

222   "At restaurants considered much less exclusive": Frank Bruni, "New Sparkle for a Four-Star Gem," *The New York Times*, January 21, 2009.

253   As it turned out: Elaine Sciolino, "Curveball Cod," Diner's Journal blog entry, *The New York Times*, January 28, 2009.

257   Unbeknownst to the team: Elaine Sciolino, "With Cowbells and Oxtails, Culinary Olympics Begin," *The New York Times*, January 28, 2009.

ACKNOWLEDGMENTS

This book could not have been written without the generosity of both time and spirit of the following people, many of whom had never met me before I embarked on this adventure. My deep and abiding gratitude to:

Team USA. Timothy Hollingsworth, this story could surely have been told with other candidates at the helm of Team USA, but I don't know how many would have opened up their lives and their hearts to a stranger the way you did. Your kindness to a writer granted access by others was extraordinary, and I'll never forget it. Adina Guest, thank you for letting me watch you work and evolve, for making time for me during a very important time in your life, and for your openness, especially about your personal life. And Roland Henin, CMC, for teaching me about the world of culinary competitions and for sharing your passion and history with me. I know that it wasn't always ideal to have a writer in the room; thanks for not holding it against me.

The Bocuse d'Or USA, especially Daniel Boulud, for receiving my original proposition with such enthusiasm, for your help in Lyon, and for all of your time in the Skybox and elsewhere. Thomas Keller, the self-described "cautious one," for your trust and for the hospitality you and your extraordinary staffs showed me at The French Laundry, Bouchon, and Per Se. It was a privilege to spend time with you and with them, and it rubbed off on me: my kitchen has never been cleaner! Jérôme Bocuse, for your support of this book, for your invaluable assistance in Lyon, for always being a willing translator between me and your father, and for a memorable visit to Orlando. Jennifer Pelka, for inviting me to meetings, copying me on e-mails, sending me piles of documents, tracking down that FCI video, getting me a seat at all the right tables at all the right dinners, making time for interviews, and for everything else. And Gavin Kaysen, for your time, enthusiasm, insights, your brain's extra gigabytes of memory (seriously, you are a fact-checker's dream), for taking me under your wing in Orlando and in Lyon, and especially for that 6:00 a.m. taxi on Game Day, even though we got by without it.

"Monsieur Paul," the great Paul Bocuse, for setting me at ease from the first moment we met and for granting me so many interviews, especially during the week of the Bocuse d'Or.

David Black, for the idea, and for almost a decade of helping me attain dreams that date back to childhood.

At Free Press, Leslie Meredith for her great excitement and tireless efforts. Martha Levin for taking the thing on in the first place. Donna Loffredo for finding answers to countless compulsive questions and for help polishing the manuscript down the home stretch. Andrew Dodds and Carisa Hays for getting the word out. And Dominick Anfuso and Suzanne Donahue for their support.

At SepelCom, Florent Suplisson for his insights and availability and Damien Gagnieux for assisting with endless requests long after the Bocuse d'Or 2009 was over.

Richard Rosendale and Hartmut Handke for making time for me during a fascinating visit to Columbus and helping me understand why chefs compete.

Kate Laughlin, for your inexhaustible patience, your time, and your support.

The team at The French Laundry and The Thomas Keller Restaurant Group: Kristine Keefer, for your hospitality in Yountville, arranging interviews on two coasts, fact-checking assistance, help with photographs, and for being a pleasure to work with. Carey Snowden, for helping me out, especially during the first days of this project; Gerald San Jose, for always being quick with the answers; and to Bertram Whitman—all good things to those who wait.

Daniel Boulud's team in New York, especially Georgette Farkas, for your help in Orlando and New York, and with photographs. And Vanessa Absil, for helping me find DB when I needed him and for priceless assistance making plans for Lyon.

Amy Tucker, for transcribing a few phone books' worth of interviews. It was fun having you along for the ride.

Florence Kahn-Ramos, for helping me find my way around Lyon, for joining me for lunch, and for being my translator and new friend.

Karen Klees, for translating help from the States.

Lisa Abend, for hanging with me in Lyon, and for help interviewing the Spanish team.

Those at The French Laundry and Per Se who graciously spent time interviewing with me: Corey Lee, Jonathan Benno, Devin Knell, Larry Nadeau, Molly Ireland, Erin Tichy, Raj Dagstani, Chloe Genovart, Ema Leftick, and Tucker Taylor.

Karen and Quentin Hollingsworth, for spending a Sunday afternoon with a jet-lagged writer, telling me about yourselves and your family.

Michel Bouit and Liz Bergin, for all those stories about the past twenty years. Wish I had room for more of them in these pages.

Susan Weaver, for sharing the story of the first Bocuse d'Or.

The U.S. candidates and commis who competed in Orlando: Richard Rosendale and Seth Warren; Kevin Sbraga and Aimee Patel; Michael Rotondo and Jennifer Petrusky; Percy Whatley and Josh Johnson; Hung

Hyunh and Girair (Jerry) Goumroian; Rogers Powell and Kyle Fiasconaro; and John Rellah and Vincent Forchelli.

The Bocuse d'Or competitors who interviewed with me before and after the big day: Ronald Bellaart, Luke Croston, Wim Klerks, Filip Langhoff, Jonas Lundgren, Philippe Mille, Geir Skeie, and David Wong.

The photographers whose images grace the insert: Will Blunt, Nora Carey, Owen Franken, Dave Getzschman, Etienne Heimermann, Deborah Jones, Justin Lewis, and Paal André Schwital. Thanks also to Joleen Hughes and the team at Level for allowing me to include the Team USA poster.

And to the many others who shared time and information: Michael Bersell; Christian Bouvarel; Terrance Brennan; Joel Buchman; Nora Carey; Alison Cullin-Woodcock; Traci Des Jardins; Marie-Odile Fondeur; Jacky Fréon; Daniel Humm; Vincent Le Roux; Frank Leake; Paul Liebrandt; Lea Linster; Regis Marcon; Ferdinand Metz; Anne-Sophie Pic; Emilie Pichon; Marco Poldevaart; Renée Richard; Alain Sailhac; Daniel Scannell, CMC; Fenny Straat; Laurent Tourondel; Alan Tsuchiyama; Serge Vieira; Jean-Georges Vongerichten; David Waltuck; and Nick Versteeg.

The *TENNIS* magazine gang (Pete, Steve, Tom, James, Ed, and the extended family of Jon, Doug, and Asad). The way you guys think and write about the athletes who play the sport we all love helped me in this cause more than you'll ever know.

The residents of Fourth Street, Brooklyn, where this book was finished to the sounds of chirping birds and barking dogs, thanks for welcoming us to our new home. Hopefully, by the time you read this, we'll have all broken bread together.

And above all, to my wife, Caitlin, who has two careers and a very full life of her own, thank you for enduring the many weeks without me, especially the half-month I spent in Lyon, and to our beautiful children, Declan and Taylor, for making it fun to work at home.

ABOUT THE AUTHOR

Andrew Friedman writes about the worlds of food and tennis, which also happen to be two of his personal passions. His articles on food and chefs have appeared in *O, The Oprah Magazine* and *The Wall Street Journal*; he co-edited the popular anthology *Don't Try This at Home*; and has collaborated on more than twenty cookbooks and other projects with many of the best chefs in the United States, including Alfred Portale, David Waltuck, and former White House chef Walter Scheib. He also coauthored, with James Blake, the *New York Times* bestselling tennis memoir *Breaking Back*, and is a contributing editor to *TENNIS* magazine. He lives in Brooklyn, New York, with his family.